DATE DUE			
Dec 16 7 7			

THE
GLOBAL
MIND

THE
GLOBAL
MIND
BEYOND THE LIMITS
TO GROWTH

LEWIS J. PERELMAN

 MASON/CHARTER

NEW YORK 1976

301.31
P41g
100551
apr 1977

Library of Congress Cataloging in Publication Data

Perelman, Lewis J
    The global mind.

    Bibliography: p.
    Includes index.
    1. Ecology. 2. Environmental protection. I. Title.
QH541.P42   301.31   76-10709
ISBN 0-88405-124-2

CONTENTS

LIST OF ILLUSTRATIONS

LIST OF TABLES

ACKNOWLEDGMENTS

committee, Gerald Lesser and Walter McCann. Many other people at Harvard provided institutional, financial, academic, and personal support without which the studies which formed the basis for much of this book would have been impossible. I especially want to acknowledge the contributions of Dean Paul Ylvisaker, and of Charles Myers and the faculty, staff, and students of the Center for Studies in Education and Development.

Dennis and Donella Meadows provided invaluable assistance at every stage of the work on this book. Many of the ideas contributed by Dennis in a paper we coauthored in 1973 have been included. At a critical moment, when I was trying to decide whether or not to tackle this enormous subject, Donella provided the encouragement that enabled me to begin. She continued to provide precious moral support at times when I was about to give up.

The Project to Study the Implications of Growth Policy for Post-secondary Education provided the opportunity to advance significantly my understanding of limits to growth and higher education. I must recognize the invaluable assistance of my colleague and co-director of the project, William Bergquist, whose contributions permeate the later chapters. Nancy Barber provided useful administrative, editorial, and intellectual assistance during the project, and afterwards, helped me considerably during the writing of the final draft of this book. I appreciate the foresight and understanding of the commissioners and staff of the Western Interstate Commission for Higher Education in sponsoring the project, and the financial support provided by the Rockefeller Brothers Fund, which made the project possible.

I would like to thank Tom Lipscomb for his faith in publishing this book. Gerda Whitney helped me through the final and most frustrating phase of writing this book with great good humor, patience, and encouragement, and for this I am extremely grateful.

Finally, there is simply no way to adequately acknowledge here the magnitude of the contribution of my family or to adequately express my gratitude. Also, I have been blessed with many great friends whose loyalty, support, encouragement, respect, and love have made possible whatever success I have known. But for the help of all these good people, this book could not have been written.

Denver, Colorado
March 1976

toward a definite goal, or upon, and that is the g...

is dynamic, who must be ever in motion to remain stable, and who has equipped and trained himself to tilt and recover, to adjust to direction and temperature and density and whatever else he may encounter. And by and large, gulls outlast pyramids, for flex and bend and change are the very essence of life, while pyramids, however impressive, are doomed to dust for the lack of ability to cope with the life-forces, the sunbeam, the rain-drop, which will destroy them.

Theodore Sturgeon[1]

PROLOG

ing apocalypse or some diffuse influence of the insidious ambiance of Los Angeles or—which is more likely—some synthesis of the two, I cannot say for sure. I suppose one could say that my whole life had contributed to the continuous evolution of my "ecological consciousness."

Certainly, growing up on the limb of New York City provided me with an excellent prospect from which to view the debilitation of a total environment through the synergetic action of pollution, crowding, poverty, and violence. But 23-odd years in that location didn't have a major effect in producing that relatively sudden crystallization of environmental awareness that took place in my head sometime in the spring of 1970. If anything, growing up in New York had only served to inure me to the symptoms of ecological devastation. I had come to accept a degraded environment as "normal." Like that of most New Yorkers, my own environmental awareness before 1970 was confined pretty much to the problem of air pollution.

Air pollution in New York was so obtrusive that one could hardly be unaware of it. Not only did it smell bad, but the long avenues lined with stalagmitic skyscrapers provided a neat, even obvious calibration of the limits of visibility. And there were enough truly *clear* days conveniently interspersed throughout the year that one was pretty constantly aware of how bad the pollution was. This was less true of water pollution, for, by fortuitous circumstance, New York enjoys one of the finest systems of water supply in the world; the fetid estuaries that embrace Manhattan Island *look* sufficiently clean that most New Yorkers are not hard pressed to be concerned about their content. To the remaining host of environmental degradations which we have more recently come to "see," we were then almost utterly insensitive. We knew about the crime, the poverty, the rundown housing, the disease, the overburdened subways, the jammed highways, etc., but we thought of these things, when we thought of them at all, as separate administrative/political problems, not yet as a skein of environmental corruption. We took these things as virtually *defining* the urban ambiance, as being in the "nature" of things, the way it was "spozed to be."

No, it was Los Angeles and Earth Day that introduced the concept of crisis to me. How I came to be in Los Angeles is too long a story to tell here, nor is it germane. Suffice it to say that in January 1970 I moved from New York to Los Angeles where I eventually took up residence in Santa Monica, not far from the UCLA campus. Not surprisingly, it was the air pollution in Los Angeles County that I associate most clearly in my memory with the birth of at least the emotional sense of crisis, which is not to say that air pollution is Los Angeles' only ecological insult, or even its worst. The air pollution of Los Angeles is, of course, renowned. It was neither unexpected nor something for which I felt unprepared. Indeed, like most New Yorkers, I took a sort of perverse pride in my capacity for tolerating the insults of urban living. I even felt, chauvinistically, that the smog of L.A. would probably pale in comparison with the copper haze of the "Big Apple."

I am not aware of any statistics which would show that the physical effect of the air pollution in Los Angeles is significantly more severe than that of New York. But from my personal experience, I have little doubt that the psychological impact of Los Angeles' smog is far greater than that of New York's.

There are a number of reasons for this, the first of which is the chemical composition of the stuff. Los Angeles smog is composed predominantly of peroxyacetylnitrate (PAN), a complex substance produced by the reaction of nitrogen oxides with hydrocarbons under the influence of intense sunlight; about 80 percent of it has its source in automobile exhaust. New York pollution, on the other hand, is much more of a mixed bag: dirt and smoke, sulfur oxides, nitrogen oxides, carbon monoxide, hydrocarbons, and so on. It emanates from various sources such as incinerators, furnaces, power plants, factories, and cars and trucks. The sensory impact (as opposed to the long-term health effect) of the two smogs is tangibly different. The New York variety smells bad and is a little hard to breathe. The suspended dirt tends to stick to one's skin, producing a grimy feeling at the end of the day. Yet the overall sensation isn't much worse than that of being in the smoking car of the Stamford local. One gets used to it. Los Angeles smog is a whole different trip, however. On a bad day—of which there are literally hundreds—the effect of the air is fright-

The impact of that day really "blew my mind." It was the first time that I perceived the *insanity* of an entire city of several million people living in a *gas chamber!*

But it wasn't just the physical discomfort of the Los Angeles smog that led to my profound change of mind; it was the smog in conjunction with the total Los Angeles environment that did it. It was the vast scale of the city and county that imploded on one's consciousness and created a sense of catastrophe. Finding one's self surrounded by ticky-tacky houses, metallic apartment towers, sprawling shopping centers checkered with a fantastic assortment of Taco Bells, Jack-in-the-Boxes and other instant eateries, all banded by eight-lane, traffic-choked freeways and immersed in a noxious soup of cream-colored air would have been unpleasant yet potentially tolerable if there were some form of relief close at hand. But when one realized that he could drive literally for hours in any direction without being able to escape the relentlessly redundant pattern of corruption, the effect was utterly and abysmally depressing. In New York it was different. No matter how blighted the central city may have seemed, one was assuaged by the knowledge that "the country" was not far away and therefore that the possibility of escape was always present. Within a half-hour's or hour's ride from midtown Manhattan one can be in a wholly different environment. Even for those who cannot readily escape, this provides a sense of hope. But the unrelenting "slurb" of Los Angeles condemns one to a growing sense of claustrophobia and ultimately of despair.

Yet the most frightening and even shocking aspect of my experience of Los Angeles was the realization that this city represented not the worst of America but ostensibly the best. After all, Los Angeles had, for most of my life at least, been touted as a kind of Mecca of the American Dream, the unofficial capital of the Golden West. Southern California (and Florida) was the land of sunshine, milk, and honey to which most Americans wanted to move. Hollywood, Beverly Hills, Malibu, and in its own special way, Disneyland: these were names that conjured up visions of the Good Life in the minds of most Americans. The rate of in-migration to this part of the country throughout the 1950s and 60s was legend. When the population of California finally surpassed that of New York State, California's victory in the demographic sweepstakes was almost ubiquitously viewed as a cause for celebration. But in the seventies, all this began to change, and thousands of Californians left the Golden State for greener lands, many of them not just to save their sanity but to protect what remained of their physical health. These expatriates from the promised land were, however, only the vanguard of a larger movement that has come to pervade every corner of America and eventually spread its influence throughout the world, a movement whose birthday will almost invariably be identified as 22 April 1970 —Earth Day.

The important thing to understand about Earth Day is that it was *not* the celebration of the birth or maturation of the environmental movement in the United States, in the sense that the first Fourth of July was the celebration of the birth of a nation. It wasn't the environmental movement that created Earth Day, but vice versa. The old conservation movement had historical roots that went back more than a hundred years. The groups and organizations that would be identified with the environmental movement after Earth Day—the Sierra Club, Friends of the Earth, ZPG, and so forth—all existed before it. Yet there was no environmental movement in the United States before Earth Day or even *on* Earth Day. It was only *after* Earth Day that the movement began.

The environmental movement is a phenomenon almost unique to the twentieth century, a cybernetic spectre that was born as an "idea," composed almost entirely of "bits" of "information," and which only subsequently acquired substance. A Harvard law student who was one of the group in Washington that orchestrated the first national celebration of Earth Day, told me later that the environmental movement was a sham, that the whole thing had been "created by the media." So I discovered that the environmental movement, like the National Football League, had literally been created by television. At first this was disillusioning, but I later came to realize that the environmental movement was not only *not* less "real" for being a child of the mass media, but that, on the contrary, the movement was endowed thereby with the most powerful kind of "reality" an entity can enjoy in this cybernetic age. From an

movement rather than being merely another member of a disaffected crowd.

A turning point as significant in the intellectual dimension for me as my first experience of bad smog had been in the physical and emotional dimensions occurred on a day in early April when I was browsing through a books-and-records store in Westwood and spontaneously decided to buy a new book called *The Environmental Handbook.*[1] I took it home and read it in one night. Just as in the old cliché, I felt as if the scales had fallen from my eyes. Up till then, I had felt that the world was screwed up, that something had to be done. But suddenly I could see more clearly just how screwed up the world really was. I could begin to perceive more accurately the kinds of things that needed doing. The ecological crisis was far more than just "dirty" air, "dirty" water, and mounting piles of garbage. It was pesticides, automobiles, the SST, rats, roaches, gypsy moths, nuclear power plants, oil spills, contraception, abortion, aluminum cans, plastic, diethylstybestrol, polychlorinated biphenyls, the Bomb, air-conditioners, skyscrapers, subways, freeways, fertilizers, dams, strip mines, male chauvinism, racism, heroin, advertising, commercial TV, the War. It was all of these things and yet more than their sum. It was a total, global system, a system that was mindlessly chewing up the Earth, her resources, and her inhabitants and spitting them out as growing gobs of "entropy."

If the cure for this pathological system was not yet evident, it was clear even then that the system could not be amended by mere cosmetic patchwork. No, the system that created the ecological crisis could not be reformed. If there were to be any real hope for planetary survival, it would have to be totally dismantled and replaced with an effective operating system for Spaceship Earth. The radical implications of "environmentalism" were largely obscured at its inception by the euphoria of Earth Day. The inchoate movement was protected in its infancy by rosy clouds of euphemism. The clouds lasted less than two years, but as they dissolved, they precipitated the movement which had begun as an idea.

Earth Day, 22 April 1970, was a typically sunny day in Los Angeles. I spent the afternoon on the campus of UCLA, manning a table and handing out literature for one of the student environmental organizations. But mostly I just observed and took part in the general activity. The walk in front of Ackerman Union was lined with the tables of various organizations, each with its own assortment of buttons, balloons, posters, bumper stickers, leaflets, and books. Some blamed the ecological crisis on the "capitalist pigs" and advocated a socialist revolution to protect the Earth. Others took the opposite view, blaming pollution on government interference with the free market and asserting that a strict return to laissez-faire and private ownership of all resources was the required solution. While one group was promoting free abortion, another was attacking all forms of birth control as "genocide." Beneath the superficial solidarity that would come to characterize that first Earth Day—the sense of unanimous determination to halt the scourge of the Earth—one could already detect the beginning of the inevitable choosing up of sides. Still, the carnival atmosphere was dominant; it was exhilarating and inspiring. The sense of a "movement" was inescapable.

I walked over to the wide lawn on the other side of the ROTC building where blue-helmeted phalanxes of Los Angeles police would soon sweep back and forth in pursuit of a vast crowd outraged by the Nixon invasion of Cambodia. But the scene this day gave no augur of the coming storm of protest. The crowd of several hundred sat quietly on the grass, eating sandwiches and hot dogs under an arcing string of black balloons while speaker after speaker went to the microphone to describe yet another parameter of the ecological apocalypse and to make yet another impassioned plea for action to save the planet. As I got there, a Hopi medicine man was performing incantations to the Great Spirit, after which a fellow Indian congratulated us whites for having finally begun to understand what his people had always known.

I got home that evening in time to catch the news on TV.

The avuncular face of Walter Cronkite came on the screen. Over his shoulder was a picture of the Earth with an enormous hand reaching out to grasp it, both overlaid with a giant question mark: "Can The World Be Saved?" Thus did "environment" suddenly become a household word. Thus was an entire movement electronically synthesized. Thus was the ecological crisis certified as "real."

1

ECOCRISIS

into four general categories, what Richard Falk calls the "four dimensions of planetary danger"[1]:

1. environmental decay
2. population
3. resources/development
4. war/violence

The decay in the quality of our environment is manifested in many ways.[2] At the lowest level is simply the loss of "amenity"—that is, what is defined as "the quality of being pleasant or agreeable."[3] People simply find their surroundings more and more unpleasant and disagreeable. "Dirty" air and water, urban blight, litter, noise, crowding, and so on all contribute to the general loss of amenity in the human environment. Beyond these annoyances there are a host of effects of environmental decay that degrade human health. Air pollution, water pollution, various kinds of unsafe working or living conditions, and other environmental hazards can lead to cancer, heart disease, lung disease, damage or degeneration of other parts of the body, injury, and infectious disease, often of epidemic proportions.

Perhaps an even graver and more insidious threat to human survival than the effects of environmental decay on individual health is that posed by genetic and reproductive effects. Anything which threatens a species' capacity to reproduce or which "pollutes" its genetic pool presents the most serious kind of hazard to the species' prospects for surviving. This might seem like a spurious concern in light of the existence of a human "population explosion," but as Sterling Brubaker observes: "if we are to limit reproduction we would prefer to do it deliberately rather than have it occur as the by-product of chemicals employed for other purposes. And if we are to toy with human genes, at least we should not do so in the spirit of Russian roulette."[4] Can the recent "birth dearth" in the United States be attributed not only to an increased sense of responsibility, women's liberation, or a sluggish economy, but perhaps also to chemicals in the environment, poisons in food, radioactive fallout, and/or medical x-rays to which the postwar generation has been exposed? This may seem a bit farfetched, but the truth is, we really don't know nor are we likely to find out until it is too late to do much about it. Yet the real threat of these genetic/reproductive effects is not so much that they are likely to extinguish the human race, but more that they are now establishing the constraining influences under which the evolution of the human species will proceed. The dismal prospect arises of a new species of "homo" which can no longer be considered "superior," resulting, as René Dubos warns, "in a form of life that will retain little of true humanness."[5]

Ultimately the most apocalyptic implications of man's degradation of his environment arise from the numerous impacts of human activities on the delicate fabric of the global ecosystem. These who predict an "eco-catastrophe" of global proportions have often been disparaged as "prophets of doom." Unfortunately the evidence mounts daily that the pessimists may be right.

Photosynthesis is now being threatened by sunlight-reducing air pollution and the proliferation in the environment of DDT and similar chemicals. There is the danger of drastic modification of the climate by the increase in atmospheric dust or carbon dioxide from various sources of air pollution. Many plant and animal species are being eradicated through the destruction of their habitats or overexploitation by man. Soil is being destroyed in wholesale quantities through overcultivation, overgrazing, and a general failure to protect it against erosion. Such environmental degradations create the peril of an ecocatastrophe not only individually but in combination. Each one may, in fact, contribute to the others.

The question ultimately arises: To what extent is the threat of an ecocatastrophe only *potential,* and to what extent is it *real?* Barry Commoner's judgment, which is hardly radical and probably falls somewhere on the optimistic side of the middle of the road of scientific opinion, is that "the present course of environmental degradation, at least in industrialized countries, represents a challenge to essential ecological systems that is so serious that, if continued, it will destroy the capability of the environment to support a reasonably civilized human society."[6]

A variety of problems associated with the size, growth, distribution, composition, and other characteristics of human population constitute the second major dimension of ecocrisis. The report of the

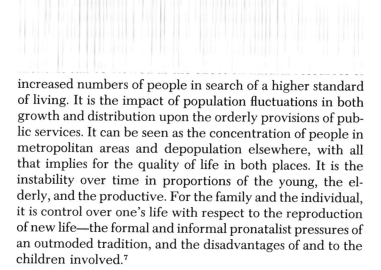

increased numbers of people in search of a higher standard of living. It is the impact of population fluctuations in both growth and distribution upon the orderly provisions of public services. It can be seen as the concentration of people in metropolitan areas and depopulation elsewhere, with all that implies for the quality of life in both places. It is the instability over time in proportions of the young, the elderly, and the productive. For the family and the individual, it is control over one's life with respect to the reproduction of new life—the formal and informal pronatalist pressures of an outmoded tradition, and the disadvantages of and to the children involved.[7]

The commission is speaking mainly of the situation in the United States, but its various interpretations of the meaning of "population problem" are pertinent to the rest of the world as well. Generally these different interpretations arise from changing the emphasis from one set, or combination, of demographic factors to another.

There is no "problem" inherent in population size, per se. The problems of population size are all comparative. They must be assessed in comparison with the availability of some "resource" or set of resources which are presumed crucial, or at least relevant, to survival, welfare, or development. The "resource" might be physical space, food, water, renewable or nonrenewable "natural" resources, energy, housing, industrial capital, "goods and services," scenery, information, "social welfare capital," or just about anything else.

The current rate of world population growth is about 2 percent per year, which implies, among other things, an approximate doubling of human population from its current figure of around 4 billion to over 7 billion by the end of this century. This growth of human numbers has come to be popularly labeled the "population explosion" or "population bomb." How apt is the metaphor?

To the physicist, an "explosion" is essentially a very rapid increase in *pressure.* The pressure of population size cannot be attributed to the size of population alone. It follows that the kind of rapid increase in population "pressure" that could appropriately be called an explosion could result not only from the rate of growth of population *size,* but additionally from the rates of change of the per capita *demand* for and general *availability* of some critical resource or resources. The pressure of population against its life-supporting environment increases not only with the size of the population, but also with the growth of demand for critical resources and/or the limitation or decline of the availability of such resources. In general, considering that two-thirds of the existing world population is impoverished and enjoys only a minor fraction of the total availability of critical resources, that furthermore, it is among the poorer sector of the total population where the rates of growth of both population size and per capita demand for resources of all kinds is the greatest, and that the aggregate availability of many critical resources has either leveled off or is already declining, it isn't hard to see why the resulting growth in population pressure is indeed rapid enough to be termed "explosive."

As the statement of the Population Commission above suggests, there are a number of additional problems associated with human population other than size and growth. Fertility and mortality are not only central to the problem of population growth, they are intertwined with several other relevant issues and problems, for example, contraception, abortion, women's liberation, the role of children and the family in society, nutrition, health, public safety, and warfare. Some of the most pressing population problems have to do with migration and distribution. Specifically, what might be called the "urban crisis" around the world—the rapidly growing concentration of population in sprawling urban centers—is a clear-cut problem of migration and distribution of population which is intimately related to the distribution of goods and services, to the psychological and social quality of the human environment, and to the impact of human settlements on the ecosystems to which they belong. Fluctuations in mortality and fertility conditions over time can produce bulges and pinches in the age structure of the population (the distribution of numbers of people over the various ages) which can have all sorts of social, political, and economic consequences. For example, there can be changes in the ratio of dependent to productive members of society, or in the relative demand for various social services by particular age groups such as children or the elderly. Some of the most complex, and in some ways ominous, population problems involve

third major dimension of the ecocrisis. It was Thomas Malthus who originally stated the dismal theory that population will grow until the scarcity of critical resources (Malthus was chiefly concerned with the limits of arable land) brought it to a halt, chiefly through the mechanism of "misery" (disease, starvation, and so on). David Ricardo modified Malthus' theory somewhat by observing that the effects of scarcity would set in, not just when the resource (for example, land) was "all gone," but would increase continuously as the *quality* of the remaining stocks of the resource progressively declined.

Food is probably the most critical resource associated with population growth. It was the limitation of agricultural productivity that prompted Malthus' apocalyptic predictions in the nineteenth century, and it was the unprecedented amplification of agricultural output by modern technology which led many to mistakenly discount the essential validity of Malthus' theory.

While agricultural productivity has increased enormously in recent years, on the whole, there seems to be little cause for optimism about the future. The record growth of agricultural production during 1965–1970 in certain less-developed areas where high-yield strains of rice and wheat and modern methods of cultivation were introduced for the first time, sparked talk of a "green revolution" that promised to save the world from famine. But the promise of the green revolution has turned out to be a cruel disappointment to those who failed to understand the economic and ecological implications of high-yield agriculture. Economically, the green *revolution* is a misnomer because it has largely failed to solve the problems of hunger and poverty in those regions where these problems are most severe. The big landowners who can afford the new technology prosper and drive the small farmers from the land. The fact is, mechanized agriculture is antithetical to the kind of revolution that is desired and needed in many less-developed countries, i.e., redistribution of land. Meanwhile, the influx of labor-saving technology into the Third World increases unemployment and thus reduces income and the ability to buy food which the displaced farmers can no longer grow for themselves. Ecologically, the green revolution could lead to catastrophe. High-yield grains are dependent for their success on artificial fertilizers, pesticides, and often extensive irrigation. Some of the perils of this kind of agriculture are dependency on nonrenewable and increasingly scarce chemical and energy resources, destruction of the natural fertility of the soil, pollution of water resources, extinction of pest-controlling predators, and the generation of poison-resistant strains of pests.

There is little question now that there is an absolute limit of food productivity for the Earth. Making some fairly optimistic assumptions, Sterling Hendricks has estimated that agricultural productivity might be theoretically increased as much as eight times. But he concludes: "While the total factor of eight is possible for the United States, it would impose severe demands on the rational use of water. Other nations will have to struggle to obtain even a twofold increase, being limited by fertilizer supply in inadequate economies."[8] As for the belief that the seas will feed the world's burgeoning multitudes for generations to come, nothing could be farther from the truth. According to John Ryther, if fish yields continue to increase at their current rate, the absolute maximum will be reached in about another decade. In a world where protein deficiency is epidemic, the available amount of fish protein per capita can be expected to *decrease* by 3 percent by the end of the century.[9] And this, of course, does not take into account the rapidly growing destruction of ocean life by various forms of pollution or the depletion of existing fisheries through mismanagement and overexploitation.

Modern technology has not obviated the Malthusian nightmare; it has merely postponed it. Hunger is a very real problem generated by the unrestrained growth of human population. In the absence of alternative actions, starvation and its cognate suffering, disease, and death threaten to be nature's solution to the population explosion.

But food is only one resource which places an obligative ceiling on human population growth. To survive as a species, man requires more than just food. To survive as a civilized and intelligent being, man demands resources far greater than the mere means of subsistence. Natural and other resources are an unyielding noose around mankind's neck that grows ever tighter as human numbers increase.

For example, while the supply of water is great, it is still limited, and abuse of this precious resource could spell disaster. Per capita daily water consumption ranges from 12 liters in many less-developed countries to 150 liters for the average Londoner and 250

metals and other minerals required by industrial society are being rapidly depleted; the sources of some will vanish by the end of this century. "Few of the developed countries have adequate internal sources of the principal minerals needed to meet current demands; and none have reserves of marginal grade adequate for the next century under current technology and without recycling."[11] No amount of technological wizardry or economic juggling will be able to compensate for the loss of these vital raw materials.

But it is the limitation of energy resources, of which the world has recently become so painfully aware, that constitutes one of the most stringent restrictions on continued industrial and/or population growth. Water power could ultimately provide as much energy as fossil fuels do now. But dams are merely temporary structures which are rendered useless by sedimentation after about a hundred years. Wind and geothermal heat could become important energy sources in some favorable geographical locations. The thermal gradient of the oceans represents a potentially vast source of energy if it could be harnessed efficiently. Solar energy seems to be the cleanest and most reliable energy source for the long run, but current technology for exploiting it is crude, at best. And the ultimate reliance on the sun as the prime source of energy would almost certainly require radical transformations in the nature of human settlements and economic activities.

For the immediate future, man will probably continue to depend on mineral fuels for most of his power. Were the rate of growth in consumption which existed until the Arab oil embargo of 1973 to continue in the future, by the end of this century 80 percent of the world's supply of petroleum would be used up, and in another 20 years almost all reserves would be exhausted. Oil shales and tar sands, if economically exploitable and if deemed worth the environmental "cost," might extend petroleum resources up to a century. Coal supplies are more abundant and could last another 200 to 500 years, depending on the rate of consumption. But coal and oil are not merely energy resources, they are also vital sources of chemicals.

Nuclear energy is a power source that promises to equal in magnitude all other energy sources combined. That promise is dependent, however, on the perfection of the "breeder" reactor—a technological problem that has frustrated some of the world's best minds for over 20 years—which through the idiosyncrasies of nuclear physics produces more nuclear "fuel" than it consumes. The ordinary atomic reactors of today are using up uranium-235 so rapidly that the reserves of high-grade uranium ore will be gone in 15 to 20 years. And the extraordinary hazards of nuclear reactors to safety, political stability, and a healthy environment are such that their proliferation is certain to be more of a catastrophe than a boon.

Hope for an abundant supply of cheap energy for the future seems to lie in the development of a feasible nuclear fusion reactor which would "burn" the virtually unlimited supply of "heavy hydrogen" available in the world's oceans. It seems doubtful, however, that such a device will be generally available anytime within the next 30 years. In any event, fusion power will not solve many of the ecological problems associated with man's use and abuse of energy.

Ultimately, the fact that the Earth is a sphere places a limit on the possibilities for continued growth, even under the most hyperbolic assumptions about the availability of resources other than sheer physical space. If the current rate of population growth were to continue indefinitely, a condition of "standing room only" over the entire surface of the earth would be reached in only 677 years, and even if all the matter in the planet could be converted into human beings, the Earth would become a writhing ball of Homo sapiens within 1,577 years.[12]

This rather cursory look at the conditions of a few critical resources out of the many that are required for human existence reveals a rather bleak picture. Not only do we find little reason for optimism about further economic "development" worldwide, but there seems to be in the current trend of rapid depletion of the earth's resources considerable cause for doubt about maintaining existing levels of human welfare—and even a real threat to mankind's chances for survival.

Were people perfectly rational and fully aware of the numerous threats to their well-being and survival which we have reviewed so far, one would expect a massive trend to "get themselves together" to meet the challenge that confronts them. Instead we find ourselves in a world that is not only violent and divided but which seems to be drifting toward ever more pervasive violence and irreconcilable division. On the whole, the planet finds itself in the grip of what Falk

that the tangible outbursts of what we conventionally recognize as violent behavior are only the tip of the iceberg.

The threats to human survival, welfare, and development posed by the overt violence of the war system are fairly easy to identify. Uppermost in our minds, of course, is the threat of nuclear war. In the 1950s and 60s that threat seemed real, especially at the time of the Cuban missile crisis. While the spectre was raised again briefly during the Mideast war of 1973, for the most part we are more and more coming to feel, as T. S. Eliot put it, that the world will end "not with a bang but a whimper." Now that a whole generation has gone from birth to adulthood living in the shadow of the Bomb, the threat of nuclear war seems less significant, especially in light of our growing awareness of the other dimensions of ecocrisis that imperil us. Yet it may well be that this very complacency and apathy is increasing the threat of a nuclear holocaust. The proliferation of nuclear power plants is creating vast, accessible quantities of weapons-grade uranium and plutonium which "crazy" governments or terrorists or criminal organizations will eventually try to exploit.

Should a total nuclear holocaust occur, it would almost certainly spell the end of human civilization as we know it and quite possibly the extinction of the human race altogether. Indeed, there is some question whether life in any form would be able to survive in the radioactive aftermath. But even "conventional" warfare has been technologically amplified to disastrous levels of destruction, as Vietnam so horribly attests. The explosive power of the aerial bombardment of North Vietnam unleashed by President Nixon during the unprecedented American offensive of Christmas 1972 exceeded that of the two nuclear devices dropped on Hiroshima and Nagasaki combined.

Vietnam, in addition to being a political, social, economic and moral tragedy, has, to an extent far greater than that of any war which preceded it, been an ecological disaster. Not only have millions been killed, maimed, and uprooted from family, friends, and homes, but the entire ecosystem of Indochina, which was once one of the richest and most fertile, has been ravaged, plundered, and destroyed with a thoroughness unprecedented in human history. To a large extent, it has been turned into a wasteland, all in the name of a political abstraction called the "domino theory."

Conventional warfare is, of course, only part of the overt violence that plagues the world. Guerilla warfare, political terrorism, torture and riots are rampant throughout much of the world. Violent crime—murder, rape, assault, and kidnapping—is on the rise in the United States and elsewhere. All of these forms of violence are the kind that capture people's attention. They are the subject of headlines and television coverage. But the dazzle of this kind of violence tends to blind people to the great dark mass of *structural* violence that pervades human society.

The forms of structural violence are myriad. Some are almost as tangible as the kinds of overt violence noted above. Fifty-five thousand Americans are killed every year by the automobile. We free the automobile industry from responsibility for this profit-motivated violence against the public by calling these "accidents." Thousands more are killed or maimed in industrial "accidents" that could be prevented by an adequate investment in job safety. Many other working men and women have their lives degraded and cut short by "occupational diseases" such as miners' black lung or asbestos workers' mesothelioma, which arise from hazardous working conditions that could be ameliorated were it not considered "unprofitable" by management.

But much structural violence is more subtle and more nearly invisible. Schools, prisons, welfare systems, and mental hospitals are a few of the ostensibly "service" institutions in our society that patronizingly do violence to the very people they are supposed to help. "Urban renewal" was a benevolent-sounding euphemism for what turned out to be a violent assault on established human communities and the poor for the profit of the real estate and construction industries and the benefit of the middle and upper classes. A policy of "benign neglect" is an instrument of callow violence in a country afflicted with the festering sores of racism, discrimination, and general inequality. The violence of the war system is manifest not merely when it makes war, for even in "peacetime" a $100-plus billion "defense" budget constitutes a malicious act of violence, through an unconscionable waste of resources, against some 25 million *hungry* Americans plus another billion or so *starving* fellow passengers on this Spaceship Earth. Repressive antiabortion statutes do violence to the bodies and minds of thousands of women, especially the poor.

of people in the world today are to a large extent openly or subtly violent. We are literally tearing each other apart at a time when all our hopes for the future depend on our capacity to come together. This is the meaning of the war system. It is the last—and perhaps most tragic—of the four dimensions of ecocrisis.

CHAPTER 2

THE ROOTS OF CRISIS

dimensions of planetary danger. But why is it that these dimensions define, as a whole, a *crisis* rather than simply a large set of discrete problems? For there is no doubt that we are now in a state of global crisis whose gravity is unmatched in human history, and that the seriousness of the threat posed by the whole is perceptibly greater than that of any of its parts.

Why, then, does this state of crisis exist? I think the answer is to be found in several key attributes of our global social/ecological system—that is, the comprehensive world system comprised of all of the myriad and complex relationships between individual, society, and environment. These attributes characterize a system which is afflicted with inherent *instability* and which is fated to generate the very kind of critical situation in which we now find ourselves.[1]

First, most material and demographic aspects of the global system are growing at a rate unprecedented in history. Until very recently in man's tenure on Earth, his population and economic activities grew globally at rates that caused them to double over periods of 1,000 to 2,000 years or more. Now population is increasing at a rate that will cause it to double within about 30 years, and the rate of global population growth itself is increasing. Resource consumption and the release of pollutants are both growing at rates that will cause them to double within the next 10 to 20 years.

Second, there are many inescapable physical limits to material growth. The capacity of the environment to absorb material or thermal emissions, the ability of the land to produce food, and the ability of the Earth to yield economically useful deposits of nonrenewable resources are all finite. Technology cannot eliminate these limits. It can only permit society to use the resources of the Earth somewhat more efficiently. These and other limits indicate that material and demographic growth will ultimately cease. It now seems likely that the transformation from growth to some kind of equilibrium will be substantially completed within the lifetime of people now living.

The third attribute has been aptly expressed by Barry Commoner: "Everything is connected to everything else."[2] No important part of the global system is completely disconnected from the others. For example, the future U.S. energy policy will influence the amount of dollars available to Mideast countries for the pursuit of their own political objectives. The policy will alter the price of oil imported to India. It will also affect the global climate, the U.S. environment, and the relative affluence and political power of several major American industries. The energy problem is not a technical problem alone; it involves aspects of the world normally sequestered within the disciplines of political science, economics, geology, business administration, regional planning, and other fields. Similarly, the solution of problems in transportation, food production, environmental protection, and housing will affect many other aspects of global society.

The fourth attribute of the global system is the long time delay inherent in cause-and-effect relationships, whether they are physical, biological, social, political, economic, or other. For example, even with U.S. birth rates at replacement levels, the population of the United States will grow for 70 years because of the momentum inherent in the age distribution of the population. Even after we begin to decrease the rate of DDT usage, the level of DDT in the marine environment will continue to rise for 20 years or more. There will still be DDT present in marine fish in significant amounts well beyond the year 2020. Having now perceived the crisis engendered by the impending depletion of its domestic fossil fuel deposits, it may take the United States five years to determine its long-term goals for energy use, 10 years more to develop the appropriate technology, and 10 to 20 years more, at a minimum, to implement those new technical capabilities so that they begin to have a significant effect on the production and consumption of energy. Social relationships may involve the greatest delays of all. For example, the U.S. has been working for more than a hundred years to eliminate racial discrimination, and the job has not yet been accomplished.

The fifth attribute is that many changes introduced into the global system tend to be irreversible. Once depleted, nonrenewable resources are, by definition, impossible to reclaim. Many kinds of radioactive and chemical contamination of the biosphere will take 10 times longer to decay than the entire span of prior human history. Once the oceans and many lakes become polluted with oil, mercury, and the like, they will remain so virtually forever. The Romans transformed the Sahara from a vast forest into a permanent desert; the Brazilians could easily do the same to the Amazon. A species of plant or animal, once extinguished, can never be restored. Once a popula-

the Middle East—it may be nearly impossible to stop short of the total destruction of one or both of the parties involved.

The sixth attribute of the global system is the prevalence—at all levels, from interpersonal to international—of "unpeaceful" relationships which ultimately lead to a process which we can call the "drive-to-breakdown." Adam Curle defines unpeaceful relationships as those that "do damage to one or more of the parties concerned, through physical violence, or in economic, social, or psychological ways."[3] According to this definition, the absence of peace may characterize many situations where overt conflict is not present. "Unpeacefulness is a situation in which human beings are impeded from achieving full development either because of their own internal relations or because of the types of relations that exist between themselves (as individuals or group members) and other persons or groups."[4] The self-relationship of an individual who lacks "peace of mind"; an unharmonious marriage that constrains the growth capacity of either or both partners; the relationships between colonizer and colonized, between privileged and underprivileged, between the "have" and "have-not" nations—these are all examples of unpeaceful relations. "War is such a relationship: it epitomizes all the evils of unpeacefulness."[5]

The ultimate result of such unpeaceful relationships is the phenomenon which Gregory Bateson observed in his anthropological studies of the society of a South Pacific island: the drive toward a breakdown in a society or a relationship, the breakdown being marked by a more or less violent, and in some sense, "orgasmic," release of tension. Bateson further identified two different characteristic paths of this drive-to-breakdown.[6] We can call these *escalation* and *submission*. In the drive-to-breakdown of escalation, a situational conflict leads A to provoke B in some way intended to resolve the conflict in A's favor. But B responds in kind and may even further provoke A. A then reciprocates, and the result is the kind of escalation characteristic of poker games, gang wars, and armaments races. On the other hand, in the submission kind of drive-to-breakdown, A's provocation is greeted by a gesture of submission or appeasement on the part of B. This, in turn, only serves to reinforce A's temerity, and A increases his provocation or aggression, only to find that B, even more intimidated, is more submissive or appeasing. Clearly, in either case, such relations must inevitably lead to an ultimate "breaking point" without the intervention of some stabilizing influence.

The seventh, and final, attribute of the existing world system is the nearly total inability of our existing social, political, and economic institutions to comprehend (and hence, to cope with) the dynamic behavior of complex systems, that is, the very kind of system which the previous six attributes describe.

These seven attributes constitute the roots from which a global, ecological crisis must stem. Instability, and therefore crisis, are simply their logical consequence. Any system will be unstable if it grows rapidly, has limits, is highly interrelated, incorporates long delays, is subject to irreversible changes, contains breakdown-inducing relationships, and is governed by institutions which are predominantly blind and hence unresponsive to these conditions. All of man's social, technological, economic, and political institutions are thus inherently unstable; that is, they have a tendency to overshoot their long-term goals. There are many illustrations of this. It is clear that the global population has already overshot the levels that would permit satisfaction of the goals of health, education, and economic opportunity for all. The Commission on Population Growth and the American Future could find no economic or social advantage in an increased population. Consider, then, by how much the populations of less industrialized areas have grown past their most desirable levels. In Europe, Japan, and the United States today, it is clear that the energy system has also overshot the current limits to its ability to produce inexpensive and environmentally acceptable energy.

Clearly it is the blindness and unresponsiveness of our prevailing institutions to various other unstabilizing attributes of our global system that form the chief obstacle to our resolving the ecocrisis in some hopeful way. It is also this fact that marks the roots of the crisis as being essentially *epistemological*—that is, deriving from the way we perceive, act upon, and learn from our environment; in other words, our manner of modeling "reality." It is Bateson who, to my knowledge, has most elaborately and perceptively posited this view that the ecological crisis is essentially an epistemological crisis:

> There is an ecology of bad ideas, just as there is an ecology
>
> eco-mental system called Lake Erie is a part of your wider eco-mental system—and that if Lake Erie is driven insane, its insanity is incorporated in the larger system of *your* thought and experience.
> . . . . .
>
> It is clear now to many people that there are many catastrophic dangers which have grown out of the Occidental errors of epistemology. These range from insecticides to pollution, to atomic fallout, to the possibility of melting the Antarctic ice cap. Above all, our fantastic compulsion to save individual lives has created the possibility of world famine in the immediate future.
>
> *Perhaps* we have an even chance of getting through the next twenty years with no disaster more serious than the mere destruction of a nation or group of nations.
>
> *I believe that this massive aggregation of threats to man and his ecological systems arises out of errors in our habits of thought at deep and partly unconscious levels.*[7]

Bateson's work will be of central importance throughout this book. But it should be emphasized at the outset that it has become more or less clear to "many people," and not just Bateson or myself, that ecocrisis is most properly viewed as an epistemological problem. This view is apparent from the perspective of many different disciplines and professions.

Biologist Paul Shepard writes:

The conventional image of man, like that of the heraldic lion, is iconographic; its outlines are stylized to fit the fixed curves of our vision. We are hidden from ourselves by habits of perception.

. . . . .

If nature is not a prison and earth a shoddy way-station, we must find the faith and force to affirm its metabolism as our own—or rather, our own as part of it. *To do so means nothing less than a shift in our whole frame of reference and our attitude towards life itself,* a wider perception of the landscape as a creative being where *relationships of things are as real as the things.*[8]

Architect and urban planner, Ian McHarg also emphasizes the importance of mental processes in ecological decay:

The western attitudes to nature and to man in nature have changed. But for all of modern science it is still pre-Copernican man whom we confront. He retains the same implicit view of exclusive divinity, man apart from nature, dominant, exhorted to subdue the earth—be he Jew, Christian, or agnostic.

For me the indictment of city, suburb, and country-side becomes comprehensible in terms of the attitudes to nature that society has and does espouse. These environmental degradations are the inevitable consequences of such views.[9]

Historian and philosopher Lewis Mumford puts it succinctly: "Nothing less than a profound re-orientation of our vaunted technological 'way of life' will save this planet from becoming a lifeless desert."[10] This same recognition is central to educator Ivan Illich's famous (or infamous) thesis on the need to "deschool" society: "The exhaustion and pollution of the earth's resources is, above all, the result of a corruption of man's self-image, of a regression in his consciousness."[11] John D. Lilly, physician and mental explorer, offers this prescription for ecocrisis: "It is my firm belief that the experience of higher states of consciousness is necessary for survival of the human species."[12] Richard Falk, Professor of International Law and Practice at Princeton, writes: *"It is not possible to reestablish the conditions for human survival without transforming, at the same time, some very basic human attitudes towards life and nature.* At present, we contaminate the world by our morality as well as by engine fumes."[13]

Also, the systems scientists who wrote *The Limits to Growth* included this comment in their conclusion:

We affirm finally that any deliberate attempt to reach a rational and enduring state of equilibrium by planned measures, rather than by chance or catastrophe, *must ulti-*

3

HARDWORLD AND

There are two fundamentally different, thought not necessarily mutually exclusive, perspectives on the nature of ecocrisis. Gregory Bateson has called them the "pleroma" and the "creatura," borrowing the terms from the work of Carl Jung. Jung once wrote a short book entitled *Septem Sermones ad Mortuos* (Seven Sermons to the Dead) during a "psychotic" period of his life when, as Bateson puts it, "Jung was going through an epistemological crisis." Bateson says that Jung

> points out that there are two worlds. We might call them two worlds of explanation. He names them the *pleroma* and the *creatura*, these being Gnostic terms. The pleroma is the world in which events are caused by forces and impacts and in which there are no "distinctions." Or, as I would say, no "differences." In the creatura, effects are brought about precisely by difference. In fact, this is the same old dichotomy between mind and substance.
>
> We can study and describe the pleroma, but always the distinctions we draw are attributed *by us* to the pleroma. The pleroma knows nothing of differences and distinction; it contains no "ideas" in the sense in which I am using the word. When we study and describe the creatura, we must correctly identify those differences which are effective within it.[1]

At a superficial level the distinction made by Bateson between the pleroma and the creatura seems similar to the dichotomy between ontology and epistemology (for example, between *being* and *knowing*). But in fact the pleroma and the creatura are both epistemological concepts; they are "two worlds of explanation" (that is, they are both "ways of knowing").

This basic concept of two different "worlds of explanation" is of considerable importance to the basic thesis of this book. But the terms *pleroma* and *creatura* are so alien that I feel compelled to replace them with terms that at least sound more familiar or conventional. In the field of computer technology, the terms *hardware* and *software* are commonly used to distinguish between the physical equipment of the computer, on one hand, and the programs and data files which guide and are the subject of the computer's operation, on the other hand. This distinction is analogous to that of Jung and Bateson. Therefore, following the example of the computer jargon, I would like to coin the terms *hardworld* and *softworld* to replace *pleroma* and *creatura,* respectively, as the labels for the "two worlds of explanation" identified by Jung and Bateson.

The hardworld description of *reality,* then, is essentially that of classical physics—although it is not necessarily confined only to the "physical," or "natural," sciences—which is basically a clockwork sort of model based on "causes and effects," or "forces and impacts." On the other hand, softworld explanation is fundamentally more like that of contemporary general systems theory, whose basis is one of "relationship" and "information," or simply "difference."

The hardworld vision of ecocrisis focuses on the tangible effects of ecological illness and seeks to discover immediate causes for those effects, obviously with an eye to curing them. The softworld approach, though, treats ecocrisis as an overall malfunction of a complex cybernetic system. It endeavors to determine the relationships between the various parts of the system and the content and structure of the information which ultimately governs its dynamic behavior. The "therapeutic" goal, in the latter case, is not to attack each of the diverse symptoms of illness but, rather, to eliminate the malfunction by restructuring the total system that generates it.

The basic thesis of this book, then, is that of these two fundamentally different perspectives on the global system—the hardworld and the softworld—it is the former which is prevalent and which accounts for the inability of our existing institutions and society in general to comprehend or cope effectively with the essential roots of ecocrisis. It is the dominance of the hardworld perspective that

makes most of our current efforts to deal with the diverse problems
of ecocrisis either unproductive or counterproductive. It is my belief
that the widespread adoption of a more softworld perspective on the
world system will be necessary if we are to meet the challenges posed
by ecocrisis successfully. Therefore the balance of this book is devoted to defining, elaborating, and promoting this other perspective.
But first it will be useful to review in greater detail some of the

First, our prevailing institutions are almost totally blind to the
extreme connectedness of today's global system. Our contemporary
leaders exhibit little or no understanding of the structure and dynamics of such complex systems. On one hand, they sometimes see connections that do not exist, as in the case of Vietnam and the "domino
theory" of southeast Asia. On the other hand, they generally fail to
see crucial connections that do exist, such as the connection between
Arabian oil and the entire American life-style; the interconnectedness of Peruvian anchovies, the Japanese diet, and America's international trade relations and domestic cost of living; the connection
between mercury dumped in lakes and rivers and mercury contamination of seafood; between the wholesale use of DDT in agriculture
and the disappearance of many species of birds.

Second, there is the prevalent tendency of our current leadership to define problems narrowly, both in time and in space. Virtually
all of our economic and political actions are based on an assessment
of only near-term consequences. Those in politics care little for the
benefits or costs of their actions, which will become apparent after
the next election. Industrialists use a high rate of interest to determine the present monetary equivalent of the future costs and benefits of current alternatives. With the interest rates commonly used
—10 to 15 percent—no consequence of an act move than five or ten
years in the future is of any economic interest to industrialists today.
Even individuals are shortsighted. All of us tend to allocate our creative energies to the problem with the closest deadline, not to issues
with the most important long-term consequences. "I'll cross that

bridge when I come to it," we say, failing to realize that in the complex world system we now live in, with its often long time lags between causes and effects, we can burn many of our bridges long before we have come to them. Our shortsightedness in time is matched by our shortsightedness in space. The importance we attach to a problem is pretty much proportional to the extent to which it affects our own home, neighborhood, town, state, or country—in that order.

Third, having defined our problems in very narrow terms, for the most part, we tend to go about solving them by looking for simple "causes" to cure. But, as has been noted, the world system that generates our most severe problems is a *complex* one, in the sense defined by Jay Forrester. Our leaders and institutions base most of their policies and actions on notions of simple problems, arising from simple causes and amenable to simple cures. Yet as Forrester notes, in complex systems the concept of "causes" and "effects," which we acquire from normal personal experience, just does not apply, and these simplistic notions become fallacious.[2]

Consider, for example, the problems associated with the deleterious effects on human health of various forms of environmental contamination or decay. Take air pollution. It is only within the last generation or so that the degrading influence of air pollution on human health has been scientifically demonstrated and has acquired significant official recognition. Even now, identifying the specific health effects of the exceedingly mixed bag of substances called air pollution is a difficult, if not impossible, task.

Barry Commoner notes that the inevitable complexity and variability of the air pollution problem make it one that "resists piecemeal analysis and eludes detailed description."[3] The hazard which air pollution poses to health is thus very difficult to evaluate. "The search for simple cause-and-effect relationships between a given air pollutant and a specific disease breaks down in a hopeless morass of complex interactions."[4]

Because it is often difficult or impossible to identify the *causes* of environmental health hazards, it becomes almost equally hard to identify the *effects* with any certainty. A man dies of lung cancer. Was this a "natural" death or was it the "effect" of cigarette-smoking? of something in the air he breathed? something in the food he ate? something he was exposed to on the job? A child is a "slow" learner. Is he "naturally" stupid? Is he "culturally deprived"? Is he "genetically inferior"? Or did he once eat lead paint chips and thereby damage his central nervous system? Or was it perhaps the lead in the automobile exhaust in city air? Could it even have been some medicine or drug that his mother took during or even before her pregnancy, which impaired his development? Did the Roman Empire fall because of its political structure or because the ruling class went crazy from drinking wine out of lead jugs? The fact is, many of the deleterious *effects* on human health from environmental degradation are hard to see as such and may often pass for "natural"

make this kind of discovery. Even when the deleterious effect is obviously teratogenic it may take painstaking research to find the causative factor.[5] The case of the "Thalidomide babies" is an example. The difficulty in establishing a causal connection between teratogenic effects and prescribed drugs such as DES or Thalidomide is considerable, but it is still small when compared to those that arise when the potential causative factor is more ubiquitously "environmental." As a greater and greater proportion of the total population becomes exposed to hazardous environmental agents, the possibility of finding a statistical "control" increasingly diminishes, and the researcher is forced to study variations in the incidence of pathology over time rather than among a variety of different populations. This makes the time lag between causes and the discovery of their effects even longer.

In general, the pitfalls and fallacies of simple cause-and-effect analysis of problems in the area of environmental health apply equally to the full spectrum of problems that comprise ecocrisis as a whole. Furthermore, what is most insidious about this form of narrowmindedness is that it ultimately leads to the creation of scapegoats and the substitution of blame for reform. The obsessive search for simplistic causes eventually degrades into a witch-hunt. The simplistic cure degrades first into aggression and ultimately into destruction.

The fourth form of the narrowmindedness that characterizes the hardworld perspective is in the general failure to recognize trade-offs. An improvement in a condition or the solution of a problem at one point in space and time may come only at the price of increasing deleterious effects somewhere else or in the future. The case of laundry detergents is a commonly used and very good illustration.

Synthetic detergents were originally introduced as a replacement for soap, with the rationale that they would increase amenities in the area of doing laundry (that is, they would clean better than soap, especially in hard water). But along with this amenity came an unexpected disamenity: the hard detergents, being biologically nondegradable, accumulated in the water supply and made drinking water foam. In response to this problem, the detergent-makers replaced the hard, nondegradable detergents with soft, biodegradable, phosphate-based detergents. But these detergents provided fertilizer for algae and thereby contributed to the ecological problem of eutrophication of lakes and streams. To alleviate this effect, the amount of phosphate was reduced; but this resulted in the loss of amenity of superior cleaning power, which the manufacturers compensated for with the introduction of enzyme presoaks and detergents which were touted as having superior stain-removing powers. Then it was found that the enzymes were producing the adverse health effect of serious allergic reactions among production-line workers and consumers of these products. Enzymes went out, and the manufacturers began to tool up to replace all of the phosphates with a nitrate-based substitute—NTA. But that innovation had to be abandoned when research disclosed that NTA could, in combination with heavy metals that commonly taint water supplies, produce birth defects in laboratory animals. Some manufacturers then brought out "nonpolluting" detergents and boasted, "No phosphates! No enzymes! No NTA!" But these detergents were found to contain compounds that were more caustic than lye and which could lead to blindness if they got in the eyes or death if they were swallowed by children.

All of these forms of narrowmindedness were exemplified in the American response to the "energy crisis" of 1973–74. First, the crisis emanated largely from the failure of the United States government to appreciate the connection of Arab oil, not only to the structure of our domestic economy, but to the full range of our international relations as well. Thus the full power of the Arab economic weapon was grossly underestimated. Once the crisis was upon us, the Nixon administration and most of the Congress and the rest of our national leadership proceeded to define the problem in the narrowest possible terms. Generally, it was implied or stated that the energy crisis was *only* an *energy* crisis; it was temporally and geographically tied to the Arab-Israeli conflict; hence, it was a short-term and localized problem whose worst effects would end with the resolution of that conflict. Therefore, it had no widespread or long-term implications that would preclude a reasonably prompt return to "business as usual." As Nixon told it, the U.S. would simply bring "peace to the Middle East" (appease the Arabs) and undertake a "crash" program to achieve "independence in energy" by 1980; and that would be

imports for more than half of its supplies of nine of thirteen basic industrial raw materials by 1985 (these include iron ore, aluminum, and tin).

Energy and mineral imports in 1970 cost the U.S. $8 billion. This figure was projected to grow to $31 billion by 1985, based on the very unrealistic assumption of constant prices.

Eleven nonindustrial members of the Organization of Petroleum Exporting Countries almost totally control the world's exportable petroleum reserves.

Most of the world's exportable surplus of copper is supplied by four poor countries: Chile, Peru, Zambia, and Zaire (Congo).

Seventy percent of all exported tin is accounted for by three other poor countries: Malaysia, Bolivia, and Thailand.

Over half of the world's proven reserves of nickel are in Cuba and New Caledonia.

Zaire, Cuba, New Caledonia, and parts of Asia have the major known reserves of cobalt.

Along with Australia, Mexico and Peru provide 60 percent of all lead exports.[6]

In light of this, Lester Brown wrote, even before the Arab oil embargo of 1973: "The success of the eleven-member Organization of Petroleum Exporting Countries (OPEC) in bargaining for improved terms for supplying petroleum to the international community is a model which other raw material exporters can be expected to attempt to emulate."[7]

Thus the "energy crisis" was a far greater problem than conventional wisdom seemed willing to recognize, or at least admit. It wasn't merely an *energy* crisis, but a crisis of an overdeveloped, industrialized economy running suddenly into limits to its insatiable growth, limits imposed by its dependence on supplies of critical resources which lay outside its geographical boundaries and beyond its political control. It was a crisis of which the Arab-Israeli conflict was at most the trigger. The oil weapon had proven its potency and would certainly be used again over issues and for purposes having nothing to do with Israel. Petroleum was only the first lever with which the "developing" countries would upset the hegemony of the industrialized countries in world affairs. In fact, the energy crisis of 1973–74 represented the beginning of a radical and permanent transformation of: the power and role of the U.S. and other industrialized nations in the governance of the world system; the life-style and standard of living in the U.S. and other rich nations; and in general, all of the economic and political goals and· assumptions that had dominated the world system since the Second World War.

The response to the energy crisis also typifies the narrowminded attempt to find simple causes and cures for complex problems. The Americans blamed it on the Arabs' "blackmail" and on the Europeans' and Japanese's acquiescence. The latter blamed it on the Americans as a clever ploy to improve America's balance of payments and strengthen the dollar. Nixon blamed the Congress, and the Congress blamed Nixon. Ralph Nader blamed the oil companies, the oil companies blamed the environmentalists, the environmentalists blamed Madison Avenue, and so on. Not surprisingly, in some places this witch-hunt eventually settled on a popular and perennial scapegoat. Bumper stickers were sighted, proclaiming, "Stop Jews, Not Oil."

That form of narrowmindedness that lies in the failure to recognize and rationally resolve trade-offs also appeared. The lessons that were learned through three years of rapidly growing "environmental awareness" were seemingly forgotten overnight. In order to expedite the production of Alaskan oil, the National Environmental Policy Act (NEPA) was castrated. The hard-won protection of the Clean Air Act was cast aside. An attitude of "environment as luxury" suddenly seemed to prevail. The tacit assumption on which most of our leaders appeared to be operating was that the critical hazards and costs of environmental degradation, which had prompted so much concern between 1970 and 1973, simply went on vacation and left us alone for awhile, because it was inconvenient and too costly to deal with them for the time being. Almost uniformly, our leaders were unwilling to state openly that the reintroduction of high-sulfur fuels and the relaxation of air pollution standards and regulations would result in increased disease and death for thousands, perhaps millions, of Americans. The ecological devastation of strip-mined coal or oil shale was suddenly treated as insignificant. The Pandora's box of

results largely from our loyalty to the very systems that spawned it. For example, one of my local Congressmen, in response to the energy crisis, proclaimed that while he recognized the urgency of the situation, he opposed any means for dealing with it—for example, rationing—which would "undermine the free enterprise system." This man *believes in* this system and has a blind faith in its capacity to solve all important problems. His attitude is typical of those who *believe in* capitalism, socialism, Catholicism, Maoism, or any of the other myriad isms with which virtually all of the political, social, religious, and other institutions that govern our world identify themselves. The great tragedy of progressive thought, from Moses to Marx, is that truly revolutionary ideas, in the very process of becoming edified, are rendered into arthritic dogma, their further evolution curtailed by their most zealous proselytes. The *belief in* fixed systems ultimately results in the convolution of ends and means. Goals are screened out and whittled down to fit the increasingly limited performance capabilities of The System. Dogmatism becomes the sacrifice of wisdom to consistency.

The alternative is not merely the substitution of new systems to believe in for the old; rather, it is the creation of new kinds of leaders and institutions that are competent in the design, management, and adaptive change of various systems in pursuit of long-term and global goals.

Another characteristic of the hardworld perspective is a kind of "technological fatalism." In general, our current leadership takes as axiomatic the equation: can equals should equals will. Once the technological possibility for some innovation—a supersonic transport, a nuclear power plant, a mechanical tomato-picker—is announced, most of our leaders jump to the conclusion that the innovation should be adopted, or, in any event, that it will be, the march of progress being quite unstoppable. The defeat of the SST was a singular reversal of this trend, but it was one that has not often or recently been repeated. The other side of this particular coin is our obsessive infatuation with the technological "fix." Given any urgent new problem, there is an overwhelming tendency among our existing leadership to see solutions in technological, financial, and logistical terms rather than in social, psychological, or philosophical terms. Confronted with crisis, the man in the street's standard response has become: "If we can send a man to the moon, why can't we_____?" To meet this demand for the technological "fix," American leaders respond with crash research programs, massive appropriations of money, and various kinds of bureaucratic juggling to create the form, if not the substance, of a new program. Ironically, this seems also to be the case even among those who perceive the problems as arising from an illness in our social structure, flaws in our mental processes, or distortions of our basic values. Thus, many American politicians and commentators, in response to the energy crisis, perceived that the roots of the crisis lay in the American ethos of materialism, growth, and affluence. They claimed to recognize the need for some fundamental change in this regard. Yet it was the Sputnik response that prevailed. The crash research program, vast new expenditures, and new bureaucracy were all dedicated to preserving or restoring the precrisis business as usual. That research effort, money, and resources might also be devoted to changing American social structure, thinking, and ideals wasn't seriously considered.

A fourth characteristic of the hardworld perspective is a *reactive* rather than *projective* responsiveness. Some call this the "rule by crisis." The phenomenon is illustrated by a parable of Dennis Meadows'. A ship is sailing in dense fog. From the bridge, visibility is only ten yards in front of the ship's bow. On his screen, the radar operator sees an iceberg ten miles ahead, lying directly in the ship's path. The radar operator runs to the bridge and warns the captain that unless he changes the ship's course, a collision will ensue. Now it might seem to us surprising and even bizarre if the captain were to condemn the radar operator as a "prophet of doom" and banish him from the bridge, but that is precisely the way most of our leaders and institutions govern today's society. In general, we are unable to act projectively. Perhaps more important, we are, for the most part, strongly *unwilling* to act on "speculation," and practically demand to be immersed in crisis before we will act to avert it. We want to hear the ice crunching on the ship's bow before we will deign to turn the wheel.

Once again, the energy crisis serves as an example. In November 1973, in its first special section on energy, *Time* magazine said:

interference in the free market; *to them planning is a dirty word.*[8]

In this instance, the Nixon administration's extreme commitment to reactive responsiveness resulted in a failure to respond effectively to an emerging crisis even when the iceberg was virtually tearing the bow off the ship. But in fairness to Nixon, it must be said that it is highly improbable that even the most popular and powerful American president could have instituted the necessary changes in American domestic and foreign policy (and, more important, in the American life-style and ethos) that would have prevented an energy crisis of some sort from occurring sooner or later. As is suggested in the quote above, neither the special interests nor the electorate would have bought it without the kind of tangible evidence of dire necessity that only emerges after the opportunity for preventive planning has passed. Even those Democrats and others who criticized the Nixon administration for its failure to plan adequately to deal with the energy crisis offered no proposal, much less legislation, to legitimize and formalize the planning function within the American system of government. (In 1975, the Joint Economic Committee of the U.S. Congress began hearings on a proposal by Senators Javits and Humphrey to do this.)

This is not meant to suggest that other governments, where planning is more formalized and plays a more central role, are necessarily superior in achieving projective rather than reactive responsiveness. Even in these countries (for example, the Soviet Union,

China, countries of eastern Europe or Scandinavia) planning horizons are rarely greater than five years, and plans regularly fail to achieve their objectives. One major reason for this failure is clear: it is in the same places where planning plays the most powerful role that dogmatism is the most virulent. The more the options available to planning are constrained, the more ineffectual planning will be. Dogmatism is simply at odds with planning, as are narrowmindedness and technological fatalism. In general, there is today virtually no government or institution that exhibits an advanced or even a significant degree of projective responsiveness.

Still another characteristic of the hardworld perspective is its overwhelming irresponsibility. Our society is dominated by what evangelist Garner Ted Armstrong has called an "I'll get mine" philosophy. The same local Congressman I mentioned above held a public hearing on the energy crisis in the fall of 1973, at which just about a hundred local citizens testified. Of these, at least 97 spoke on how the energy crisis affected them as individuals, on why they needed or deserved special consideration or exemption from whatever regulations might be created to deal with the crisis, and in general, why their burden should be shifted to somebody else—in short, the "I'll get mine" philosophy in action.

But this kind of irresponsibility is not due simply to an individual lack of moral fiber; it is even more characteristic of the institutions and leaders that govern our society than it is of individual citizens. In fact, it mainly results from a general failure to create *systematic* accountability and hence responsibility in the structuring of our social institutions, whether these are individual offices such as the presidency or corporate entities such as conglomerate business firms, political parties, and universities. Whenever an actor cannot be held accountable for his actions, there is systematic irresponsibility. Such irresponsibility on the grand scale of governments, corporations, and other organizations creates not only the inspiration but the necessity for a similar self-indulgence on the part of the individual citizen. When the oil companies, OPEC, labor unions, the Mafia, and the President of the United States can get away with murder, we can hardly blame the little guy for saying "me first" too. If this attitude is not entrenched in some countries as much as it is in the U.S., it is still typical of the philosophy of international relations that has existed for several centuries. It is characteristic of an outlook that dominates our world system.

The final characteristic of the hardworld perspective I want to mention here is the pervasive acceptance of violence. This entails an insensitivity to and a legitimization of violence in both its overt and its more "structural" forms. To a large extent, the acceptance of violence is the result of a combination of the previously mentioned characteristics of the hardworld perspective. In general, our prevailing narrowmindedness blinds us to our true "communities of interest" with other persons, living things, the planet as a whole. It seems that a prerequisite to any form of vio-

makes us acquiescent to the violence of its side effects. Our naive faith in the technological "fix" makes us apathetic in addressing the real roots of human suffering. By being predominantly reactive rather than projective in our responsiveness to problems, we allow a crisis atmosphere to evolve in which the use or tolerance of violence apparently becomes more legitimate than it otherwise would be. Finally, irresponsibility simply *is* violence.

These characteristics form a mosaic from which a vision of the world, from the hardworld perspective, emerges. It is this vision that leads human actions within the global system as a whole to be either impotent or harmful. If ecocrisis is not to end in catastrophe, a new vision will be needed.

The Softworld Perspective

The softworld perspective is an alternative vision of the world and reality. It is a vision whose widespread adoption will be necessary if the resolution of ecocrisis is to lead to a better world. The essential characteristics of the softworld perspective may initially be viewed as simply the complements of those of the hardworld perspective.

The first of these—and the one which, to some extent, embraces all of the others—is what can be called *holistic thinking*. Holistic thinking is the ability to recognize and deal with all the important components and feedback relationships of complex systems. This is an ability not only to think rationally about the interactions among the parts of a complex system, but to develop an intuitive feel for the dynamic behavior of such a system *as a whole*. Holistic thinking implies a concept of reality that spans artificial boundaries and projects to the most distant horizons of time.

The second is a kind of *flexibility;* that is, the antithesis of dogmatism, the ability to design, create, manage, and change systems, as opposed to inflexible belief in a given system.

The third characteristic might be called many things, but perhaps *sophistication* best expresses it. This is in contrast to the tendency to ascribe critical problems to simple causes and to search for simple cures. The effective leader must be more sophisticated. He must be able to perceive the complex causes that underlie most critical problems and to design treatments that are tailored to this complexity.

The fourth is a *projective responsiveness.* This is the ability to avert crises by planning ahead, shaping the future rather than simply reacting to it.

The fifth is a kind of *technological skepticism.* This is not merely the antitechnological bias of some elements of the counterculture. It involves, first, a constructively critical attitude toward technological innovation. This requires the ability to make crucial value and political judgments about whether a given technological change should or should not, will or will not, be proliferated. Second, it involves the recognition that while technology may often make a useful contribution to the solution of many problems, there are almost never any completely technological "fixes." Indeed, technology, by itself, is rarely the major part of the solution to any significant problem in a complex social/ecological system.

The sixth is *responsibility.* Responsibility not only involves the individual's capacity for empathy, or "sense of responsibility," but it involves the ability to design and create systems that permit (and hopefully, require) responsible behavior.

The last is *peacefulness.* Following the thinking of Adam Curle, something far more positive is implied here than merely the absence of overtly aggressive, violent behavior. Peacefulness involves being at peace with oneself, enjoying peaceful relations with one's family, friends, colleagues, and community, and perhaps even beyond these, the skills of the peacemaker.

But these complementary characteristics give only a hint of the softworld perspective. The softworld vision is not merely a reaction to the hardworld; it is a growth *beyond* it. It is my purpose in the remainder of this book to contribute to the development of this new vision. In general, there are certain requirements that must be met if we are to acquire this alternative perspective on the world system.

First, we will have to learn to deal with the structure and dynamics of complex systems. We will need to understand the causes and consequences of growth in a finite world. This provides the motivation for the adoption of a new *paradigm*—the softworld perspective —appropriate to the age of equilibrium that must inevitably succeed the age of exponential growth.

We will have to have some understanding of basic systems con-

cation. We will have to learn how to create a world of learning systems that incorporate the softworld vision.

4

THE LIMITS

crisis and thereby formulating a general prescription for its cure. This is largely because the hardworld approach did not adequately comprehend the dynamic behavior of the complex system that generates the myriad symptoms that make up ecocrisis as a whole. This deficiency has been overcome with the development of the system dynamics methodology of Jay Forrester and his associates. But if system dynamics represents the highest level of sophistication of the hardworld approach to ecocrisis, it also constitutes a transition from the hardworld to the softworld approach. In fact, system dynamics could be considered a hybrid of the two approaches.

The culmination—so far at least—of the system dynamics approach to ecocrisis is the report of the Club of Rome's project on the predicament of mankind, entitled *The Limits to Growth*.[1] The project, which was directed by Dennis Meadows, then at MIT, and which was based on Jay Forrester's work in the application of system dynamics to the problem of a global ecological crisis, undertook to develop a viable computer model of the complex world system, comprised of such critical variables as population, food production, industrialization, pollution, and consumption of nonrenewable resources. Meadows and his team improved and augmented Forrester's *World Dynamics* model.[2] They have used it to identify the general trends in the behavior of these important variables over a 200-year period (1900–2100) and to test the probable results of various policies that might be proposed to deal with the problems suggested by these trends. The general conclusion of the Club of Rome study is that, if the existing trend of exponential growth in all of these critical variables is allowed to continue, the result will be a severe, perhaps even catastrophic, decline in both world population and industrial capacity, probably within the next century.

The severity of this potential decline cannot be underestimated; it boggles the mind. We are talking about the potential of up to *seven billion people,* or about twice the current population of the globe, dying off in the span of one generation, and of a drop in world economic production roughly equal to today's annual world output, occurring over the same span of time. All of the wars ever fought, all of the famines, all of the economic depressions in history, combined, shrink to insignificance when compared to the magnitude of such a global catastrophe. It is important to note that the model used by Meadows and his associates does not account for many social and political factors that might only serve to hasten the apocalypse—the gulf between the rich and the poor, racial and national animosity, and the prospect of nuclear war. The project's model is not particularly pessimistic in its basic assumptions and has actually been made to include virtually all of the most optimistic assumptions and assertions that are commonly used to disparage the warnings of the "prophets of doom." Rigorous pollution control, worldwide adoption of birth control, discovery of nonrenewable resources several times greater than known world reserves, recycling, the green revolution, and all the others have been taken into account and have been found inadequate to stave off the ultimate decline.

The Club of Rome report concludes that, in the long run, no patchwork or ad hoc solution to the global ecological crisis can work. The report finds that only the establishment of a state of global equilibrium, or the *stationary state* (a state in which population and capital are maintained at nearly constant levels), can save us from the inexorable decline and fall. The project team has tested and suggests a number of policies that might be adopted, in concert, to achieve the goal of world homeostasis (dynamic equilibrium):

1. Population is stabilized by getting birth rate equal to death rate. Industrial capital is similarly stabilized by having investment rate equal to depreciation rate.

2. To avoid a shortage of nonrenewable natural resources, resource consumption per unit of industrial output is reduced to a fraction of its current value.

3. To reduce depletion and pollution, economic preferences are shifted away from material products and toward services.

4. Pollution production per unit of industrial and agricultural output is reduced to a fraction of current levels.

5. Capital is diverted to food production, and/or existing inequalities in distribution of food are reduced.

6. The further capitalization of agriculture would lead to greater erosion and depletion of soil fertility; therefore agricultural capital and technology are altered to place

respects desirable, to implement such policies with all deliberate speed. However, it is clear that the longer we delay and the more lax we are in establishing the conditions for global equilibrium, the larger will be the stable population that is achieved and the lower will be the average standard of living. There appears to be a critical point, certainly by the year 2000, beyond which the adoption of these stringent policies would come too late to prevent an eventual decline. The clear implication of the Club of Rome report is that if mankind is to have any sort of future worth looking forward to, we must prepare to establish a state of global equilibrium. At the very least, this means, first, zero growth in population and capital, and second, minimal rates of input and output (or throughput) of these stocks.[3]

The Meadows report has not been unanimously endorsed. It has been greeted with considerable criticism, some of which is legitimate, much of which is misguided, and a good deal of which is pure contumely. In the latter category is the reaction of a number of old-line economists who attacked the report almost immediately after its publication, some of whom had not even read the report before leveling their guns at it. The initial reaction of these economists seemed to be that no sane or morally straight person could seriously question the demigod, Growth, and furthermore, if there were a conflict between economic policy and natural law, nature had better move over. It reminded me of a satirical article that appeared in the April fool's issue of a student newspaper a few years ago, which reported that legislation had been introduced into the U.S. Congress to repeal the law of gravity. The need for such legislation was clear: gravity was "keeping down the poor," it was a major factor in the high cost of ballistic missiles and space research, and it was generally responsible for keeping the economy from "getting off the ground."

But most of the criticism is not sheer bombast, and it usually has at least a veneer of rationality. For example, the critics frequently charge that the MIT model is not really representative of "reality," since some parts of it, in the absence of adequate supporting research, have had to be based on "best guesses" rather than substantive data. This criticism demonstrates an ignorance of the system dynamics methodology itself, which holds that the validity of a model is more dependent on the authenticity of the simulation of feedback structure than on the quantity of hard data. Forrester writes:

> In the social sciences failure to understand systems is often blamed on inadequate data. The barrier to progress in social systems is not lack of data. We have vastly more information than we use in an orderly and organized way. The barrier is deficiency in the existing theories of structure. The conventional forms of data-gathering will seldom produce new insights into the details of system structure. Those insights come from an intimate working knowledge of the actual systems. . . .
>
> A shortage of information is not a major barrier to understanding . . . complex systems. The barrier is the lack of willingness and ability to organize the information that already exists into a structure that represents the structure of the actual system and therefore has an opportunity to behave as the real system would. When structure is properly represented, parameter values are of secondary importance. . . .[4]

Meadows and his associates are the first to admit that their model of the world system has its flaws and is as yet incomplete, that there is much room for improvement. Yet three years of subsequent experimentation and refinement by research groups throughout the world have not substantially altered the basic policy implications of the original model. What the critics either avoid or fail to recognize is that all of our concepts of "reality" are, in fact, based on models of one sort or another. Most often, these are mental or intuitive models that exist in the human mind. As Forrester explains:

Every person in his private life and in his community life uses models for decision making. The mental image of the world around one, carried in each individual's head, is a model. . . . The question is not whether to use or ignore models. The question is only a choice between alternative models.

. . . . .

What may be most remarkable about the MIT model is that it contains as much hard data as it does. To the extent that parts of it are based on conjecture, it is in that respect that it is most like the mental models that exist in the minds of those who accuse it of being "unreal." We have to take this criticism from these eminent economists with a large grain of salt, considering that the model of "reality" they have persisted in using for many years and on which much of their criticism is based, is one in which the Earth is represented not as a sphere but as a flat, infinite plane capable of sustaining infinite growth and of tolerating unlimited exploitation.

The real issue, then, is not whether or not the Meadows model is real, but rather, whether it is *more* real than the model of the "flat-earth" economists who criticize it. The dialectic here is analogous to the confrontation between the Ptolemaic and the Copernican models of the universe, as a clash between an anthropocentric and a naturalistic vision of reality. It is said that Galileo, harangued by the church into publicly renouncing his belief in the heretical notion that the earth revolves around the sun, was afterward heard to mutter, "But still, it *moves!*" So today, some of us may have to whisper, beneath the shouts of our economic pontiffs proclaiming that the earth has no bounds, "But still, it is *round!*"

Much of the criticism of the Club of Rome report is more pointed and substantive than this kind of broad rejection, but it is not necessarily more legitimate. A representative example is the review of *The Limits to Growth* published in the *New York Times Book Review* and written by three economists (of the flat-earth school, I think), Peter Passell, Marc Roberts, and Leonard Ross. In general, Passell, Roberts, and Ross disparaged the complex system dynamics model on which *Limits* was based as "a kind of intellectual Rube Goldberg device— one which takes arbitrary assumptions, shakes them up and comes out with arbitrary conclusions that have the ring of science."[6] They noted that "economists also use simulation," but, they argued, "simulation models have a rather spotty record" in making even short-term predictions of national income, employment, and so on.[7] So they had little respect for a model which presumed to project the future a century hence.

Their essential point was this: the Meadows model stacks the deck against technology—which, as any good economist knows, can solve any problem—in order to make zero population growth (which they endorsed) and zero economic growth (which they condemned) appear as the only solution to the ecological crisis (which they claimed to recognize). As they put it, the MIT world model "hypothesizes exponential growth for industrial and agricultural needs," but the model "places arbitrary, non-exponential, limits on the technical progress that might accommodate these needs."[8] Granting that exponential growth could not continue indefinitely if technology did not keep pace, these authors asserted that "there is no particular criterion beyond myopia on which to base that speculation."[9] History had proven Malthus wrong, they believed, and it would prove the neo-Malthusians wrong too.

The apparently reasonable criticism by these three economists is simply wrong. Their backhanded rejection of computer technology and "systems jargon" reveals a general lack of understanding of systems theory in general and systems dynamics in particular. And their blanket dismissal of the utility of "simulation models" demonstrates an ignorance of Forrester's caveat: "The question is not whether to use or ignore models. The question is only a choice between alternative models."

It is also not true that the Meadows model assumes nonexponential growth of technology. In fact, the authors of *Limits* assumed that technology is able to grow at as exponential a rate as the problems it is supposed to solve. It turns out to be not true that exponential growth cannot go on forever *only* if technology fails to keep up. In the last example in the chapter entitled "Technology and the Limits to Growth," the authors assumed that technology does all that can be expected from it, and they show that exponential growth still cannot go on forever. In the simulation run of the world model used for the example, a technological policy was utilized in every sector of the model in order to circumvent the limits to growth. The model pro-

duced nuclear power, recycled resources, and mined the most remote reserves; it pushed agricultural yields to "undreamed-of
heights"; and it produced only "actively wanted" children. Still, the
result was an end to growth by the year 2100, caused by a nexus of
three crises: land erosion, resource-depletion, and pollution.[10]

The blind faith of Passell, Roberts, and Ross in the ability of
technology to provide a geometrically enlarging escape hatch from

silk from which it realized a return on its investment of many billions
of dollars. Aching to repeat this success story, in the 1960s Du Pont
came out with "Corfam," a synthetic substitute for leather. Du Pont
gambled over $100 million that it could repeat the "progress" of
nylon—and lost. The company abandoned the product in 1971 and
sold off the inventory at a considerable loss. The moral of this story,
Hardin says, is that the "dogma of Aladdin's lamp tells us that since
we can dream of something better than real leather, we must be able
to invent it. Possibly the dogma is false."[11]

Passell, Roberts, and Ross claimed that there exists "no . . .
criterion beyond myopia" on which to base the expectation that
continued exponential growth of technology is not inevitable. "The
best econometric estimates," they said, indicate that technology "is
indeed growing exponentially."[12] On the contrary, it is their position
that is myopic, for they cannot see, as Hardin does, that "technical
progress" is becoming ever more costly—in terms of both internal
and external costs—and is not only slowing down but may even be
going backward if one considers the way each new technological
"fix" seems to create more problems than it solves. Their confidence
in the "best econometric estimates" seems especially ingenuous. In
fact, there exists no theoretical basis for making predictions of future
technological development, and there is reason to doubt whether
there ever will be. As Donald Schon has pointed out, the problem
with a theory that presumes to predict invention is that "a prediction
of invention *is* invention, and the prediction fulfills itself."[13] Of
course, a theory of technological change may only attempt to predict

some characteristic or objective of future invention, for example, the ability to control human aging or an electric automobile with a range of 200 miles and a top speed of 70 miles an hour. But as Schon has noted, such predictions share the fallibilities of all predictions of the future of complex social/ecological systems.[14] Technological forecasts may be among the weakest of all exercises in futurology, given the essentially inscrutable and unpredictable nature of the invention process itself.

This is not to deny that technological inventions will probably come along which will be helpful in solving many of the critical problems that now concern us. Nor should technological research and development related to the problems of ecocrisis be discouraged. But equal to the likelihood that useful inventions will appear is the likelihood that most of them will carry social, economic, political, or environmental costs that will be equal to or outweigh their benefits. The claim that technology can be relied on to save us from the dangers of ecocrisis is nothing more than an exercise in wishful thinking, as insulated from the tests of logic and scientific validation as the claim of papal infallibility.

Passell, Roberts, and Ross further charged that the MIT model fails to account for the benevolent effects of the pricing system. In the "real world," these economists claimed, rising prices act to conserve scarce resources, creating incentive for the substitution of cheaper materials for more expensive ones, provoking research on saving resource inputs, and increasing the profitability of exploration for new reserves of resources. "In fact, natural resource prices have remained low, giving little evidence of coming shortages. . . . Technical change has dramatically reduced exploration and extraction costs, while simultaneously permitting the substitution of plentiful materials for scarce ones—plastics for metal, synthetic fibers for natural, etc."[15]

This optimistic statement was written in early 1972. It seems naive in the light of subsequent economic events. But these economists should have known better even then. In 1969 Thomas Lovering wrote in *Resources and Man:* "Unhappily the widespread belief that technology is continually lowering unit costs while allowing us to work deposits of ever lower grade is contradicted by the trends revealed in the copper industry. . . . Unit costs are not declining, nor have they been for a decade."[16] As for the success of the pricing system in increasing discovery and production of new mineral reserves, Lovering noted: "The average consumption of mercury in the United States has increased at a rate of 3 percent per year for 20 years, equivalent to a doubling in consumption every 23 years, but, to meet this demand, in the same period, the price of mercury has increased by more than 500 percent."[17] Projecting this trend into the future, Lovering pointed out that if the current price of mercury were increased by five times again, the result would be a ninefold increase in the economically recoverable reserves of mercury. But if consumption of mercury were to continue to grow at the rate of 3

new discovery is required that, together with technological innovation, will develop reserves of mineral resources at an exponential rate until population control and relatively constant or decreasing per capita demand can be achieved—both inevitable requirements on our finite earth."[21]

It is ironic that the very technological fixes that Passell, Roberts, and Ross hold out as the solution to the problem of resource scarcity (for example, the substitution of plastics for metal and synthetic fibers for natural) are the factors that have been indicted by ecologist Barry Commoner as *the* major cause of critical environmental pollution. So these economists seem also to be ignorant of one of Commoner's cardinal laws of ecology: "There is no such thing as a free lunch." Perhaps the greatest irony, however, is that we find economists lionizing the powers of technology to solve all our problems in direct contradiction to a report emanating from MIT, the mecca of American technology.

The critique of *Limits to Growth* is simply erroneous, but this is not to suggest that the Club of Rome report cannot legitimately be criticized. The report must be criticized substantively and on its own level, which means delving into the Meadows model and assessing not merely the parametric data but the total feedback structure of the system.

I am convinced that the MIT model, in spite of its imperfections, is still a reliable model of the general world system with which it deals. I feel that the flat-earth economists are first going to have to vindicate their own peculiar model of the real world before they will be able to legitimately disparage the impressive achievement of Meadows and his staff.

I find it hard to believe that condemning natural laws and the disasters they sometimes lead to, as unfair, undemocratic, and discriminatory is going to reduce the number of hurricanes, earthquakes, or volcanic eruptions significantly. Similarly, I do not recall that the sheer force of hubris was enough to keep the *Titanic* from going down. And I am equally skeptical that the bombast of our prestigious economists will be of much avail on a shipwrecked Spaceship Earth. In the case of the planet, as in the case of the ill-fated *Titanic*, I am inclined to believe that adequate prior planning, based on a realistic assessment of the hazards that confront us, is likely to have far greater value in insuring our survival over the long haul than all of the phony confidence, flamboyant rhetoric, and groundless optimism combined.

5

BEYOND THE LIMITS

other leading scholars who have been concerned with the "limits to growth," a considerable amount of controversy and debate has been generated about the nature of such limits and their impact on the behavior of social/ecological systems. Chapter 4 contains a sample of this extensive and continuing "growth debate." Yet even while the debate about limits to growth goes on, I believe there has emerged a school of thought that has gone beyond the limits to growth.

The members of this emerging school are less concerned with the elementary question of *whether* there are limits to growth than they are with the far more challenging problem of developing detailed and viable *alternatives* to conventional patterns of growth (that is, with developing models of potential equilibrium systems) and effective *means* for making those alternatives realizable. The attitude of the "beyond limits" school is represented by Kan Chen and his colleagues at the University of Michigan in their fine study, *Growth Policy*, in which they say that, rather than debate what they call the "world macroproblem" (that is, the limits to growth), "we assume its existence *so that we can go on to explore methods of coping with it.*"[1] The rapid maturing of the "beyond limits" school, or movement, is symbolized by the creation of the Mitchell Prize and the series of biannual conferences on limits to growth, beginning in Woodlands, Texas in 1975, both of which were designed not merely to continue the growth debate but to promote the search for solutions to the critical problems of growth and equilibrium.

Why has a "beyond limits" school emerged? Partly because the problem of creating an alternative, equilibrium society is too intriguing for creative minds to ignore, but mainly because of the nature of the growth debate itself.

THE GROWTH DEBATE AS PARADIGM CONFLICT

The growth debate is a controversy, or dialectic, that is not the sort that can ultimately be resolved simply through rational debate of the nature or meaning of discrete facts. This controversy exists on a higher plane, on the level of what scientific historian Thomas Kuhn called a "paradigm shift." This is a subtle and complex, but crucial, notion.

Essentially, what Kuhn postulated in his radically innovative thesis, *The Structure of Scientific Revolutions,* was that, contrary to what classical historians of science almost uniformly implied, the evolution of western scientific thought was not a gradual, continuous process of incremental accretion of knowledge. Rather, the evolution of western science was marked by two distinctive and recurring phases. One was "normal science," the practice of which Kuhn suggested was analogous to puzzle-solving. Characteristics of this phase are: (1) the definition of what problems are and their priority are almost uniformly known and subscribed to by the practitioners of the science; (2) the general heuristics, or "rules of the game," of problem-solving are uniformly known and subscribed to; (3) there is a definite, underlying confidence among practitioners that the solutions to problems do, in fact, exist and hence that the normal practice of science lies in puzzling out the actual solutions; (4) therefore, the polemics of normal science center on the validity of data or the actual carrying out of problem-solving procedures, but they do not generally center on the definition of problems, the existence of solutions, or the validity of the normal problem-solving procedures of the science themselves. In short, the *paradigm* of normal science is not intentionally challenged in the common practice of normal science.

However, Kuhn says, from time to time anomalies arise, problems that do not yield to the conventional puzzle-solving practices of normal science, problems that seem to demand, for their solution, a radical transformation of the essential paradigm of normal science itself. If these anomalies are sufficiently stubborn, they give rise to the second distinct phase of western scientific development: scientific revolution.

The essential characteristic of these occasional eras of scientific revolution is that a new paradigm or paradigms emerge to challenge the old. The ranks of the practitioners of normal science undergo a schism as a general choosing up of sides among competing paradigms occurs. For the practitioners involved, this era of paradigm shift may be marked by considerable stress, anxiety, and bitter controversy. "Reality" itself seems to be, and in fact is, in doubt. In Yeats' words,

Kuhn went on to try to analyze how, in fact, the scientific revolution was resolved, that is, how sides were actually chosen and how the ensuing dialectic was carried out to a conclusion. His conclusion seems somewhat uncertain to me, but it does contain one observation that impresses me as being profoundly relevant to the controversy surrounding limits to growth and to the rise of the "beyond limits" school. Specifically, Kuhn says that debates involving competing paradigms are not really about the comparative success of conflicting paradigms in past or even present problem-solving, although superficially this is what the controversy may seem to imply. Rather, the underlying concern in paradigm debates is for the *future* of the science. The real issue "is which paradigm should in the future guide research on problems many of which neither competitor can yet claim to resolve completely."[3] Established facts cannot resolve the debate, and existing experience provides little guidance for the individual who is compelled to choose between conflicting paradigms. So, one who embraces a new paradigm at an early stage must do so with the belief that the new paradigm will succeed, yet only with the knowledge that the conventional paradigm has, perhaps in but a few cases, failed. A "decision of that kind can only be made *on faith.*"[4]

Some historical examples of this process of scientific revolution are the rise of Copernican astronomy, the establishment of Newtonian mechanics, and the subsequent overthrow of Newtonian mechanics and the ascendancy of modern quantum mechanics and relativity theory. These revolutions were sparked by the existence of anomalies which the established paradigms of the then normal sciences were unable to resolve or assimilate. Today, new anomalies have arisen which threaten to undermine the establishment of contemporary normal science, for example, the discovery of the anomalous astrophysical phenomena of quasars and pulsars, and the whole set of inexplicable but demonstrably real phenomena of parapsychology.

The question arises whether Kuhn's notion of paradigm shift can be justly applied outside of the natural sciences. Do similar revolutions occur in the social sciences? Even more germane to this discussion is the question, do they occur in the more applied branches of social science, what might be called the "helping/governing" sciences (for example, government, public health, social work, management, and education)?

The fact is that some have suggested that the concept of paradigm shift is not properly applied to the social sciences. The reason given is fairly simple: in the social sciences, it is argued, paradigms are in a constant state of conflict and flux. Since no one paradigm ever becomes sufficiently established to become "normal," no climactic "revolution" ever occurs. For some fields of social science—for example, some areas of psychology—this is probably true; but I am inclined to believe that this is not so much true in the area of what I call above the helping/governing sciences. It seems to me that in this area a fairly concrete and nearly ubiquitous paradigm has been operating at least since the end of World War II and that this dominant paradigm is now being challenged by at least one newly emerging paradigm. As evidence of this contention, I return to the characteristics of "normal" science described above and suggest what I think are their analogies in the normal helping/governing science.

First: *the definition of what problems are and their priority are almost uniformly known and subscribed to by the practitioners of the science.* I would suggest that in the recent postwar era, most practitioners of normal helping/governing science were in substantial agreement about what were problems and what were important problems. Some problems that were generally recognized to be important were economic development; cancer; crime; nuclear war between the U.S. and the U.S.S.R., or, in fact, anything concerning relations between these two countries; national power, prestige, and independence; landing a man on the moon; unemployment; drug addiction; Vietnam; individual mental health; educating children; and pest control.

Second: *the general heuristics, or "rules of the game," of problem-solving are generally known and subscribed to.* This is a little harder to give examples of, but some of the tacit or overt assumptions of conventional helping/governing science problem-solving are: problems are attacked through "programs"; crises are

when we come to it; problems can be solved or at least alleviated by disseminating money, resources, information, and services *from* a central distributor *to* a passive recipient population; problems arise from simple causes that are amenable to simple cures; solutions that work in the short term, on a small scale, will work in the long term on a large scale.

Third: *there is a definite, underlying confidence among practitioners that the solutions to problems do, in fact, exist and hence that the normal practice of science lies in puzzling out the actual solutions.* This has obviously been true of the normal helping/governing science of the postwar period. It is reflected every day in our newspapers and broadcast news programs. Most of the news deals with problems of public recognition and concern. The protagonists in public problem-solving—political parties or factions, government agencies, special interest groups, and so on—may attack each other's competency to solve or even analyze publicly recognized problems. Some may occasionally argue that a publicly recognized problem is not really serious or perhaps that it is not even a problem. But it rarely happens that a public official or business manager will openly declare that a problem widely considered to be genuinely important is simply insoluble. To do so would subject the individual to charges of pessimism, defeatism, and by implication, incompetence.

Fourth: *therefore, the polemics of normal science center on the validity of data or of the actual carrying out of problem-solving procedures, but they do not generally center on the definition of problems, the existence of solutions, or the validity of the normal problem-solving procedures of the science themselves.* I repeat, this has been generally characteristic of the normal practice of helping/governing science in the last 30 years or so. It has begun to change significantly only in the last few years, primarily because of the emergence of new, challenging paradigms.

There has been considerable debate over the years about how best to solve the problem of narcotics addiction, but recently some have begun to question whether narcotics addiction is a serious problem and, in fact, have suggested that the attempted solutions to this alleged problem have been far more pernicious than the problem itself. There has long been plenty of controversy over how schools could be made more effective, efficient, and productive, but now a body of thought has emerged which perceives schooling not as a solution but as the problem itself. The long-standing arguments about how to build better prisons, mental hospitals, interstate highways, skyscrapers, supersonic transports, and nuclear weapons have been undercut by the more basic questions posed by the proponents of newly emerging paradigms about whether the solutions are not, in fact, the paramount problems.

It seems, then, that the controversy surrounding "limits to growth" is symptomatic of the emergence of a new paradigm challenging the basic paradigm of conventional helping/governing science. I believe this new paradigm is emerging in a different way on all of the fronts mentioned above, as well as many others. I suspect that the "growth debate," as a forum for the confrontation between the old and new paradigms, may be of somewhat greater importance than any of the others because the issues it raises seem to be the most urgent, immediate, global, and radical in their implications.

Something important needs to be said about what the growth debate is *not.* It is not what is commonly perceived to be a conflict between developers and environmentalists, or, to put it in more extreme terms, between "ripper-offers" and "eco-nuts." In the news media the lines seem to be drawn between opposing political forces, and growth issues are centered on discrete projects such as power plants, highways, airports, housing developments, and so on. What must be clearly understood is that the polarization between conflicting paradigms lies in a completely different dimension than the polarization between growth and antigrowth or development and antidevelopment political factions which the media seem to define. The fact is, the schism of paradigms in helping/governing science divides the ranks of both the developers and the environmentalists, albeit not exactly equally.

Ultimately the growth debate is the clash between two paradigms competing for control of the future navigation of Spaceship Earth. The old paradigm is the hardworld perspective; the new is the softworld perspective. This conflict is not the kind that can be resolved through simple changes in knowledge, attitude, or behavior;

6

A SOFTWORLD PRIMER

This chapter is devoted to a primer on these fundamental concepts, explicating each of them in some detail. The reader who is already familiar with most of these concepts and who feels confident of his grasp of them, may wish to skip ahead to Chapter 7 and use this chapter as an appendix to refer back to as the need arises. Before doing so, however, I strongly advise reading at least the section on learning. The discussion there is of central importance to the rest of this book. It is based heavily on Bateson's concept of the learning hierarchy and may present some ideas that are unfamiliar even to those with some cognizance of conventional learning theories.

In general, the fact that these concepts are basic should not be taken to imply that they are therefore simple. Many are quite complex, and the uninitiated reader may find even the following rather lengthy discussion unsatisfying. Therefore, some of the references cited in the notes should be turned to when a fuller explanation is wanted.

SYSTEM

System is an interesting word because it is one that really defies definition. Perhaps it is so hard to define what a system *is* because it is nearly impossible to define what it *isn't*. That is, anything can be described as being a *system,* and conversely, there is nothing that could not be described as being a system. More importantly, there is nothing that one could point to as a good example of a *nonsystem,* not even nothing itself. Consider the following typical definition of the word:

SYSTEM—An assembly of components united by some form of regulated interaction to form an organized whole.

Like most definitions offered for *system,* this one is verbose and redundant. "Assembly," "united," and "organized" tell us nothing, since ultimately everything in the universe is *organized* in some way. If we accept the basic proposition that there are "laws of nature," then *regulated interaction* could also apply to anything at all. And "components" is just a fancy word for "parts." How many *parts* must a system have? Two? One? None?

The flaw in the definition above is that it implies that a system is a *thing* (hardworld) when it is actually an *idea* (softworld). I suggest that the only word in this definition that has any relevance is *whole.* A group (including a group of one or even none) of objects, ideas, forces, impressions, stimuli, perceptions, processes, events, and so forth *is a system,* if one simply thinks of the elements of the group as being a *whole.* In other words, a system is a conceptual reality, not a physical one.[1] The only thing required for an orange, a volcano, a transistor radio, and the city of Detroit to be a *system* is that I or someone else consider them as one.

Furthermore, we should observe that there is a common distinction made between *open* and *closed* systems. First, every system has a *boundary* which sets it apart from the rest of the *universe* or the system's *environment.* An open system is one in which *interaction* or *exchange* occurs between the system and its environment across or through the boundary. A closed system manifests no such interaction or exchange. Therefore a closed system is considered *isolated* from its environment.

As the reader may already have realized, there is no such thing as a closed system in the real world, since the laws of physics assert that everything in the physical universe is affected by its environment. Why, then, the concept of a closed or isolated system? Because, first of all, many systems are approximately closed systems, their interaction with the environment being either negligible, or at least well defined. Secondly, and more important, scientists and engineers could not accomplish much without the concept of a closed system. The reason is not hard to see. If a scientist wants to explain why chemical X reacts in his test tube with chemical Y to produce chemi-

be replicated.

Nearly all of our scientific and technical knowledge, then, is based on a fallacy: that there is a closed system. Generally, this need not bother us since the fallacy is useful; it helps us solve many problems where the approximation to a closed system is a good, or at least acceptable, one. Unfortunately, many of the problems that concern us today, especially the kind of problems that are the subject of this book, involve systems so complex that the attempt to isolate a subsystem and consider it as a closed system is indefensible and invariably leads to grievous error.

Again, the case of laundry detergents is a good example. The chemical engineer who developed a "hard" detergent was treating a washing machine as a closed system. His successor who invented biodegradable detergent enlarged the system to include the water supply but left out the algae, which led to the eutrophication problem. And so on, until now the relevant system has been enlarged to the point where it seems virtually impossible to develop a detergent that will satisfy all the constraints imposed by the system. The obvious answer is simply to go back to soap flakes, a product that didn't have any of these problems attached to it. But it is a general truism of systems that changes are not often reversible. To assess the possible reintroduction of soap flakes, we cannot shrink the "laundry system" back down to the washing machine or turn it back to the predetergent era. To evaluate the effect of this innovation we would have to expand the boundary of our system still more. We have to consider how the decimation of the detergent industry would affect the entire domestic economy. We also will have to consider how the loss of advertising revenue from this industry would affect the entire mass communications system. These effects, in turn, will interact with the political and social structure of American society and ulti- mately, therefore, affect the impact of human activity on the global ecosystem. In fact, take almost any problem of interest today to social scientists, to engineers, and even to many physical scientists, and one will generally find that the only system of relevance to that problem that can meaningfully or safely be considered closed is the biosphere as a whole.[2]

INFORMATION AND ENTROPY

Information and entropy are the two most powerful and impor- tant concepts in softworld thinking. I have put them together be- cause, as we shall see, one can be understood only in terms of the other; in fact, they are complementary.

I am using the term *information* here in a very special sense, and the reader must be wary to strip away his conventional connota- tions of the word:

> In ordinary speech we use the word "information" as a synonym for news, knowledge, intelligence, report, and so on. It is an amalgam of so many vague and imprecise mean- ings that a scientist has to purify from the blend of its diverse connotations the one he requires for his purpose, very much as a chemist purifies a substance in order to study its behav- ior. In the communication engineer's purification of the term the stress is on the quantitative aspect of the *flow* in a *network* of an *intangible* attribute called *information*. It is measured . . . by its "news" value, that is, the extent of surprise it causes the recipient.[3]

This statement by Singh conveys the most salient elements of the concept of "information": it is quantitative, yet it is intangible, and it flows.

Let us deal first with the quantitative aspect of information. The unit in which the *information content* of any message is measured is the *bit,* which is a contraction of the term *binary unit* or *binary digit.* This derives from the fact that the simplest possible code in which information can be conveyed is the binary code of two symbols

("0" and "1"). The information content of a message is equal to the negative of the logarithm (to the base 2) of its *probability* of selection. The logarithm is used because we expect the information content of a sequence of messages to be *additive*.[4] The probability of a given message is the reflection of what Singh alludes to above as its "news value." Our measure of the information content of a message is such that the greater the probability of a given message, the less

ences. In the hardworld, when a man kicks a dog, the dog's behavior can only be described in terms of the change in the dog's momentum resulting from the force of the kick. In "reality" we know that the dog's behavior is likely to be more complex. The dog may lie down in the corner and sulk or it may bite the man's leg, but its behavior is more likely to be determined by the information conveyed by the kick than by the impact. The kick conveys information to the dog because the difference in the relationship between man and dog manifested by the kick makes a difference to the dog. If we anesthetize the dog so that it has no perception of being kicked, the difference represented by the kick makes no difference to the dog and no information is conveyed.

Now we can begin to see why information is inherently intangible. Information is news of a difference, and *difference cannot be localized.* Look closely at a newspaper photograph or TV picture and you will see that the picture is composed of a matrix of black and white dots. The information conveyed by the picture lies in the *difference* between the black dots and the white dots. But the information is not *in* the black dots nor *in* the white dots; therefore the information is not *on* the paper nor *on* the television screen.

Where is the information? It is nowhere, or perhaps it is everywhere. We can't answer the question because information has no location, because difference cannot be localized. This seems paradoxical. I've used the term *information content* which seems to imply something *inside* of something. Yet I have also said that information is nothing (literally, "no thing") and that it is *nowhere*. We all know that there are *places* or *people* who have more information than others—libraries, the information desk, the information operator. Therefore if there is someplace to go to get information, there must certainly be someplace where the information *is*. But this isn't so; the paradox can be explained by the fact that we are getting our conventional connotations of the word *information* mixed up with the precise scientific meaning of the term. This brings us to the third key attribute of *information,* mentioned in Singh's statement, namely, that information *flows*.

First of all, when we speak of *information content,* we are talking about the information content of a *message,* and a message is not a *thing.* In fact, a message is a difference or set of differences. A message is not information because information is a difference that *makes a difference.* Just how much difference a message makes is, in fact, our measure of its information content. What is stored in a library or a telephone directory or in a computer's memory is not information but rather a set of differences—ink marks on paper or blobs of magnetic flux on a ferric matrix—that are potential messages. But the potential messages contain no information until they are *transmitted* (that is, until they begin to *flow* from one place to another through some kind of channel or network). The messages contain no information until they make a difference. Even though information may (in fact, *must*) "flow" from A to B, the information is never "at" A nor "at" B nor "at" any point in between. When the man kicks the dog, the information the dog receives does not originate in the man's brain, flow down the man's body into his toe, thence into the dog's posterior, up the dog's spinal cord and into the dog's brain, although a train of *differences* may, in fact, follow some such path. The information is *in* the kick and the dog's knowing or perceiving being kicked. To be more precise, we should replace the term *in* with *immanent.* Information is immanent in the flow of differences, but it is not *in* the flow.

If this is confusing and perhaps a bit disturbing, it is probably because our minds are so commonly steeped in hardworld thinking. The hardworld seems to offer us the solid ground of ontology —the knowledge of "reality"—on which to stand. But the softworld provides us only with the filmy images of epistemology— the knowledge of "knowing"—with which to orient ourselves; furthermore, it not only withholds ontology but denies its possibility. As Bateson puts it:

This world, of communication, is a Berkeleyan world, but the good bishop was guilty of understatement. Relevance or reality must be denied not only to the sound of the tree which falls unheard in the forest but also to this chair which I can see and on which I am sitting. My perception of the chair is communicationally real, and that on which I sit is, for me, only a message in which I put my trust.[5]

discussing information, let us first look at the younger of these two concepts, that of information theory.

In 1948, Claude E. Shannon, the father of modern information theory, created the informational concept of entropy in his famous paper, "The Mathematical Theory of Communication." Shannon's entropy is defined by the following formula:

$$S(Q|X) = - K \sum_{i=1}^{n} p_i ln(p_i)$$

S is the symbol that stands for "entropy." Q is a "well-defined" question (a question for which all the possible answers are known). X is the set of all possible answers (n) to the question Q; therefore X could be called the "state of knowledge," or, more aptly, the "state of ignorance." To each of the possible answers X_i to the question Q, there corresponds a certain probability of that answer being correct, p_i. The entropy, then, is defined as the sum of the logarithms of the probabilities of each possible answer being correct, weighted by the same probabilities (K is an arbitrary constant which makes the units of informational entropy come out *bits*).

The properties of this definition are such that if one knows the correct answer to the question Q with complete certainty, the probability of that answer is 1 and that of all other answers is 0, with the result that the entropy is 0. On the other hand, if one is completely ignorant of what the correct answer might be, then all of the probabilities are equal, and the entropy turns out to be maximum. The entropy, then, is clearly an index of the state of our ignorance.

For a given question Q there could be many different possible probability distributions over the set of possible answers and therefore many different possible states of ignorance. If a message is received which changes our state of ignorance from X to X', how do we know whether we are more or less ignorant as a result of the message? Shannon's entropy provides an exact measure of our ignorance in a given state. Therefore he defined *information* as being precisely equal to the change in entropy caused by a message: $I = S(Q|X) - S(Q|X')$. Information in the mathematical theory is equivalent to a *decrease* in entropy; therefore information can be considered *negative entropy*, or, as it is sometimes called, *negentropy*. Now we can see more clearly what Bateson meant in defining information as "a difference that makes a difference": the difference that information makes is a decrease in entropy.[6]

Observe that the mathematical definition of information has, in fact, the epistemological significance noted by Bateson above. Specifically, Shannon's entropy depends on the existence of a question and on a state of ignorance described by the probability distribution over the set of possible answers. But this means that the measure of the entropy depends on (a) what is the question? and (b) who is asking? Therefore, information requires the existence of an informee. Furthermore, the information content of a message depends entirely on the state of ignorance of the recipient; different recipients may well derive different amounts of information from the same message.[7]

This brings us to the older, thermodynamic, concept of entropy. Thermodynamic entropy derives from the Second Law of Thermodynamics. A complete derivation of the Second Law is beyond the scope of this discussion, but we can consider the fundamental statement of the law and something of the nature of the concept of entropy that emerges from it.

The Second Law was initially motivated by the observation that it was impossible to construct a "perpetuum mobile" (perpetual motion machine) of the *second kind*. The First Law said that all work ultimately becomes heat (this ruled out a perpetuum mobile of the first kind, one that would never "run down"), but a perpetuum mobile of the second kind would essentially recycle the heat generated by the work it produced back to its power plant and thereby be able to run forever. The fact that this is impossible leads us to Lord Kelvin's statement of the Second Law:

A transformation whose only final result is to transform into work heat extracted from a source which is at the same temperature throughout is impossible.

The Second Law was restated by Clausius as follows:

A transformation whose only final result is to transfer

$$\sum_{i=1}^{2} \frac{}{T_i} = 0$$

where the system comes in contact with n sources of different temperature T_i and exchanges an amount of heat Q_i with each. When the distribution of sources is continuous, this sum becomes an integral and each increment of heat becomes infinitesimal:

$$\oint \frac{dQ}{T} = 0$$

The sign $\oint$ indicates that the integral is taken over a *closed* path (this is what we mean by a *cycle*). But this, in turn, implies that for two different paths or curves, I and II, joining two states of the system, A and B, then:

$$\left(\int_A^B \frac{dQ}{T}\right)_{\mathrm{I}} + \left(\int_B^A \frac{dQ}{T}\right)_{\mathrm{II}} = 0$$

This enables us to define a *function of state*, which will be called the "entropy", S, as follows:

$$S(A) = \int_O^A \frac{dQ}{T}$$

where the equilibrium state O is arbitrarily chosen as a standard state and S is therefore entirely a function of the state A. The entropy change of the system following a transformation from state A to state B is then simply:

$$S(B) - S(A) = \int_A^B \frac{dQ}{T}$$

This assumes that the transformation from A to B is reversible. If it is not, the equation becomes an inequality and the left side is greater than the right side.

The practical significance of this thermodynamic concept of entropy is still unclear. But if we consider a completely isolated, closed system, the last equation becomes simple. For such a system there is no exchange of heat (or anything else) possible with the environment; therefore $dQ = O$ and we have:

$$S(B) \geqq S(A)$$

This means that any transformation that occurs in an isolated system will be such that the entropy of the final state is never less than that of the initial state. This is true only for a completely closed system. A system can undergo a transformation which decreases its entropy by borrowing negative entropy from an external system; but if the two systems are considered in combination as a closed system, the net result of the transformation is to increase the entropy of the system as a whole. An erroneous implication that has often been drawn from this is that the universe as a whole must be "running down" (that is, its entropy must be continuously increasing). But this begs the question of whether the universe can be considered a closed system. There is mounting evidence in modern astronomy that it cannot.

Another important implication of this formula is that when an isolated system is in a state of maximum entropy (consistent with its energy), no further transformation is possible, since any transformation would imply a decrease in entropy, something that is not possible. It follows that *the most stable equilibrium state for an isolated system is the state of maximum entropy.*

It was Leon Brillouin, following work by Leo Szilard, who finally proved that the informational and thermodynamic entropies are, in fact, the same. Without getting into the details of Brillouin's proof, we can observe the basic motivation for it in his explication of the paradox of Maxwell's Demon.

Imagine two isolated boxes of gas, both at the same temperature and pressure, joined by an insulated partition that has a small trapdoor in it. Maxwell proposed that a demon could stand at the door and operate it in such a way that it would allow only fast-moving molecules to pass through the door from the left and only slow-moving molecules to pass through the door from the right, with the result that the temperature of the gas on the left side of the door would be lowered and that of the gas on the right side raised. This

In other words, there is no *difference* in the radiation, no matter where the demon looks, and therefore the radiation conveys no information. In order to sort the fast- and slow-moving molecules, the demon needs some kind of "torch" to enable him to see them. If the energy for the torch comes from inside the system, it turns out that the energy used by the torch would increase the entropy of the system faster than the demon's sorting could decrease it. If the energy for the torch comes from outside, the system is no longer isolated and the Second Law permits a reduction in the thermodynamic entropy. The latter case is most interesting, though, because it turns out that the minimal amount of "information" (negative entropy) needed by the demon to sort the molecules is just equal to the amount of negative thermodynamic entropy that results from the sorting. The two entropies are thus the same.[8]

COMMUNICATION

We were talking about communication when we discussed information, particularly the flow of information. It is not information itself that "flows" but rather, the differences or messages. Information is immanent in the flow of messages. By its very definition, then, information implies communication. Conversely, we can now assert that communication implies information. This is the difference between a communications network and a heating system. Both convey energy, but the former is designed to transmit maximum information and minimum entropy, whereas the latter is designed to do just the opposite.

But there is more to the concept of communication than just the basic flow of messages. First, Shannon broke the basic communication process down into a number of essential elements. These are shown in Figure 1 which illustrates an elementary communication system. The basic structure is simple and largely self-explanatory. Note that, except in the strictly idealized case of a noiseless system, there is always a decrease in the information content going from initial message to transmitted signal to received signal to final message. The reason we discriminate between source/destination, on one hand, and encoder/decoder, on the other, is that the *language* of any communication channel is not necessarily the same as (in fact, is virtually always different than) the language of the source and/or that of the destination (the language of the source and the destination, also, need not be the same).[9]

Critical to the effectiveness of the process of communication is the element of *redundancy*. Redundancy is simply the repetitiveness of a message or set of messages. It might seem at first that redundancy in communication is uniformly a bad thing. We know that the more frequently a message occurs, the greater its probability, and the greater its probability, the less its information content. If efficiency in the transmission of information were the sole criterion of optimal communication, it would seem that we should want to always minimize redundancy. But, in fact, efficiency is only a secondary criterion in communication, and we are generally concerned primarily with effectiveness. That is, we usually would like *all* of the information we send out to be received without error. Clearly, the way to protect against the information-eroding effect of noise is through redundancy. Essentially, redundancy allows us to reconstruct the information contained in lost or erroneous messages from the *context* in which those messages occur. It is the redundancy of a language, then, that insulates it against the errors introduced by noise.

Let us consider English as an example. The English alphabet actually consists of 27 symbols (26 letters, plus the blank space between words). Were English to use these symbols with perfect efficiency, each symbol would contain 4.76 bits of information ($\log_2 27$). Because the symbols do not occur with equal probability (*e* is the most probable, *z* the least), the information content per symbol is reduced to about four bits. But the effect of redundancy in the actual use of the language is to reduce the information content per

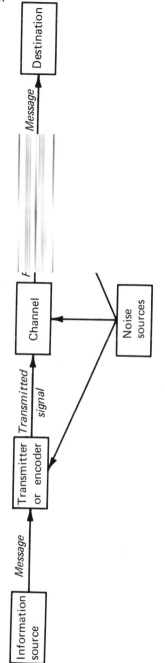

FIGURE 1. THE ELEMENTARY COMMUNICATION SYSTEM

symbol to about two bits. One can gauge the degree of redundancy by playing a simple game. Take a paragraph of common English prose and recite it to someone else, letter by letter (or symbol by symbol if you want to include the blank), asking the listener to guess the next letter before it is revealed. The accuracy of the guesses will be less at the beginning of the paragraph than at the end, but on the average, the listener can be expected to guess about half of the letters. Tests of this kind reveal the redundancy of English to be about 58 percent. This is not a bad thing, because it is this redundancy that enables us to read manuscripts replete with typographical errors or to read bad handwriting. But neither is too much redundancy a good thing, since it leads to boredom, to cliché and ultimately to the complete loss of information. Effective communication is therefore a delicate balance between redundancy and efficiency.[10]

FEEDBACK AND CONTROL

Norbert Weiner, the great mathematician who invented the science of cybernetics (from the Greek word, *kybernetes,* meaning *steersman*), defined the concept of feedback and, furthermore, asserted that the major function of feedback is to control entropy.

There are two kinds of feedback, positive and negative. Negative feedback is goal-seeking and stabilizing; positive feedback is growth-producing and unstabilizing. A thermostat works on the principle of negative feedback. The colder a room gets, the more heat a thermostat allows to flow in to maintain a (nearly) constant temperature. An example of positive feedback which almost everyone is familiar with is what happens when a microphone is placed in front of the speaker of its own amplifier. The more sound that goes into the microphone, the more that comes out of the speaker to go back into the microphone, and so forth, until the system reaches its maximum capacity. The net effect has impressed itself on anyone who has ever heard it.

Figure 2 illustrates the structure of an elementary control system. The controlled quantity could be anything from pupil dilation to steam pressure. The fundamental cybernetic structure of any control mechanism is always the same. In order to control the level of some variable quantity or quantities (v_1, v_2, . . . , v_n), the control system must, first of all, be able to sense or perceive the level of the variable or variables. The sensor function must then translate this perception into a sensor signal (which will obviously be some function of the v's) to be transmitted to a comparing mechanism, or comparator. The comparator then compares the sensor signal to some reference level (usually simply by subtraction). If there is a difference in the sensor signal and the reference level, the comparator sends a signal containing information about the magnitude and sign of the error to the effector function. The effector function then produces some quantitative output which either increases or de-

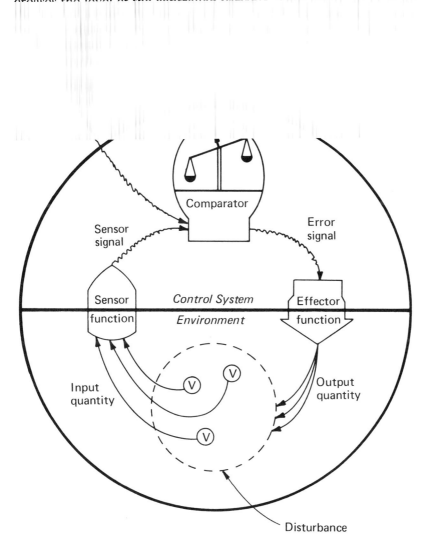

FIGURE 2. THE ELEMENTARY CONTROL SYSTEM

The elementary control system, to be a *control* system, must be based on a *negative* feedback loop. This means that the effector function will produce an output opposite in sign to any error detected by the comparator. For example, an increase in ambiant light intensity will cause the iris in my eye to decrease the amount of light that is allowed to pass through the lens to the retina, and vice versa. This is not to deny the existence of positive feedback loops or their potential usefulness. In fact, positive feedback loops are commonly present in more complex control systems and are important in permitting the reference levels of controlled variables to be shifted quickly to higher or lower levels. But a system that is solely under the influence of or merely dominated by a positive feedback loop cannot actually be said to be "under control." Indeed, whether the result of such influence is monotonic growth or monotonic decay, such a system is clearly "out of control" and is probably headed for some kind of crash if there are any limits to the size of the key variable(s).

It should also be noted that the system/environment boundary shown in Figure 2 is placed somewhat arbitrarily so as to divide the feedback loop into an *internal* and an *external* part. Such boundaries probably make little sense in cybernetics. An example of this (which, again, I get from Bateson) is the case of the blind man with a cane. Where is the "boundary" between the blind man and his "environment"? Is it at the handle of the cane? At the tip? Halfway between? The fact is, in the cybernetic softworld, the only meaningful boundaries are those that enclose whole loops or circuits.

Note also that the control system may be either internal or external to the dynamic system that it controls. For example, a rocket may be controlled from the ground via radar and telemetry or its guidance system may be completely built in.

From Figure 2 it is clear that the only things that are actually external to the closed feedback loop of the elementary control system are the source of disturbance of the controlled variable(s) and the reference signal which provides the reference level for the comparator. The fact that these are external creates both the possibility and the necessity for *hierarchies of control*.

To see how and why control systems are hierarchical, let us consider an example used by Powers.[11] A soldier is ordered to point his arm at a target. The position of the soldier's arm is now under the control of a simple negative feedback loop. We can test this by seeing what happens when we try to disturb the position of the soldier's arm. For example, if we hang a one-pound weight on his wrist, we observe that he provides a one-pound counterforce—just sufficient to maintain the position of the arm. The same thing happens if we try to displace the arm in any direction away from the target.

Now we attach the target to a helicopter and order the soldier to continue to point at the target. The helicopter flies around while the soldier's arm constantly follows the moving target. But his arm is no longer controlled simply by a single feedback loop. If we tell the

produce matching variations in the arm's velocity such that the arm is able to constantly track the target. But why doesn't the position-control system produce a counterforce to resist the influence of the velocity-control system? Because the velocity-control system does not control the muscle forces that govern the position of the arm. Rather, the system controls the *reference level* of the position-control system by providing a reference signal to the lower-order system's comparator. The velocity-control system's reference level is, in turn, derived from a still higher level of control (for example, the order of the soldier's superior). This is how and why control systems are hierarchical.

It is also important to note that for a complex (multilevel) control system to function effectively, the various levels in the hierarchy of control must be well matched in terms of energy and characteristic time of response (or *lag time*). Otherwise, such systems tend to become unstable. In general, the more energy a given feedback loop controls, the greater the instability of control. For example, one is more likely to slip up carving his name into hard wood with a gouge than writing it on paper with a pencil. Instability also results when the lag time of a higher-order control system gets close to or even less than that of a subordinate, lower-order control system. This is why people who are highly tense or stimulated may tremble: their movement-control systems are sending reference signals to their position-control systems faster than the latter can respond to them; the result is continual overshoot and undershoot in position control, which creates oscillation or trembling.

The hierarchical structure of feedback and control systems is significant. Expanding the levels of control extends the range of explanations of behavior. More behavioral types and longer time periods are included. The question of ultimate causes is redefined by every extension of the hierarchy, as each new reference signal level presents goals of greater generality. Going *up* a level in the hierarchy is equivalent to asking *why*. That is, what purpose is being served by the attainment of a set of lower-order goals? Going down a level is equivalent to asking *how*. How must a system behave to control a given variable or set of variables?[12]

The general purpose of any system of control, no matter how simple or complex, is always to try to maintain some kind of stable equilibrium state of the variable or system of variables that is under control. This tendency of control systems, to maintain a state of equilibrium, was labelled *homeostasis* by the American physiologist, Walter B. Cannon. The term has become popular in spite of being something of a misnomer. In fact, the equilibrium states of most "real" systems are rarely static, but rather, dynamic. Indeed, it is the very dynamism of such systems that makes the processes of feedback and control important and interesting.[13]

SIMPLE AND COMPLEX SYSTEMS

The essential difference between simple and complex systems is explained by Forrester:

> A complex system—a class to which a corporation, a city, an economy, or a government belong—behaves in many ways quite the opposite of the simple systems from which we have gained our experience.
>
> Most of our intuitive responses have been developed in the context of what are technically called first-order, negative-feedback loops. Such a simple loop is goal-seeking and has only one important state variable. For example, warming one's hands beside a stove can be approximated as a first-order, negative-feedback loop in which the purpose is to obtain warmth without burning one's hands. The principal state variable of the loop is the distance from the stove. If one is too close he burns his hands, if too far away he receives little heat. The intuitive lesson is that cause and effect are closely related in time and space. Temperature

depends on the distance from the stove. Too much or too little heat is clearly related to the position of the hands. The relation of cause and effect is immediate and clear. Similarly, the simple feedback loops that govern walking, driving a car, or picking things up all train us to find cause and effect occurring at approximately the same moment and location.

tive, goal-seeking loops. In the complex system the cause of a difficulty may lie far back in time from the symptoms, or in a completely different and remote part of the system. In fact, causes are usually found, not in prior events, but in the structure and policies of the system.[14]

The message to be derived from Forrester's work in industrial, urban, and world dynamics is that it is a perilous mistake to treat a complex system like a simple one. The problem-solving techniques we learn from our experience with simple systems break down when applied to complex systems, yielding "counterintuitive" results. I should note that Forrester's use of the word *intuitive* may be misleading. The word *intuitive* is a common piece of mathematical jargon which usually refers to steps in the solution of a problem or in the proof of a theorem which are presumed to be so obvious as to require no overt substantiation. By contrast, *intuition* often has the connotation of a thought process that is somehow illogical or irrational (what Forrester might well refer to as being *counterintuitive*). To say, then, that the behavior of a complex system is counterintuitive is not to say that it is incomprehensible, but rather that the behavior is not obvious even when the relationships that govern the behavior are obvious.

Not only is applying simple-system problem-solving techniques to complex systems hazardous, but the reverse is also true. One may well need an IBM 370 computer to govern a corporation or a city, but it would clearly be counterproductive and even dangerous to rely on the same kind of sophisticated control technology to govern such activities as walking or picking up an object.

The point is this: the problem-solving habits that we derive from ordinary experience and that work well in most common applications do not produce correct answers in other, more complicated, situations. To put it simply, common sense works but not always. It is important to know when it does and when it doesn't. The magician gives most of us our first introduction to the counterintuitive behavior of complex systems, in which the obvious solutions to problems paradoxically and inexorably fail.

Consider this example. A woman is placed in a large wooden box, with only her head and feet sticking out the ends. The box is closed, and a man proceeds to saw the box in half. What happens? The obvious, or *intuitive*, solution to this problem is that the woman is killed. This is true even if you have seen the trick done and know that the box can be sawed in half with no harm coming to the occupant. In fact, this is true of all magic tricks: unless you know how the trick was done, you are confronted with a frustratingly counterintuitive solution to what seems to be a simple problem. The reason for this is that the system of which the trick is comprised seems to be simple but is actually more complex. The problem-solving techniques which apparently ought to apply, do not work, and one is left puzzled.

Once one has had some exposure to acts of magic, he learns the magic trick as a complex system from such contextual cues as the magician's costume, his mannerisms, the stage, or the setting. As we mature, we learn, often from harsh experience, that the marketplace, the polling place, and various other social situations contain circumstances or contexts in which we may be tricked. While in many cases we never learn how the trick is done, we do learn many cues in dealing with merchants, politicians, and others which at least put us on our guard. However, more often than not, most of us fail to identify complex-system problems as such. Our individual and collective attempts to solve these problems turn out to be unproductive or counterproductive, and the overall result is the kind of frustration and bewilderment that characterize contemporary society and which is a central aspect of ecocrisis. As time goes by, we can expect that the failure of those who govern human society to distinguish between simple and complex systems and to adopt the problem-solving strategies appropriate to each, will have consequences that are even more disastrous than those we are experiencing today.

SYNERGY

Buckminster Fuller writes: *"The word 'synergy' means 'Behavior of whole systems unpredicted by behavior of any of the systems' parts.'"*[15] When we say, "The whole is greater than the sum of its parts," we are essentially defining the concept of synergy. Fuller's definition is better. Synergy may be evident when the whole i̶ ̶ ̶ ̶

[illegible/damaged text]

̶p̶r̶o̶p̶e̶r̶t̶y̶, all systems are synergetic with respect to at least one property.

Perhaps the classic illustration of the phenomenon of synergy is Fuller's geodesic dome. The geodesic dome is a structure whose impressive strength is practically unpredictable from the properties of the relatively flimsy struts and plates that comprise it. The strength of the geodesic dome is vastly greater than that of any of its parts taken separately. The same phenomenon is illustrated in reverse by an ancient Chinese fable. The story was that an aging mandarin could not decide which of his three sons should inherit his wealth after his death. The old man finally summoned his three sons to his chamber and presented them with a bundle of 12 sticks. He told them that whichever of them could break the bundle of sticks in half would be the one most fit to inherit his title and fortune. Two of the sons each tried with all of their strength to break the bundle in two, but to no avail. The third son simply untied the bundle and broke the 12 sticks one at a time.

CONNECTEDNESS

The complexity of many of the systems that concern us—especially social/ecological systems—which implies a hierarchical structure of feedback and control and resulting synergetic interaction of the systems' various components, is manifest in a simple concept—connectedness. As Garrett Hardin explains it, our modern mythology is built around a dream that is the reciprocal of the dream of the "philosopher's stone." The philosopher's stone was an entity that could solve all problems of a general type. The contemporary dream, on the other hand, is of "a highly specific agent *which will do only one thing.*"[16] To illustrate the fallacy of the modern myth, Hardin recalls "The Monkey's Paw," a story by W.W. Jacobs, which was used to similar effect by Rachel Carson in *Silent Spring.*

In the story, a man is given a monkey's paw and told that it will grant him three wishes. Incredulous at first, the man decides to wish for money. The next day the man's son falls into some machinery at the mill and is killed; he receives a sum of money as compensation for his son's death. Dismayed, the man wishes that his son were alive again. That night, the son returns home, looking as he would after such an accident. Finally, the desperate father wishes that everything return to the way it was before he was given the monkey's paw. Hardin's statement of the moral of the story sums up the concept of connectedness in a phrase: *"We can never do merely one thing."*[17]

The fallacy inherent in the failure to comprehend the connectedness of the global ecosystem is one of the chief roots of ecocrisis. This fallacy—or dream, as Hardin calls it—is what Bateson was describing when he said: "When you narrow down your epistemology and act on the premise 'What interests me is me, or my organization, or my species,' you chop off consideration of other loops of the loop structure." The result of this single, pervasive epistemological error is essentially the whole list of problems enumerated in Chapter 1.

LEARNING

The theory of learning is another of those subjects of which a complete discussion would go way beyond the scope of this book. What I mainly want to discuss here is learning as a softworld, or cybernetic, concept, especially Bateson's concept of the learning hierarchy.

We must begin with a brief consideration of Bertrand Russell's theory of logical types.[18] Essentially, what Russell's theory says is that it is a logical fallacy to consider a class as a member of itself. Thus, for example, the *class of chairs* is not a chair. But neither is the class of chairs a member of the *class of nonchairs.* Classes of things are different from the things they classify and the difference is one of logical type. Furthermore, this difference is clearly hierarchical (that is, classes of classes are of a different logical type than classes, and so on).

As Bateson notes, to commit an error of logical type is like eating the menu instead of the dinner. This kind of error is of great importance and is the subject of the next and last section of this softworld primer. For now, we need only keep in mind that there is this hierarchy of logical types of messages and information.

Corresponding to this logical hierarchy in the structure of information, Bateson asserts that there is a similar hierarchy in the struc-

[text obscured]

... will be talking not only about the learning of human beings but also about the learning of machines and other kinds of organisms.

Learning 0 is exactly what I referred to earlier as *control*. It can be represented in its simplest form by the elementary control system illustrated in Figure 2. Fundamentally, zero-learning is characterized by *specificity of response*. That is, the response to disturbances by an organism or system that is capable of no higher level of learning than the zero level is essentially *built into* the structure of the control system. It is always specific to the given disturbance and is always the same, no matter how often the disturbance is repeated.

Any simple control system, therefore, evidences Learning 0. But even highly complex control systems may "learn" at the zero level and, in fact, are often capable of no higher level of learning than Learning 0. For example, most computers are designed for no more than zero-learning and respond to instructions and commands strictly and slavishly according to the way they have been programmed. Unless the computer is capable of changing its programming according to the outcome of its performance, we can say that it is *hard-programmed* and capable only of zero-learning. Many living organisms exhibit this zero level of learning. The honeybee, for example, performs a complex dance to communicate to its fellow workers the location of its food (flowers). But the dance and the interpretation, or decoding, of it are not learned through instruction or cultural transmission. Rather, they are hard-programmed into the bees' nervous systems and are incapable of adaptation or change (except through the genotypical process of evolution).

Another kind of zero-learning in living organisms is the imprinting demonstrated by various kinds of animals, especially birds. A duckling, for example, will become imprinted on its mother shortly after birth and from that moment on will follow its mother wherever she goes. If the duckling is exposed to a human being or a toy boat or any other object after birth, it will become imprinted on that object and will treat it as its mother.

Learning I, or *proto-learning,* is the subject of most "learning theories." Proto-learning includes both of the major kinds of learning discussed in modern psychology, "classical conditioning" (Pavlov) and "operant," or "instrumental conditioning" (Skinner). Both kinds of learning, or conditioning, are based on an "S-R," or "stimulus/response," model. In classical conditioning, new stimuli are conditioned to produce the same response, whereas in operant conditioning, a given stimulus is conditioned to evoke or shape a new response.

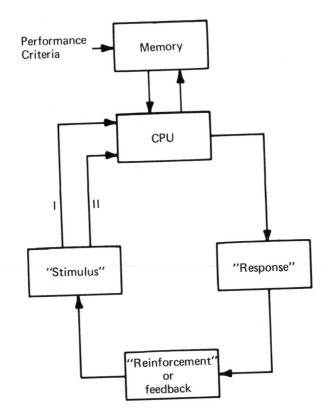

FIGURE 3. LEARNING I

Figure 3 presents a simple schematic model of the elementary process of Learning I, which includes both classical and operant forms of conditioning. The similarity in structure between this model and the one given in Figure 2 for the elementary control system is not merely coincidental, since the difference between Learning I and "control," or Learning 0, is fundamentally one of logical type. The learning system must be presumed to be

[illegible] the sensory functions of the control system.[19] News of this signal, or "stimulus," is then sent to a function which, for lack of a better term, I will call the "CPU," or "central processing unit," borrowing from the vocabulary of the computer scientist.

The CPU functions in the learning system in a manner similar to, but far more complex than, the way the comparator functions in the control system. First, the stimulus signal may be enormously complex. At the very least, it must contain two distinct parts: (1) news of the stimulus itself, and (2) news of the *context* in which the stimulus occurred. (In other words, the stimulus signal defines a *gestalt*.) Second, the output of the CPU does not depend merely on a simple matter of subtraction of signal from reference level. The CPU must make some kind of a *decision* about what to do about this stimulus, and its decision may be difficult, imprecise, and frequently wrong. A crucial and distinctive part of the learning system, therefore, is the *memory unit* attached to the CPU. The CPU must first *store* the stimulus signal in its memory before it can decide what to do about it. The CPU must then scan its memory to find out what possible responses are available, what criterion of performance (criterion of optimization) applies to this stimulus, what responses have been matched with this "stimulus" in the past (if any), and what their outcomes were. From all of this information, the CPU will either select the appropriate response from the set of alternatives or, if it has insufficient history on which to base such a choice, choose a response more or less arbitrarily from the set of alternatives; or it may even synthesize a new response and add it to the list of alternatives. Having gone through its decision-making process, the CPU will output instructions to the control system to implement its chosen response.

Changes in the control system corresponding to the CPU's response instructions will eventually be manifested in changes in the performance of the control system which will then be *fed back* to the CPU via new stimulus signals. This feedback is essential to the Learning I process. In the operant conditioning case, this feedback constitutes the reinforcement that is an intrinsic part of that kind of learning. The CPU evaluates an operant response according to the appropriate performance criterion or criteria. If the response is found to be insufficient or erroneous, the learning loop may be repeated any number of times until the criteria are met. This is why the essence of Learning I can be considered the process of *trial and error* when these terms are properly defined. Even in the classical conditioning case we can probably safely assume that there are performance criteria built into the learning system which define some optimum scheme of sensory information processing and which therefore finds some modes of sensory integration more reinforcing than others.

I have suggested that the term *learning* might refer to some kind of change. Now it should be clear that Learning I is, in fact, defined by changes in the performance of a control system resulting from a cyclical process of trial and error. In other words, the very specificity of response that characterizes Learning 0 is exactly what is changed in the process of Learning I. It must be emphasized, though, that these changes need not be deterministic but may be— in fact generally are—probabilistic. That is, any change in the probability of a given stimulus being matched with a given response will be evidence of Learning I.

Since the process of proto-learning involves both a change in the Learning 0 or control system and a change in the Learning I system itself, it is interesting to ask what the entropy changes associated with the transformations in these respective systems are. The answer is that the entropy change in the control system resulting from the proto-learning process may be either positive, negative, or zero, but that *this change must be associated with a negative entropy change in the Learning I system.* The reason for this is not hard to see. I have already said that any change in the probabilities associated with the pattern of response of the control system will be taken as evidence of Learning I. Therefore it doesn't matter whether these changes result in an increase, decrease, or no change in the entropy of the control system. Both learning and unlearning, or conditioning and deconditioning, require the same process of Learning I. The Learning I system, however, must "remember" every change in the control system (at least for a short while), regardless of its entropic valence. But this means that *information* must be added to the Learning I system at the end of each cycle, which is equivalent to a *decrease in entropy*.

Let us also explore in greater detail the difference between

difference is also one of logical type. Since in both systems *feedback* emanates from a set of secondary sensor signals following the output of the various effector functions, it follows that the difference between feedback in Learning I and feedback in Learning 0 is the same as the difference just mentioned between stimulus signal and sensor signal. And *error* in Learning I is actually an integration, classification, or interpretation of the errors of the control system, as referenced to the performance criteria of the Learning I system. Thus no (an absence of) errors in Learning 0 can correspond to an error in Learning I, no feedback in Learning 0 can correspond to a feedback in Learning I, no sensory disturbance in Learning 0 can correspond to a stimulus in Learning I, no effector output can result from a response in Learning I—all because of the difference in logical type between Learning 0 and Learning I.

But the difference in logical type between the various levels of learning depends even more on the importance of *context* in learning. I mentioned above that the stimulus signal to the CPU contains information not only about the stimulus itself but about the context in which the stimulus occurs. This information is crucial, for in the vast majority of instances, the same stimulus will have many different meanings according to the context in which it occurs. The CPU would have no way of resolving this ambiguity and therefore would be incapable of either choosing a response or of evaluating the resulting feedback without this knowledge. In other words, the CPU *responds* not to a *stimulus* but to a *gestalt* of *stimulus-in-context*.

From this it follows that for learning to occur, it must be assumed that not only is the stimulus itself repeatable but that the context in which the stimulus occurs must also be repeatable. If not, then each stimulus-in-context is unique and each response of the control system is specific, and therefore Learning I becomes indistinguishable from Learning 0. On the other hand, the assumption of repeatable context makes the logical typing, and resultant hierarchical order, of learning inevitably follow, since the concept of context itself is subject to logical typing. As Bateson observes:

> Either we must discard the notion of "context," or we retain this notion and, with it, accept the hierarchic series —stimulus, context of stimulus, context of context of stimulus, etc. This series can be spelled out in the form of a hierarchy of logical types as follows:
> Stimulus is an elementary signal, internal or external.
> Context of stimulus is a *meta*message which *classifies* the elementary signal.
> Context of context of stimulus is a meta-metamessage which classifies the metamessage.
> And so on.
> The same hierarchy could have been built up from the notion of "response" or the notion of "reinforcement."[20]

To see the relationship between the hierarchy of contexts and the hierarchy of learning more clearly, let us consider some examples.

First, consider the example of a dog that has been trained to "heel." When the master utters the appropriate command, the dog will move to the master's left side and sit or walk close to that side until a contravening command is given. The dog has presumably "learned" to respond to the stimulus of the word *heel* with the complex behavior known as *heeling.* The importance of the context in this example may not be immediately apparent, but it is crucial. Careful observation will disclose that the dog does not always respond to the word *heel* by heeling. If the dog is lying in the corner while the master is sitting on the couch engaged in conversation, we will note that the master may say the word *heel* many times without evoking the heeling response, for example, "My shoe needs a new *heel*"; "The cut will soon *heal.*" The utterance of the word *heel* will only evoke the heeling response in a fairly well-defined context. It usually must be the master who says the word, the master must be standing or walking, the word must be preceded by a prefatory signal which the master thinks of as the dog's name, and the word must be uttered with the intonation of a command. Similarly, in the human sphere, many of us who drive have "learned" to respond to a red light by stepping on the brake. But again, this stimulus only evokes this response within certain well-defined contexts: the car we are sitting in must be moving, we must be the person who is driving, the red light must be part of a traffic signal, or the taillight of another

of "Yummies." In this context, the dog learned not merely to respond to various command stimuli but also "learned-to-learn" as she gradually discovered that the behavior associated with Learning I would itself be reinforced in this context. This leads us to the next level of Bateson's learning hierarchy—Learning II, or "deutero-learning."

The simplest thing we can say about Learning II is that it functions the same way as Learning I, except that it is at the next higher level of logical type. In short, if Learning I is what we conventionally call *learning,* then Learning II is learning-about-learning, or learning-to-learn. The schematic structure of Learning II is essentially the same as that of Learning I depicted in Figure 3, except that where the Learning I system was "plugged in" to the Learning 0 or control system, the Learning II system is "plugged in" to the Learning I system.

While not all organisms are capable of Learning II (just as not all are capable of Learning I), its existence is well documented in the psychological literature. For example, "reversal learning" experiments often reveal the existence of Learning II. In these experiments, subjects are trained to respond one way to one stimulus (say, a red light) and another way to a second stimulus (a green light). Then the "meanings" of the two stimuli are reversed, and the subjects are trained to reverse their responses accordingly. If the reversal is repeated several times, many higher organisms, and most people, will require fewer and fewer trials to learn the new reversed meaning of the two stimuli. This is evidence of Learning II. Another example is that of rote learning, where people are given sequences of symbols to memorize. As the tests are repeated on the same subjects, most people become more proficient at memorizing new sequences.

The significance of deutero-learning is more than just academic. Bateson suggests that most of the terms we use to describe human "character" (dependent, hostile, competitive, passive, fatalistic, perfectionist, and so on) all actually describe various results or premises of Learning II. He proposes that the premises of Learning II "punctuate" human interaction. By this he means that in the interaction (or "transactions") between two individuals, A and B (or between A and his environment), whether a given behavior of A's will be a stimulus, response, or reinforcement in relation to B's behavior will depend on A's and B's understanding (or misunderstanding) of the *context* in which the interaction occurs. In other words, the stream of interaction between A and B $(a_1b_1a_2b_2 \ldots)$ will be punctuated into the subsequences (stimulus-response-reinforcement) of Learning I according to the context of the context of the mutual stimuli. It follows that for A and B to have the same understanding of the context of their interaction, in order to punctuate the stream of their interaction in the same way, they must exchange meta-metamessages that define the context. What these meta-metamessages will be and how they will be interpreted will depend on previous Learning II.

Perhaps the most important thing that follows from this is that errors of communication at the level of Learning II can have extremely unstabilizing results that may be considered pathological. For example, the forms of aggressive behavior that characterize *fighting* or *playing* between two dogs are virtually indistinguishable. Therefore, whether two dogs are fighting or playing depends almost entirely on how they mutually understand the context of their interaction. Since the dogs cannot actually say to each other, "This is only play," they must exchange symbolic signals at the outset (for instance, tail-wagging) to indicate to each other that "the aggressive behavior we are about to engage in will be considered play." It is not uncommon to see two dogs engaged in play suddenly forget that they are only *playing* and start *fighting*. Usually a sharp yelp or submissive lying on the back by one of the participants is sufficient to redefine the context as *play*. But it is also not uncommon to see two dogs engaged in aggressive behavior where one thinks it is playing while the other thinks it is fighting, usually with more or less pathological results for the "player."

This kind of crossing of wires lies at the heart of Bateson's "dou-

ble bind" theory of schizophrenia. Without getting into an exhaus-
tive discussion of the theory here, essentially, it hypothesizes that the
state of mind commonly labeled *schizophrenic* may result from epistemological stress which derives from contradictions between messages at the levels of Learning I and Learning II. The person diagnosed as schizophrenic may be the victim of paradoxical communication resulting from irreconcilable contradictions between

... acute schizophrenic episode was visited in the hospital by
his mother. *He was glad to see her and impulsively put his
arm around her shoulders, whereupon she stiffened. He
withdrew his arm and she asked, 'Don't you love me any
more?' He then blushed, and she said, 'Dear, you must not
be so easily embarrassed and afraid of your feelings.'* The
patient was able to stay with her only a few minutes more
and following her departure he assaulted an aide and was
put in the tubs.

Obviously, this result could have been avoided if the
young man had been able to say, 'Mother, it is obvious that
you become uncomfortable when I put my arm around you,
and that you have difficulty accepting a gesture of affection
from me.' However, the schizophrenic patient doesn't have
this possibility open to him. His intense dependency and
training prevents him from commenting upon his mother's
communicative behavior, though she comments on his and
forces him to accept and to attempt to deal with the complicated sequence. . . .[21]

This interaction contains a host of complications and paradoxes for
the schizophrenic victim, but essentially they boil down to this: "The
impossible dilemma thus becomes: 'If I am to keep my tie to mother,
I must not show her that I love her, but if I do not show her that I
love her, I will lose her'."[22]

Bateson was primarily concerned with intrafamily communication in his initial work on the double-bind theory of schizophrenia.

More recent research suggests that schizophrenic behavior can be provoked by any kind of "stress" (as measured physiologically), and the propensity in a given individual toward this form of behavior probably has a significant genetic component. This does not, however, vitiate the potential validity of Bateson's double-bind theory, since Bateson recognized the relevance of genetic factors, and his theory asserts primarily that it is the epistemological stress induced by the "double bind"—and not necessarily the particular characteristics of the double bind of intrafamilial communication—that is schizophrenogenic. After all, stress, even when measured physiologically, is a subjective and not an objective phenomenon, since we know that different individuals in the same environmental circumstances will experience different degrees of stress. It seems reasonable to assume that even purely physical stress (for example, pain) is likely to be schizophrenogenic in a given individual to the extent that it poses a double bind for him (for example, "I can't stand it" and "I can't stop it").

It is also important to note that the state of mind which may result from the double bind and which western medicine calls *schizophrenia* is not intrinsically pathological. Its pathological aspect depends on its social context, as well as how the victim deals with it. As Bateson observes:

> In the Eastern religion, Zen Buddhism, the goal is to achieve enlightenment. The Zen master attempts to bring about enlightenment in his pupil in various ways. One of the things he does is to hold a stick over the pupil's head and say fiercely, 'If you say this stick is real, I will strike you with it. If you say this stick is not real, I will strike you with it. If you don't say anything, I will strike you with it. We feel that the schizophrenic finds himself continually in the same situation as the pupil, but he achieves something like disorientation rather than enlightenment. . . .[23]

To get back to the relationship between Learning II and Learning I, the question arises: how does the Learning II system effect changes in the Learning I system? The Learning I system effects change in the Learning 0 or control system by altering the reference levels of the comparators of that system. Similarly, the Learning II system changes the Learning I system by altering the *performance criteria* of that system (see Figure 3). Also, just as the negative entropy change essential to Learning I could be associated with a positive, negative, or zero entropy change in the Learning 0 system, the same thing holds true for Learning II. Specifically, an increase in Learning II could result from a decrease in Learning I (that is, a positive entropy change in the Learning I system), as long as the Learning II system *remembers* the change (and therefore is capable of reversing or repeating it). These statements also hold true for all of the higher levels of learning and their relationship to their subordi-

tions of this learning that can be tested against reality. It is like a picture seen in an inkblot; it has neither correctness nor incorrectness. It is only a *way* of seeing the inkblot.[24]

In short, the self-validating nature of the results of Learning II is such that (a) the premises of Learning II tend to be, in some sense, "unconscious," and (b) the results of Learning II in early childhood tend to persist throughout adulthood and to be resistant to change.

Learning III is, by definition, learning-to-learn-to-learn. Essentially, Learning III throws open the largely unexamined premises of Learning II to question and change. Bateson offers some examples to illustrate the concept of Learning III:

(a) The individual might learn to form more readily those habits the forming of which we call Learning II.

(b) He might learn to close for himself the "loopholes" which would allow him to avoid Learning III.

(c) He might learn to change the habits acquired by Learning II.

(d) He might learn that he is a creature which can and does unconsciously achieve Learning II.

(e) He might learn to limit or direct his Learning II.

(f) If Learning II is a learning of the contexts of Learning I, then Learning III should be a learning of the contexts of those contexts.[25]

The most profound implication of the nature of Learning III is that it inherently implies a redefinition and perhaps a complete negation of the concept of self:

> Learning III . . . may lead either to an increase in Learning II or to a limitation and perhaps a reduction of that phenomenon. Certainly it must lead to a greater flexibility in the premises acquired by the process of Learning II—a *freedom* from their bondage.
> . . . . .
> But any freedom from the bondage of habit must also denote a profound redefinition of the self. If I stop at the level of Learning II, "I" am the aggregate of those characteristics which I call my "character." "I" am my habits of acting in context and shaping and perceiving the contexts in which I act. Selfhood is a product or aggregate of Learning II. To the degree that a man achieves Learning III and learns to perceive and act in terms of the contexts of contexts, his "self" will take on a sort of irrelevance. The concept of "self" will no longer function as a nodal argument in the punctuation of experience.[26]

There are relatively few people who have, like the great Yogis and Zen masters, attained the level of Learning III, although more and more people are now embarking, via drugs and meditation, on "trips" to that level. It is unlikely that Homo sapiens is capable of Learning IV, but Bateson suggests that the phylogeny of this latter group represents its existence.

Finally, it should be emphasized that while both learning and control are hierarchical, the hierarchies of learning and of control are not the same. Thus, while the first stage of the learning hierarchy is the control system of Learning 0, that control system may be either simple or complex (that is, it may contain either first-order feedback loops or feedback loops of one or several higher orders). Conversely, the most complex control system may be utterly incapable of any more than zero-learning.

However, what was said earlier about the "hierarchy of control" is also true of the "hierarchy of learning." That is, going up a level in the hierarchy is equivalent to asking *why* a certain learning process is taking place (what are the performance criteria for this level of learning?) and going down a level is equivalent to asking *how* it is being carried out (what changes are effected in lower-order systems that evidence learning at this level?).[27]

REIFICATION

A typical dictionary definition of the term *reification* would say that reification is the treatment of an abstract mental construction, or "idea," as a "real thing." Since in the softworld there is no distinction between a real thing and an idea, this kind of definition is not useful here. However, reification can be defined simply as the ge-

Parsimony, or the Law of Occam's Razor. This law is often stated as: "There shall be no unnecessary multiplication of explanatory principles." The term *explanatory principle* is ironic because an explanatory principle is merely a label for those things that remain unexplained or unknown. The fallacy of reification occurs whenever the label for that which is unexplained is used as if it were an explanation. This is an error of logical type (that is, the confusion of a class with its members). It took the physical sciences many years to rid themselves of reified concepts (for example, *phlogiston, ether,* and *vital humors*), but the younger, social "sciences" are still replete with them *(ego,* the *invisible hand, dialectical materialism, need for achievement,* and *minimal brain damage).*

This is particularly true in the field of psychology and psychotherapy (the *psyche* itself is a reified concept, which is perhaps one reason why Skinner prefers to use the term *science of behavior* rather than *psychology*) where there is a fairly well-marked dichotomy between a host of schools that can be called "psychodynamic" and which are all guilty of reification to some extent, and another school which is generally called "behavioral," or "behaviorist," and which is fairly stringent in its adherence to the Law of Occam's Razor.

Albert Bandura illustrates the reification of much contemporary "psychodynamic" psychology and psychotherapy with the metaphor of what he calls "zoognick theory." Such a theory is born when some set of asocial, or perhaps illegal, behaviors are designated as the external expressions of a *zoognick,* which is inferred to be an autonomous agent functioning "intrapsychically"; that is, inside the mind. While the hypothetical zoognick is endowed with causative power, the observed behavior from which its existence was originally inferred is passed off as mere "superficial behavioral manifestations." Psychological tests are created to measure zoognick strength. These, in turn, form the basis of diagnoses which identify the action of the underlying zoognick as the cause of individuals' deviant behavior. It is assumed that "patient variables are not conceived to be behaviors, but constructs concerning internal constellations." Proceeding on this assumption, the goals of psychotherapy are stated in terms of removing the pernicious zoognick. But attempts to directly modify the deviant behavior are considered superficial—maybe even dangerous—since the *symptoms* of the zoognick, if eliminated, may only be forced to reemerge in other, equally if not more pernicious forms. A "sufficiently charismatic exponent" of zoognick theory is readily able to attract zealous followers, convinced of the vital importance and etiological potency of zoognicks. And finally, would-be humanists will "embrace zoognick theory as more befitting the complexities of human beings than those simplistic mechanistic doctrines that stubbornly insist that the zoognick is the deviant behavior rechristened."[28]

If these intimations by Bandura seem at all hyperbolic, one need only consider the enormous commercial success of such books as Janov's *The Primal Scream* or Harris's *I'm OK, You're OK* to realize their essential validity.

If these considerations seem tangential to the subject of this book, let it be clearly asserted that they are not. They are of central importance. There are as many "zoognick" theories of eco-pathology as there are of psycho-pathology, and in moving from an understanding of ecocrisis toward some long-range solution, we will have to be wary of the pitfalls of reification if we want to attain useful results.[29]

It would be easy to demonstrate the relevancy of the concepts discussed in this softworld primer to our understanding of ecocrisis. The importance of the processes of communication, control, and learning in the dynamics of the global ecosystem could be illustrated by countless examples. Every organism, great or small, must communicate with its environment and other organisms. It must maintain some kind of equilibrium or homeostasis between itself and its environment. And it must adapt to new contingencies, if it is to survive and reproduce and endure. Therefore we would find that from the level of the individual cell to that of the organism to that of the population to that of the community to that of the ecosystem as a whole, the same fundamental cybernetic principles are crucial to the existence and maintenance of life. Such considerations alone would probably justify advocacy of a softworld approach to the problems of ecocrisis.

CHAPTER 7

EVOLUTION

adaptations and their form. Surely, the minimum requirement for an attitude to nature and to man is that it approximate reality. Clearly, our traditional view does not. . . . The
earth has been the one home for all of its evolving processes
and for all of its inhabitants; from hydrogen to man, it is only
the bathing sunlight which changes. The planet contains our
origins, our history, our milieu—it is our home. It is in this
sense that ecology, derived from oikos, is the science of the
home. *Can we review physical and biological evolution to
discern the character of these processes, their direction, the
laws which obtain, the criteria for survival and success?* If
this can be done, there will also be revealed an intrinsic
value system and the basis for form. This is the essential
ingredient for an adequate view of the world: a value system
which corresponds to the creative process of the world and
both a diagnostic and constructive view of human adaptations and their form.[1]

McHarg's question is crucial, for if indeed this can be done, it
implies something far more profound than McHarg's apparently
modest "value system" and "basis for form." A "diagnostic and constructive view of human adaptations and their form" is nothing less
than *the solution* to the ecological crisis. If ecocrisis results from
mankind being in violation of "nature's plan," then clearly it is essential to find out just what that plan is in order that we may bring
human behavior back into conformity with it. Having perceived

ourselves to be in a condition which seems headed down the dead-end street of extinction, it is only logical to ask where the path of survival and continued evolution lies, in the hope that we may yet get back on the right track.

Underlying this quest is an ancient imperative, to harmonize human activity with the exigencies of a capricious and often apparently cruel *nature.* This imperative lies at the heart of all religions. It was the same imperative that motivated the eighteenth-century *philosophes* to discover and articulate the "Laws of Nature," the body of which quickly grew to comprise the edifice of nineteenth-century classical "science." But as Becker observed, the "heavenly city" of the eighteenth-century philosophers was based no less on *faith* than the "heavenly city" of St. Augustine which it presumed to supplant.[2] Except for a change of "city manager" from Jesus to Newton, the two were not that much different. The laboratory and the university gradually replaced the cathedral and the monastery, but those who claimed knowledge of the rules of an orderly *nature* did so with no less zeal and self-righteousness than those who earlier had claimed insight into the obscure wisdom of an omnipotent *God.* The rise of modern science, and specifically the development of quantum mechanics and relativity theory, turned the edifice of classical science upside down, exposed ontology as a will-o'-the-wisp, and vindicated Kant's demand for a "critical" epistemology. When an absolute and deterministic reality was supplanted by a relativistic and statistical reality, the role of faith became increasingly irrelevant and its domain became constricted not even to the unknown, but to the unknowable.

The philosophical implications of modern physics troubled even Einstein who, while he accepted the mathematical necessity of Heisenberg's uncertainty principle, clung tenaciously to his faith that "God does not play dice with the universe." Nevertheless, Einstein, as well as every other modern "scientist" deserving of the title, was compelled to accept *reality* as an epistemological and not an ontological concept. *Reality* became a conceptual model for the rational integration and interpretation of "sense impressions."

> Science is not just a collection of laws, a catalogue of unrelated facts. It is a creation of the human mind, with its freely invented ideas and concepts. Physical theories try to form a picture of reality and to establish its connection with the wide world of sense impressions. Thus the only justification for our mental structures is whether and in what way our theories form such a link.[3]

In short, *reality,* in the perspective of modern science, is no longer what *is* but what *works. Reality* is a model, the validity of which, as Forrester keeps reminding us, can ultimately be assessed only in terms of its *usefulness.*

Therefore, McHarg's assertion that the minimal requirement for a functional attitude toward the relationship between man and nature is that it "approximate reality," is valid to the extent that we interpret it within the context of modern science. This means that

The evolution of the world reveals movement from more to less random, from less to more structural, from simplicity to diversity, from few to many life-forms—in a word, *toward greater negentropy.* This can be seen in the evolution of the elements, the compounds, and of life. . . . We can now see the earth as a process by which the falling sunlight is destined for entropy, but is arrested and entrapped by physical processes and creatures, and reconstituted into higher and higher levels of order as evolution proceeds. Entropy is the law and demands its price, but while all energy is destined to become degraded, physical and biological systems move to higher order—from instability towards steady-state—in sum, to more negentropy. Evolution is thus a creative process in which all physical processes and life forms participate. *Creation involves the raising of matter and energy from lower to higher levels of order. Retrogression and destruction consist of reduction from the higher levels of order to entropy.*
. . . . .

We can look at the world and see our kin; for we are united, by living, with all life, and are from the same origins. Life has proceeded from simple to complex, although the simplest forms have not been superseded, only augmented. It has proceeded from uniform to diverse, from few to many species. *Life has revealed evolution as a progression from greater to lesser entropy. . . .* Evolution has revealed a progression from simple to complex, from uniform to diverse, from unicellular to multicelled, from few to many species, from few to many ecosystems, and the relations between these processes have also evolved toward increased *complexity.*

. . . . .

If evolution has proceeded from simple to complex, this was accomplished through symbiosis. As the number of species increased, so then did the number of roles and the symbiotic relationships between species. If stability increases as evolution proceeds, then this is the proof of increased symbiosis. If conservation of energy is essential to the diminution of entropy, then symbioses are essential to accomplish this. *Perhaps it is symbiosis or, better, altruism that is the arrow of evolution.*

This view of the world, creation, and evolution reveals as the principal actors, the sun, elements and compounds, the hydrologic cycle, the plants, decomposers, and the animals. . . . Man has little creative role in this realm although his destructive potential is considerable. *However, energy can as well be considered as information.* The light which heats the body can inform the perceptive creature. When energy is so considered, then the apperception of information as meaning, and response to it, is also seen as ordering, as antientropic. Noise to the unperceptive organism, through perception becomes information from which is derived meaning. In an appraisal of the world's work of apperception, it is seen that the simpler organisms, which create the maximum negentropy, are low on the scale of apperception which increases as one rises on the evolutionary scale. *Man, who had no perceptible role as a creator of negentropy, becomes prominent as a perceptive and conscious being.* . . . That which integrates either the cell in the organism or the organism in the biosphere is a symbiotic relationship. In sum, these are beneficial. This then is the third measure, the third element, after order and complexity, of the value system: the concession of some part of the autonomy of the individual in a cooperative arrangement with other organisms which have equally qualified their individual freedom toward the end of survival and evolution. . . . Man is superbly endowed to be that conscious creature who can perceive the phenomenal world, its operation, its direction, the roles of the creatures, and physical processes. Through his apperception, he is enabled to accomplish adaptations which are the symbioses of man-nature. This is the promise of his apperception and consciousness. . . .[4]

In summary, McHarg writes:

sis. This reveals an intrinsic value system with a currency: energy; an inventory which includes matter and its cycles, life forms and their roles, and cooperative mechanisms.[5]

The theory enunciated here by McHarg is powerful and profound in its implications. Were it valid, it would open up the possibility, not only for a comprehensive way of understanding the nature of the ecological crisis, but, more importantly, for a prescriptive approach to its solution. But something so basic cannot be accepted casually or cavalierly; consequently we proceed to a critical examination of the basis of McHarg's theory. In doing so we will discover some important epistemological errors in McHarg's thesis which, when corrected, will lead us to what I believe to be a more useful general theory for extracting constructive guidance from the scientific understanding of evolution.

THE MEANING OF ENTROPY

The keystone of McHarg's theory is the assertion that *negentropy is the measure of the direction of evolution.* We will examine this contention in greater detail in the next section of this chapter, but for now, let us simply accept it as given. What follows from this is McHarg's whole "intrinsic value system." His system is based ultimately on a *subjective interpretation of the meaning of entropy.* The interpretation contained in McHarg's thesis is summarized in Table

1. Thus the alleged negentropic direction of evolution is associated with a trend toward complexity, diversity, interdependence, stability, and high number of species, or what McHarg calls "health."[6] At the heart of his subjective interpretation of the meaning of entropy is the consistent practice of equating decreasing levels of entropy with "higher levels of order." This equation is, in fact, an error, but one which is so widespread and which has such a long tradition that there are many who would probably not recognize it as one.

In a discussion of the laws of thermodynamics, Witold Brostow calls this idea that "entropy is a name given to a quantitative measure of disorder" a "persistent myth" and points out that such phrases are meaningless, "except perhaps in the three special cases of mixtures of perfect gases, mixtures of isotopes, and crystals at temperatures near thermodynamic zero." While some scientists have tried to clarify the concept of entropy, the myth continues to live. "The reason for this seems to lie in the fact that one tries to connect an indeed quantitative and exact notion—entropy—with something called disorder, which is loose and subjective and for which no definition exists."[7] Three cases are possible and seem to have been taking place.

The three cases are merely those that cover all of the logical possibilities. The first is that in which there exists no general consensus about whether a transformation in a system and a resulting change in entropy represents an increase or a decrease in "disorder." The second is when the myth, as a *rule,* seems to hold (that is, where there is a general consensus that there has been, say, an increase in the "disorder" of the system, and this actually corresponds to a mea-

TABLE 1. McHARG'S INTERPRETATION OF THE MEANING
OF ENTROPY

	HIGH ENTROPY		LOW ENTROPY
	disorder		order
ILL HEALTH	simplicity	HEALTH	complexity
	uniformity		diversity
	independence		interdependence
RETROGRESSION		EVOLUTION	(symbiosis)
	instability		stability (steady state)
	low number of species		high number of species

sured increase in entropy). The third case is that to which Forrester's term *counterintuitive* might well apply. The consensus holds that a *decrease* in disorder has occurred, while, paradoxically, measurement indicates an *increase* in entropy, and the rule is violated.

An example of the latter which is most commonly cited by those who have punctured the myth of "entropy as disorder" (which, of course, is the same as *negentropy as order*) is that of the precipitation

crystal in the direction of both decreasing entropy and increasing order—and hence, the *apparent* violation of the Second Law—result from a simple fallacy: considering the crystal, by itself, as a closed rather than an open system. The Second Law does not rule out *local* spontaneous decreases of entropy within the domain of a larger closed system, but asserts that such processes, if and when they occur, must result in a net increase in the entropy of the system as a whole. This is why Maxwell's Demon, even with the help of his "torch," could not diminish the entropy of the system of the boxes of gas as a whole, even in the process of "ordering" it, using only energy sources that were internal to the system.

Jacques Monod, the Nobel laureate biochemist, asserts that the alleged evolution of the biosphere in the direction of negative entropy is virtually analogous to the preceding example. He cites a biological experiment that is almost an exact parallel of the growth of the crystal. In a small quantity of water containing some dissolved sugar and mineral salts, several billion bacteria such as Escherichia coli can be grown within 36 hours. In this process, 40 percent of the sugar is converted into cellular constituents, and the remainder is oxidized into carbon dioxide and water. If the experiment is carried out in a calorimeter, a thermodynamic balance sheet can be drawn up which will show that the entropy of the entire system (bacteria plus medium) increases slightly more than the minimum predicted by the Second Law. Thus, just as in the case of the growth of the crystal, the multiplication of the highly ordered bacterial cell creates an entropy debt that inevitably is paid.[8]

The fact is that not only "order," but the whole list of factors presented in Table 1 that McHarg tries to correlate with high versus low levels of entropy, represents only a subjective approximation of the meaning of entropy in ecological systems. This is useful perhaps as a general rule of thumb, but it is unreliable in any specific application.

Certainly it would be cumbersome to have to carry out an elaborate measurement and calculation to determine whether the net result of any given process in a complex ecological system were a positive or negative change in the entropy of the system. One should be able to gauge at least the direction of the transformation more easily than that. An adequate guide to the meaning of entropy in living systems requires greater precision than McHarg's "shopping list." As Brostow notes, ". . . if one insists on explaining entropy, a very good way is to turn to information theory."[9]

As indicated in Chapter 6, the informational and thermodynamic entropies are functionally identical. But the informational entropy seems considerably easier than the thermodynamic entropy to gauge qualitatively. To estimate the effect of a particular process on the entropy of a given system, it is enough to ask whether the *information content* of the system (which is also a direct measure of our ignorance of the state of the system) is likely to be increased or decreased by that process. If our understanding of the concept of information is reasonably astute, the resulting judgment is likely to be reliable. Also, it is only a short step from this qualitative estimation to the exact quantitative determination of the entropy of the system, whereas even a quantification of most of the subjective factors mentioned by McHarg would not yield any better approximation to the actual entropy of the system.

It appears clear that our best measure of the entropy (or negentropy) of a system, or of the entropic "direction" of evolution of a system, is, both qualitatively and quantitatively, the information content of the system.

THE SECOND LAW AND EVOLUTION

The evolution of the biosphere and the fact of the emergence of life on earth itself seem to constitute a paradox, even to some, a "miracle." In some way that seems contrary to the edict of the Second Law of Thermodynamics, a collection of atoms and molecules which should only become more shuffled and disarrayed actually seem to make time run backward—just like the motion-picture trick which can make a house of cards spring up from a jumbled pile or spilled milk jump back into the bottle—and organize themselves into structures which not only resist decay but which grow and develop. Even though we can resolve the paradox by separating the quantitative concept of entropy from the subjective notion of "order" and by carefully discriminating between open and closed systems, this does

solved this riddle. The role of Maxwell's Demon is played in the process of life by a set of globular proteins called *enzymes*. It is the enzymes that sort and assemble the building blocks of living tissue according to the blueprints contained in the DNA of the genes and which also provide the control system that enables the living cell to regulate its metabolic processes and maintain a condition of homeostasis.

How the cellular enzymes perform these functions is too complex for this discussion. Essentially, the enzyme's performance hinges on its capacity to form *noncovalent bonds* and on its *stereospecificity* (that is, the capacity of a specific enzyme to "recognize" and bond only to specific molecules). These properties allow the enzymes to *catalyze* reactions between other molecules which could not otherwise occur at environmental temperatures.

This catalytic function enables the enzymes to produce three of the processes most vital to the living cell. First, they enable the living organism to burn the energy stored in its food; in this sense, as Singh notes, life can be considered "an infinitely attenuated flame."[10] Second, enzymes play the central role in the synthesis of new protein which is essential to growth and reproduction. And third, a special class of enzymes, the allosteric enzymes, provide the crucial feedback mechanisms that permit the thousands of enzymes in a "simple" cell to carry out interweaving chains of thousands of complex chemical reactions with matchless harmony and efficiency.

Just like Maxwell's Demon, the cellular enzymes use information to transform the free energy of chemical potential into the negative entropy of biological structure. A crucial part of the necessary information comes from the DNA molecules of the cell's genes. The double helix of the DNA molecule is comprised of two twisted chains, each link of which is one of four bases, or nucleotides. The sequence of the nucleotides in the DNA chain constitutes the code in which genetic information is stored. On the other hand, each protein is a polypeptide chain, each link of which is one of 20 amino acid residues. Thus we can view one of the most fundamental processes of life —the synthesis of protein—as a process of translation, or more generally, of communication. This process could be represented by a schema essentially like that of Shannon's basic communication process depicted in Figure 1, except that there would be many intermediate stages where the messages conveying the information of the genetic blueprint were progressively transformed from the initial 4-letter DNA code to the final 20-letter polypeptide code.

Since each living cell contains thousands of different enzymes and other proteins, it is evident that the DNA molecules of the genes must contain a prodigious amount of information. Indeed, while a single amino acid contains about as much information as a word of language, and the polypeptide sequence of a single protein molecule may contain about as much information as a paragraph of prose, the DNA molecule of even a "simple" single-celled organism like the bacterium Escherichia coli amounts to about 10 million bits, or the equivalent of about 100 sets of the *Encyclopedia Britannica*.[11]

As impressive as this amount of information may be, however, it is still not enough to describe the entire structure of this organism. Scientific research indicates that about 200 billion bits of information would be required to describe the three-dimensional configuration of atoms in one Escherichia coli bacterium. In other words, the complete physical structure of E. coli contains about 20,000 times more information than is encoded in its DNA molecules.[12] Thus we have the apparent paradox of "genetic enrichment."

A somewhat simpler example of this paradox is offered by Monod who notes that the amount of information required to specify the linear sequence of amino acids in the polypeptide chain of a typical globular protein would be about 2,000 bits, whereas the amount of information that would be required to specify the entire three-dimensional structure would be vastly greater. But as Monod makes clear, the apparent enrichment of information derives from "the fact that genetic information (represented by the sequence) is expressed under strictly defined initial conditions (aqueous phase, narrow latitude of temperatures, ionic composition, etc.)." Consequently, while

many different structures of the globular protein are theoretically possible, only one is actually realized. In addition to the genetic information, information representing the initial ambient conditions under which the synthesis of the protein takes place is incorporated in the final globular structure. The initial conditions do not specify a unique shape but simply eliminate all of the alternative possible structures, thereby rendering unequivocal the interpretation of a
potentially equivocal message.[13]

synthesis of new protein (that is, just the information that is lacking in the chemical soup of the cell's protoplasm), while the translation mechanism, as a whole, is sufficiently *redundant* to insure accurate transmission of the genetic message with an extremely small probability of error.

The paradoxes which seemingly make the existence and evolution of living structures miraculous—the growth of living things counter to the direction of the Second Law and the genetic enrichment of the reproductive process—can, in fact, be resolved in a manner wholly consistent with physical law and scientific method. The strangeness, the "counterintuitiveness" of the multiplication of living cells, arises from neither a paradox nor a miracle but, as Monod observes, from something else:

> There is . . . no physical paradox in the invariant reproduction of these structures: invariance is bought at not one penny above its thermodynamic price, thanks to the perfection of the teleonomic apparatus which, grudging of calories, in its infinitely complex task attains a level of efficiency rarely approached by man-made machines. This apparatus is entirely logical, wonderfully rational, and perfectly adapted to its purpose: to preserve and reproduce the structural norm. And it achieves this, not by departing from physical laws, but by exploiting them to the exclusive advantage of its personal idiosyncrasy. It is the very existence of this purpose, at once both pursued and fulfilled by the teleo-

nomic apparatus, that constitutes the "miracle." Miracle? No, the real difficulty is not in the physics of the phenomenon; it lies elsewhere, and deeper, involving our own understanding, our intuition of it. There is, really, no paradox or miracle, but a flagrant *epistemological contradiction*.[14]

THE "PURPOSE" OF EVOLUTION

The "epistemological contradiction" mentioned by Monod begs for our attention because it turns out to be the central flaw in McHarg's theory, which seriously impairs its validity and hence its usefulness.

The two most essential aspects of the peculiar phenomenon known as life are what Monod calls *invariance* and *teleonomy*.[15] Invariance is simply the reproduction or transmission of a specific body of genetic information from one generation to the next, with no error or variation. Teleonomy is merely Monod's name for something that is characteristic of every control or learning system, something we might call *purposefulness*. That is, all control/learning systems exhibit some purpose in their behavior. Going up a level in either the hierarchy of control or of learning was seen as equivalent to asking the question *why*. Since all living organisms contain necessary control systems (and many contain learning systems), the processes of life are endowed with implicit purpose.

But this teleonomic behavior seems to contradict one of the epistemological keystones of the scientific method, what Monod calls the "postulate of objectivity." This is simply the assertion that "true" knowledge cannot be arrived at by ascribing phenomena to "final causes," that is, to supernatural or metaphysical "purposes" such as "God's will" or "fate." Monod's postulate of objectivity is a corollary to the Law of Parsimony, and *teleological principles* (that is, the kinds of "final causes" just mentioned) are merely a special variety of those explanatory principles which have been excised from the body of scientific knowledge by Occam's Razor.

As Monod notes, this postulate of objectivity is too central to the scientific method to be relaxed or suspended, but

objectivity nevertheless obliges us to recognize the teleonomic character of living organisms, to admit that in their structure and performance they act projectively—realize and pursue a purpose. Here, therefore, at least in appearance, lies a profound epistemological contradiction.[16]

The resolution of this apparent contradiction can, according to Monod, be achieved only one way; hence there is only a single hypothesis that modern science can deem acceptable to explain the apparent purposefulness of life:

> This is the essence of the Darwinian explanation of the evolution of living organisms: living structures which *already possess the property of invariance* ~~~~~~ ~~~~~~."

is entirely *random*. That is, *any* sequence of nucleotides is possible in one strand of the molecule; therefore any error or change introduced in this sequence will be reproduced as faithfully as the original.

Each strand of the DNA molecule is the exact complement of the other, and each strand, therefore, contains exactly the same information as the other. When the molecule splits, each strand forms bonds with other nucleotides in such a way as to produce two perfect copies of the original molecule. Thus each base in the double helix strictly determines its lateral partner, while the longitudinal sequence of bases is totally arbitrary. The redundancy of each strand is therefore exactly zero, while the redundancy of the molecule as a whole is exactly 50 percent. The result is a communication system that transmits genetic information from one generation to the next with enormous effectiveness. Monod estimates that the probability of a bacterial gene undergoing a "significant" mutation is between one in a million and one in a hundred million per generation. But in a bacterial culture with a cellular population running into the billions, the occurrence of such mutations becomes not the exception but the rule. Even in more complex multicellular organisms such as man, the number of genes in the genome is so much larger, and the number of cellular generations in the germinal line is sufficiently large that, even though the populations are much smaller, significant mutations still occur with frequencies approaching one in a hundred thousand or even one in ten thousand. Thus it is chance—actually *noise* in the transmission of genetic information from generation to generation— that is the source (the *only* source) of all of the innovations in the genetic blueprint which have, in the course of time, differentiated one species of organism from another.

The "necessity" comes from the purposeful function of the teleonomic apparatus of every living organism. Monod asserts that the essential purpose of the teleonomic apparatus is to insure the reproduction of the invariant content of the genetic blueprint from one generation to the next. This amounts to working for the survival of the individual organism and ultimately of the species. Hence, the preservation and reproduction of the innovations introduced by chance are, to the teleonomic apparatus of the living organism, a "necessity."

It is not the environment alone, but the functioning of the teleonomic apparatus in conjunction with the environment that provides the essential filtering mechanism by means of which the process of natural selection occurs. Only those innovations of chance are permitted to survive which either enhance the function of the teleonomic apparatus or at least do it minimal damage. The great majority of the changes in the genetic blueprint introduced by chance are contrary to the purpose of the teleonomic apparatus, and these are discarded either by the apparatus itself or, if they are sufficiently deleterious, by destroying the organism that carries them, thereby terminating their reproduction.

In contrast to Monod's objective theory of evolution, there is a host of alternative theories, each of which is based on some kind of teleological principle, each of which imputes some kind of transcendant purpose to biological or to physical and biological evolution. Monod classifies these into two camps: *vitalist* theories which discriminate between living and nonliving entities and see a teleological principle active only in the former; and *animist* theories which posit a *universal* teleogical principle, operative within the biosphere and throughout the rest of the cosmos as well. In the former category, Monod places the theories of Bergson and Elsässer and Polanyi and in the latter, those of Leibnitz, Hegel, Teilhard de Chardin, Spencer, Marx, and Engels. All of them are infected with the same epistemological weakness; all of them are based on the same kind of teleological principle—anathema to truly "scientific" knowledge—as Bergson's "élan vital." But as Monod puts it:

> . . . where Bergson saw the most glaring proof that the "principle of life" is evolution itself, modern biology recognizes, instead, that all the properties of living beings rest on *a fundamental mechanism of molecular invariance.* For

modern theory, *evolution is not a property of living beings,* since it stems from the very *imperfections* of the conservative mechanism which indeed constitutes their unique privilege. And so one may say that the same source of fortuitous perturbations, of "noise," which in a nonliving (i.e., nonreplicative) system would lead little by little to the disintegration of all structure, is the progenitor of evolution in the

never encompass the biosphere, its structure, and its evolution as phenomena *deducible* from first principles." As he explains, a universal theory would have to include relativity and quantum theory, a theory of elementary particles, and a cosmology predicting the general evolution of the universe. But modern scientists know that such predictions could only be statistical. Rather, Monod's thesis is that "the biosphere does not contain a predictable class of objects or of events but constitutes a particular occurrence, compatible indeed with first principles, but not *deducible* from those principles and therefore essentially unpredictable."[19]

It is important to understand that Monod is *not* saying that phenomena cannot be *explained* in terms of fundamental scientific principles or "laws," but simply that specific occurrences cannot be *deduced* from them or, what is the same thing, deterministically predicted by them. For example, if one picks up a pebble on a beach, the configuration of atoms in that particular pebble is entirely *consistent* with the laws of physics and chemistry, but is not in any way deducible from them. This particular object, as Monod puts it, "is under no obligation to exist; but it has the right to."[20]

Monod's explanation of the process of evolution which shows it not retrograde to but entirely compatible with the operation of the Second Law in the biosphere, raises a dilemma. It implies that it is impossible to discern the *true* path of evolution in contrast to the current course of ecocrisis because both are consistent with the Second Law (both are proceeding in the same "direction" in time). In general, as we have just seen, both ecocrisis and evolution (which, in fact, is no longer even a meaningful distinction) are only particular occurrences which can neither be deduced nor predicted from any general theory or set of first principles. As Monod says, it is *noise* that produces evolution and not any "élan vital." Therefore, the International Paper Company evolved through the same process as the forests it destroys and the lakes and streams it pollutes. One is no more *natural* than the other, and *nature* does not care (that is, it has no *intrinsic* criteria for discriminating) whether one, both, or neither survives or perishes.

If there is a tendency within the biosphere as an *open* system in the direction of negentropy, it is the result, as Monod explains, of "chance and necessity": the preservation of random changes through the selection process of the teleonomic apparatus. The teleonomic apparatus is not *teleological;* its purpose is endogenous, not exogenous. The meaning of evolution is in whatever evolves. If the ecosystem collapses, evolution means collapse; if it survives, evolution means survival. When the system is moving in the direction of negative entropy, evolution means movement toward negentropy; when the system moves the other way, evolution means the opposite.

McHarg's theory, however unconsciously, is therefore, like those of Bergson and the other vitalists and animists, ultimately *reified.* It takes the behavior of the biosphere—in fact, of only the nonhuman part—as evidence of some transcendent purpose or "preferred direction." But this is an error of logical type, a violation of Monod's postulate of objectivity and of Occam's Razor. McHarg's general theory is based on an epistemological error.

Contrary to McHarg's aspiration, there is no *"intrinsic* value system" operative in the biosphere on which to base a "diagnostic and constructive view of human adaptations and their form." Does this mean, then, that we can only sit back and watch how things proceed to evolve, that we can only wait and see whether the planet survives or perishes? The answer is no, and the reason is profoundly simple: we humans do not have the option of being spectators to the process of evolution because, like it or not, we are inexorably participants in the process. In fact, at this stage at least, we seem to be the most powerful part of it. There is no way, in this situation, that any of us can "do nothing."[21]

The fact that the value system posited by McHarg is not intrinsic (in the sense of having some transcendental or divine mandate) does not necessarily render it useless. It was, after all, the *usefulness* of McHarg's theory, and from that its implicit value system, that was our major concern here. It seems evident that *if* there is to be further evolution in the direction of negative entropy, then McHarg's value system, or one essentially like it (a value system in which the cardinal criterion is negative entropy or information), will probably have to dominate human behavior. Restated in this *hypothetical* form, McHarg's theory acquires essential validity.

So what is needed are *ecological ethics.* The essential elements of ecological ethics stem from three basic attributes of the ecosystem and its evolution: synergy, symbiosis, and negentropy.

balance of the whole complex system of life and death is thrown out of equilibrium.

Symbiosis means *living together.* Its moral lesson is that we must live harmoniously, not only with each other, but with the entire living biosphere. Symbiosis is ecological cooperation. It means that we must adopt a cooperative relationship with our own life-support system in place of our historically antagonistic one. It means that we view man's role on earth as one of stewardship and not of dominion.

Finally, negative entropy provides an ethical compass to guide human behavior toward survival, welfare, and development. It suggests as being unethical any action that tends to give rise to greater entropy, for example, to ignorance, war, destruction, erosion, impoverishment, ugliness, disease—in short, to waste.

The test of whether the "meaning" of evolution will continue to be "system change toward negative entropy" will depend, to a large extent, on whether McHarg's kind of value system, as espoused by others, will be able to compete successfully with other, contradictory value systems in the world of ideas (the softworld). This leads us to a broader conception of evolution as an epistemological rather than merely biophysical process. In fact, this book itself can now be viewed not merely as a reflection on that process, but as a part of it.

THE EVOLUTION OF "IDEAS"

In Chapter 1 I offered a quotation from Gregory Bateson which began: "There is an ecology of bad ideas, just as there is an ecology of weeds. . . ." The intervening discussion has brought us to the point where we are now on the verge of seeing the profound significance of this statement as the very essence of the softworld conception of ecocrisis. All that remains to be done in order for us to achieve this perspective is the full recognition of *evolution* as a process involving not merely organisms and environments but *ideas*. This extension of the biological concept of evolution to the world of ideas is not uncommon, but questions can be raised about the extent of the validity of the analogy which need to be addressed. Monod makes the basic analogy in this way:

> For a biologist it is tempting to draw a parallel between the evolution of ideas and that of the biosphere. For while the abstract kingdom stands at a yet greater distance above the biosphere than the latter does above the nonliving universe, ideas have retained some of the properties of organisms. Like them, they tend to perpetuate their structure and to breed; they too can fuse, recombine, segregate their content; indeed they too can evolve, and in this evolution selection must surely play an important role. . . . This selection must necessarily operate at two levels: that of the mind itself and that of performance.[22]

The nature of the evolution of ideas has been a subject central to the theoretical (as opposed to empirical) work of B. F. Skinner for at least 25 years, from *Walden Two* through the recent *Beyond Freedom and Dignity*. Skinner prefers to talk about the evolution and design of "cultures," and specifically eschews the term *idea* in favor of *cultural practice*, since, he observes, the "ideas" of a culture are only abstractions induced from the actual behaviors and artifacts that define a culture. Still, because *idea* is a briefer and more generic term than *cultural practice*, I will continue to use it here, while respecting Skinner's caveat and guarding against any implied reification. Skinner extends the concept of evolution to embrace cultures, thus:

> The fact that a culture may survive or perish suggests a kind of evolution, and a parallel with the evolution of species has, of course, often been pointed out. It needs to be stated carefully. A culture corresponds to a species. We describe it by listing many of its practices, as we describe a species by listing many of its anatomical features. Two or

more cultures may share a practice, as two or more species may share an anatomical feature. The practices of a culture, like the characteristics of a species, are carried by its members, who transmit them to other members. In general, the greater the number of individuals who carry a species or a culture, the greater its chance of survival.[23]

like the chromosome-gene mechanism in the transmission of cultural practice."[24] The same objection is raised by Bateson, who writes:

> ... There is a profound difference between the processes of cultural change and those of phylogenetic evolution. In the latter, the Weismannian barrier between soma and germ plasm is presumed to be totally opaque. There is no coupling from environment to genome. In cultural evolution and individual learning, the coupling through consciousness is present, incomplete and probably distortive.[25]

The distortion alluded to by Bateson is just that which makes consciousness—at least conventional consciousness—incapable of comprehending the "cybernetic nature of self and the world."[26] It is, in fact, exactly the same phenomenon that Forrester refers to as the "counterintuitive" behavior of complex systems.

What is interesting here is the contention by both Skinner and Bateson that the analogy between genetic and cultural evolution is limited, at least partly, by differences in the mechanism of transmission. I do not believe that the differences between genetic and cultural evolution are as important as they claim, but the proposition requires further examination.

Perhaps the most important point is that genetic evolution is inherently *irreversible* because of the biochemistry of reproduction, which provides no mechanism for the introduction of "acquired characteristics" into the genetic blueprint of the DNA molecule. The only source of all genetic innovation, as Monod explains, is *noise.* As Skinner notes, cultural evolution may sometimes proceed by an analogous process of selection of randomly introduced innovations. For example, "The Egyptians, reconstructing boundaries after the annual flooding of the Nile, developed trigonometry, which proved valuable for many other reasons."[27] But the analogy between genetic and cultural evolution seems to break down with the process of *conversion,* or "diffusion of innovations." That is, the proliferation of genetic "ideas" is through the survival/extinction of the organisms that carry them. In some instances the proliferation of cultural ideas is through the same mechanism (as in the passing of ancient civilizations or the genocidal eradication or physical displacement of one cultural group by another), but it may also occur through the conversion of individuals from one cultural practice to another or even from one entire culture to another. Any process in the biosphere that is analogous to the latter seems to be proscribed by the strict functional separation of germ and soma. As Skinner points out, the antelope, observing that the giraffe's long neck may be a "good idea," has no way to adopt it.

Now, the apparent fact that cultural evolution permits the possibility of "acquired characteristics," while genetic evolution prohibits the same, does not, in itself, pose much of a problem. Whether an idea, genetic or cultural, is proliferated through direct diffusion or through differential reproduction, the idea will still survive or perish according to its ability to meet the survival contingencies established through the interaction between some teleonomic apparatus and its environment. Whether the choice is made by individuals or by nature, a process of selection will occur, and the success or failure of an idea will be determined by the extent to which it is helpful or harmful to the system in which it operates.

No, the real problem posed by the apparent possibility of acquired characteristics in cultural evolution is that they seem to imply that cultural evolution is *reversible.* This would not only make cultural evolution dramatically different from genetic evolution but would force us to ask whether the term *evolution* could be applied to cultural change at all. I will assert that irreversibility is so essential to the notion of evolution that reversibility would render the concept of cultural evolution bankrupt. It is troubling, therefore, that the process of conversion does, on the surface, seem to admit the possibility of reversibility in cultural change. After all, if an individual or a group can be converted to a new cultural practice, why can't they be converted back to the original practice? This is what we called earlier, "reversal learning," and we know that it can occur. But our apparent dilemma is resolved by Bateson's "deutero-learning," or Learning II, which we also know exists, at least among higher organisms and certainly among most humans. The existence of Learning II implies an inevitable element of hysteresis, or memory, in the conversion process (which is essentially Learning I). Consider the case of the peasant caught in an area whose control is repeatedly exchanged by forces of a revolutionary group and the central govern-

always learn something about the conversion process itself from the experience and thus a new cultural innovation, a new *idea*—however meager—will be *added* to the "old" culture, invariably making it different from what it was before. Cultural change is never reversible; therefore, we can speak meaningfully of cultural *evolution*.

But we can avoid much of the difficulty posed by conversion even more easily by simply noting, from the overwhelming weight of our common experience, that conversion is never really *total* anyway, but actually represents, to a greater or lesser extent, the synthesis of old and new cultures, or "ideas." From this point of view, cultures ought not be thought of as *species,* as Skinner says, but as *races/strains* of a single species which are therefore capable of *crossbreeding.* We can also think of a culture in combination with its total environment as an ecosystem, in which case cultural evolution becomes analogous to "ecological succession."

On the other hand, to look at our analogy from the other end for a moment, I believe that one may find in the evolution of the biosphere processes at work which are, at least in some rudimentary way, comparable to conversion in cultural evolution. The parallel results from the importance of *context* in the evolution of ideas, whether cultural or genetic. First, we must note that the process of conversion is poorly modeled by the notion of *injecting* new ideas, like some serum, into virgin individuals. Rather, we should view conversion as a process which essentially imposes a new *context* on an individual or group which, the converter hopes, is antagonistic to the old idea and conducive to the new one. Similarly, in the biosphere it often appears that the environment creates a context which demands the evolution of a certain genetic idea almost independently of the genetic "givens." Thus:

The dolphin and the shark, creatures with vastly different genetic makeups and histories, have evolved essentially similar morphological features in the context of the same aquatic environment.

Charles Darwin found that the finches which had been introduced to the Galapagos Islands had evolved into a diversity of morphological types—equipped with a wide variety of different bills—to fill ecological niches that in other ecosystems would have been taken by a number of different species.

The Tasmanian wolf of Australia looks, acts, and functions much like a wolf but is actually a marsupial.

This list could be extended indefinitely, but the point should be clear. In biological evolution the environment or context of evolution may coerce, or demand, the development of a certain form or function in much the same way the cultural context may coerce or demand the adoption of certain cultural practices.

But let us not emphasize the importance of environment or context to the point where we discount the significance of the individual's or organism's *behavior* in the process of either cultural or genetic evolution. If the horse has no horns, a single hoof, and a body built for speed, it is at least partly because its ancestors made a behavioral choice: to run away from predators rather than stand and fight. The alligator may seem well adapted to the swampy environment of the Everglades, but the Everglades, as an ecosystem, is no less highly adapted to the alligator's behavior. Specifically, the alligator digs holes in the mud which provide an essential refuge for fish and a host of other organisms during dry spells and without which the entire ecosystem would collapse. In the cultural sphere, of course, it is almost a cliché that the behavior of one or a few individuals can affect the course of cultural evolution.

In short, the process of evolution, cultural or genetic, poses a continual chicken-and-egg problem. Is it the teleonomic apparatus or the environment that is the chief mechanism of selection? The answer is, both. It is the interaction between the two that generates the contingencies for survival or extinction. Thus it is obvious that the horse's hoof evolved to fit the prairie, but it is no less certain that the prairie had to evolve to some extent to meet the contingencies imposed by the horse's hoof. Confronted with the contingencies for survival, the teleonomic apparatus of any organism can either attempt to adapt itself to the environment or attempt to adapt the environment to itself. All organisms are, to some extent, capable of both and do both. It is clearly man, however, who, vastly more than any other creature, does the latter. The processes of genetic and cultural evolution are invariably interactive, closed-loop processes of

forest. Similarly a nation may be dominated by a Communist ideology even though only a small percentage of the population may belong to the party.

We can strengthen the analogy between cultural and genetic evolution even more by noting that a culture has the essential attributes which Monod attributes to all living systems: invariance and teleonomy. A culture is defined by its invariant information content, just as is a genotype or species. Every culture is endowed with the teleonomic apparatus of a complex control/learning system whose essential purpose is to insure the invariant reproduction of the cultural blueprint from generation to generation.

All things considered, then, I would suggest that the analogy between cultural and genetic evolution is not only a good one, but is sufficiently strong that we can omit the distinction in most instances and simply speak of evolution in general.

THE ECOLOGY OF "MIND"

The final key to the softworld vision of ecocrisis is Bateson's conception of the ecology of "mind." As we shall see, central to this conception is the virtual identity of genetic and cultural evolution, or what we can refer to collectively as the *evolution of ideas*.

Since we did not actually define *idea* explicitly above, I will backtrack for a moment to point out that Bateson defines an *idea* simply as a "difference" or a "transform of a difference" (that is, an idea is just what was called a *message* in Chapter 6). The reason Bateson calls a *difference* an *idea* is that difference cannot be localized. The difference between the color of my pen and that of my desk is not in the pen or in the desk, nor, as Bateson says, can it be "pinched" between them. A difference cannot be localized in space because it is "only" an *idea*.

One can now define a *mind* in terms of the flow of ideas in a cybernetic network. Bateson offers the following list of "essential minimal characteristics of a system" which shall be taken to describe a mind:

> 1. The system shall operate with and upon *differences*.
> 2. The system shall consist of closed loops or networks of pathways along which differences and transforms of differences shall be transmitted. . . .
> 3. Many events within the system shall be energized by the respondent part rather than by impact from the triggering part.
> 4. The system shall show self-correctiveness in the direction of homeostasis and/or in the direction of runaway. Self-correctiveness implies trial and error.[28]

Bateson goes on to assert: "these minimal characteristics of mind are generated whenever and wherever the appropriate circuit structure of causal loops exists. Mind is a necessary, an inevitable function of the appropriate complexity, wherever the complexity occurs."[29]

Clearly the "appropriate complexity" does not exist merely in the network of neurons and synapses that constitute the human brain. Many mechanical, social, and biological cybernetic systems have the essential characteristics of a "mind"; a corporation, a government, an ecosystem all demonstrate the necessary complexity.

The second point in Bateson's definition carries with it the important implication that the *boundary* of what may appropriately be considered a *mental system* will depend to some extent on the function of the system. A corollary of this point is that the boundary of a mind or a mental system cannot cut any of the pathways of communication which are relevant to its function. Thus, for the function of walking, the mind of a blind man cannot be bounded at either the handle or the tip of his cane but must include the man, the cane, and the street; for the function of eating, however, the cane may be omitted. In short, a mental system *must always be defined as a cybernetically closed system* (it may be a materially or energetically open system).

In answer to the question, "Does a computer *think?*" Bateson points out that the computer, by itself, does not generally have the appropriate complexity of a mind; but the system computer plus man plus environment does, in many of its functions, demonstrate the essential characteristics of a mental system.

therefore, is a name for the actual mental behavior of the complex global control/learning system and is not an animist concept, not just another "élan vital."

What follows from this concept of Mind is that the analogy between genetic and cultural evolution explored earlier now becomes an identity. Bateson explains:

> Now we begin to see some of the epistemological fallacies of Occidental civilization. In accordance with the general climate of thinking in mid-nineteenth-century England, Darwin proposed a theory of natural selection and evolution in which the unit of survival was either the family line or the species or the sub-species or something of the sort. But today it is quite obvious that this is not the unit of survival in the real biological world. The unit of survival is *organism* plus *environment.* We are learning by bitter experience that the organism which destroys its environment destroys itself.
>
> If, now, we correct the Darwinian unit of survival to include the environment and the interaction between organism and environment, a very strange and surprising identity emerges: *the unit of evolutionary survival turns out to be identical with the unit of mind.*
>
> Formerly we thought of a hierarchy of taxa—individual, family line, subspecies, species, etc.—as units of survival. We now see a different hierarchy of units—gene-in-organism,

organism-in-environment, ecosystem, etc. Ecology, in the widest sense, turns out to be the study of the interaction and survival of ideas and programs (*i.e.*, differences, complexes of differences, etc.) in circuits.[30]

This equation between the unit of evolution and the unit of mind has profound implications, ethical as well as epistemological. Specifically, Bateson comes to a conclusion which echoes the views of McHarg and White,[31] but via a far more parsimonious route. He finds that the traditional Occidental dichotomies between man and nature, between mind and body, between God and creation, constitute deep epistemological errors that must invariably lead to ecological disaster. Bateson says:

> If you put God outside and set him vis-à-vis his creation and if you have the idea that you are created in his image, you will logically and naturally see yourself as outside and against the things around you. And as you arrogate all mind to yourself, you will see the world around as mindless and therefore not entitled to moral or ethical consideration. The environment will seem to be yours to exploit. Your survival unit will be you and your folks or conspecifics against the environment of other social units, other races and the brutes and the vegetables.
> If this is your estimate of your relation to nature *and you have an advanced technology,* your likelihood of survival will be that of a snowball in hell. . . .[32]

The alternative, on the other hand, is to accept the vision of individual mind as part of global Mind. This expansion of the concept of mind implies a reduction of the scope of the conscious self which leads, in turn, to what Bateson calls a "certain humility" at being a part of something much larger, a "part of God."

Because Mind is immanent and not transcendant, it is neither all-knowing nor perfectly rational; hence is only too susceptible to insanity. Ecocrisis is precisely this: the driving of the global Mind to madness.

A basic concern of this chapter is the man-nature dichotomy. It may seem useful to talk or think in terms of man and nature separately; it is common and comfortable to do so. But logically it tends to be subversive. In the softworld perspective, such a boundary makes no sense. If, indeed, ecocrisis emanates from the conceptual separation of man from nature and the implied dominance of man over nature, a theory which calls for reintegration of the two, however laudable, still may serve to reinforce the dichotomy. It is not the dichotomy between man and nature that is the culprit, but the *idea* of the dichotomy. To urge that we "design with nature," as McHarg does,

What is the difference between *artificial,* or *unnatural,* and *natural?* Essentially these terms define the poles of a continuum of disruption or disturbance. Something is *natural* to a system to the extent that it is harmonious, nondisruptive, to the system. An intervention or innovation in a system is more or less *unnatural,* or *artificial,* depending on the degree to which it disturbs the system in which it is introduced. To put it simply, what we generally perceive as *natural* is whatever we are *used to.*

McHarg's notion of "designing with nature" is that human settlements should be planned to have minimal disruptive impact on the ecosystems to which they are introduced. This is unquestionably sage advice, and I would generally endorse it. But the implication that such settlements are *intrinsically* more natural than other, uglier alternatives—other than in the sense of *natural* that I have just mentioned—is fallacious. Again, *natural* is, for the most part, what we are used to.

We are used to thinking of the southwestern United States as "naturally" arid and barren, therefore the recent increase of greenery and humidity due to irrigation seems to many an "unnatural" intrusion. But these deserts were vast green prairies when the conquistadores discovered them. It was overgrazing by horses and later cattle which the white man brought to the region that transformed it to what many of us are inclined to consider its natural state.

Similarly, we are inclined to think of the Indians, riding ponies and hunting buffalo, as a natural part of the North American environment that was destroyed by the invasion of the white man. But it was the Spaniards who gave the Indians their horses. The fact is that the Indians' ancient ancestors, who immigrated from Siberia during the last ice age, decimated and in many cases extinguished the indigenous populations of wild game with their fire-drive method of hunting, and actually transformed the "nature" of the North American continent hardly less radically than did the white man.

Sometimes our notions of what is "natural" are not even based on what we are used to but on what we think we *were* used to. In spite of the fact that most of my generation were raised on, and should be used to, food grown with "artificial" pesticides and "artificial" fertilizers and prepared with "artificial" colors, flavors, preservatives, vitamins, many of us are turning back to "natural" foods grown and prepared without these accoutrements. This is generally a good thing, but it often leads to rather hyperbolic gestures, as when people pay several times more for "natural" than for "synthetic" vitamin C.

Barry Commoner considers most man-made organic chemicals such as pesticides and plastics as being "unnatural." These *are* unnatural in the sense that the biochemistry of most existing ecosystems is not adapted to assimilating these new chemicals; is not used to them, hence it is disrupted by them. But there is no absolute sense in which we can say that one chemical is natural and another is not. The fact that existing organisms cannot metabolize DDT does not rule out the possibility that future organisms may evolve that can.

The ancient Mesopotamians lived in an environment that was erratic and unpredictable, sometimes productive and sometimes afflicted with plague, flood, and drought. The Egyptians, on the other hand, lived in an environment that was perennially fertile and productive, sustained by the regular flooding of the Nile, stable and predictable. Not surprisingly, the gods of Mesopotamia were callous and capricious, demanding assiduous worship and sacrifice, yet providing little security in return. The gods of Egypt were generally benevolent, loyal to their people, constant and generous. The Mesopotamians' and Egyptians' concepts of nature reflected what they were used to.

In the modern era a similar dichotomy in the vision of nature can be detected. Charles Lyell's uniformitarianism is a scientific postulate which views nature as essentially stable, constant, and uniform. Lyell asserted that the processes of nature which we observe on the Earth and in the present are the same that obtain throughout the universe and throughout time. But Immanuel Velikovsky's modern catastrophism sees nature as unstable, radically changing at times, and irregular. Velikovsky contends that a giant comet collided with the earth only a few thousand years ago, giving rise to the plagues and other disasters that befell the Egyptians at the time of the exodus and permanently altering the nature of the Earth.[34] At this point it is impossible to say conclusively which of these conflicting hypotheses are correct, since there is evidence that supports each.

Our modern conceptions of nature and hence of evoluti

to nature is to commit the animist fallacy. Values, as ideas, can only be considered intrinsic to the global ecosystem to the extent that we recognize the human mind as only one constituent of the global Mind which comprehends all ideas, genetic and cultural, equally.

All ecosystems are endowed with a teleonomic control/learning system that is inherently *purposeful.* We may induce the inherent purposes of such a system from observations of the system's past performance. We may recognize these inferred purposes as ideas and even go so far as to call them *values.* In systems that are largely dominated by man, we may call these values *cultural;* in those relatively isolated from human influence, we may say the inferred values are *instinctive* or *genetic.* This is relatively harmless labeling, but if we go on to say that genetic or instinctive values are more natural in some absolute sense than cultural values, we will be committing a grievous error.

In saying that genetic and cultural evolution are virtually identical, I do not mean to assert that the two are completely indistinguishable, only that they are functionally coequal and inseparable. Culture began as a set of genetic ideas: upright posture, enlarged brain, and an oral cavity well structured for making a wide variety of distinguishable sounds. These genetic innovations made the evolution of culture possible and to some extent necessary. But culture, once realized, became a part of the teleonomic apparatus which created the selection rules for both human and nonhuman genetic evolution. The genetic endowment of both men and the organisms on which they depended for their survival made the difference between cultures surviving and perishing. Cultural practices led to the extinction of some species and the cultivation of others which otherwise could not have survived. Cultural evolution and genetic evolution are not separate melodies but rather two contrapuntal themes within the evolutionary symphony. There is only a single evolution of which both genetic and cultural ideas are equal constituents, and that is the evolution of the global Mind.

McHarg's theory can be very useful and creative within the scope of landscape architecture or urban planning, but its epistemological weaknesses render it inadequate as a basis for solving the long-term global problems of ecocrisis. A value system like that which McHarg proposes will acquire its validity not by being intrinsic to nature but by its capacity to survive and proliferate in the world marketplace of ideas, that is, by its ability to *work* within the global Mind.

What must be designed—and is de facto being designed now—is not human adaptation to nature, nor, as the technocrats would have it, the adaptation of nature to man. What must be designed is the global, interactive gestalt of man-in-environment. We must decide what the future evolution of the global Mind is to be. Yet as "we" decide, it is simultaneously the global Mind that is in the process of deciding, and that process *is* its own evolution.

Now we can perceive ecocrisis not as a fork or splitting in the path of "true" evolution, but as a bend in the path of only a single, indivisible evolution—the evolution of the global Mind—toward a colossal "reductio ad absurdum."

The alternative to this ecological insanity, we can, along with Bateson, call *wisdom.* Wisdom is the functioning of a mind that is respectful of its own boundary and processes. A mind that arbitrarily severs its own feedback loops or communication pathways, or which makes improper connections between different levels in the hierarchies of control/learning, introduces epistemological errors into its circuits which inevitably lead not only to its own insanity but to the insanity of the larger Mind of which it is a part. Such a mind lacks wisdom.

We have seen that evolution is characterized by the essential trial-and-error process of learning, and conversely, that all learning —by any mind, human or otherwise—contributes to the evolution of the global Mind. This implies that the "cure" for ecocrisis—the progressive displacement of insanity by wisdom—is a process that might well be called *education.*

•

Ecocrisis is global Mind being driven insane by the epistemological errors of human consciousness. This is the essence of the softworld perspective. But this may yet seem too abstract. We need to see how this is reflected in contemporary human experience. That is the subject of the next chapter.

CHAPTER

8

CONSCIOUSNESS:

The Oglala Sioux call the white man "Wasichu." In John Niehardt's account, the Oglala medicine man, Black Elk, said this of the Wasichus:

> As I told you, it was in the summer of my twentieth year (1883) that I performed the ceremony of the elk. That fall, they say, the last of the bison herds was slaughtered by the Wasichus. I can remember when the bison were so many that they could not be counted, but more and more Wasichus came to kill them until there were only heaps of bones scattered where they used to be. The Wasichus did not kill them to eat; they killed them for the metal *that makes them crazy,* and they took only the hides to sell. Sometimes they did not even take the hides, only the tongues; and I have heard that fire-boats came down the Missouri River loaded with dried bison tongues. *You can see that the men who did this were crazy.* Sometimes they did not even take the tongues; they just killed and killed because they liked to do that. When we hunted bison, we killed only what we needed. And when there was nothing left but heaps of bones, the Wasichus came and gathered up even the bones and sold them.[1]

DISSONANCE

The psychologist Leon Festinger has developed a theory of what he calls "cognitive dissonance."[2] His theory is based on the universally recognized fact that man is a hypocritical creature. Psychologists—and before them philosophers, artists, and other observers of the human scene—have long recognized contradictions and inconsistencies, not only among various human attitudes and beliefs but also between attitudes and beliefs, on one hand, and actual human behavior, on the other. Festinger theorizes that as people become aware of these contradictions a certain cognitive dissonance is generated which, as it grows in severity, increasingly motivates people to resolve the implicit conflicts, either by modifying their behavior or, as is more generally the case, by modifying their attitudes, or even by trying to escape from the situation which generates the dissonance altogether. While Festinger's cognitive dissonance may, to some extent, be a reified concept, his theory, nevertheless, discloses a real phenomenon: people do experience conflicts among their knowledge, attitudes, and behavior, and these conflicts do generate effects.

When the degree of stress resulting from such conflicts is not too great, we generally observe the effect noted by Festinger. That is, a person caught in a moderate conflict between his attitude toward something and his behavior toward it will act to modify either his attitude or his behavior or both, in order to reduce or eliminate the conflict. But when the conflict becomes severe, and especially when it is *logically irreconcilable,* we are escalated from the level of Festinger's cognitive dissonance to that of Bateson's double bind, and the resulting stress may have effects that are so pervasive and devastating that they represent not merely selective modifications of discrete attitudes and behaviors, but a transformation of the total consciousness of an individual (or a collective) mind. The dissonance which embraces this full spectrum might be better called *epistemological dissonance,* since it arises from contradictions and conflicts not only within a given system of cognition, but also between different levels in the learning hierarchy and therefore between different ways of knowing.

The current state of the world, and especially of the United States, is one of profound and severe dissonance, resulting largely from the epistemological errors and inadequacies of the dominant Occidental culture. Of course this culture has been what Black Elk calls "crazy" for a long time, probably from its very beginning. But throughout most of its history the fallacies and paradoxes of Occidental culture generated significant dissonance for the most part only among those who were outside of it (the American Indian and the Black Africans). The short-term material benefits of Occidental culture insulated most of its adherents (with the exception of a few visionaries like Rousseau, Wordsworth, and Thoreau) from its contradictions for a long time. It has been only perhaps in the last hundred years or less that, with the closing of the frontier, which gave the culture its veneer of success, the internalization of its inconsistencies

tion that Alvin Toffler has called "future shock."[3] This current state of extreme dissonance is unprecedented in human—or so far as we know—planetary history. There are no valid historical models to guide us in this situation. For the first (and probably last) time in history, the fundamental premises of Occidental culture are being plugged into a global network which, with each new disaster, each emerging crisis, is systematically proving to the culture itself that it is unworkable and fallacious. Turning to traditional concepts, tenets, and models is not only of no avail, it actually exacerbates the crisis. The result is a massive, multifaceted double bind that is affecting not only large and growing numbers of individual minds, but the minds of their collective organizations and ultimately—inevitably—the global Mind as well.

•

Here are just a few examples/symptoms of the dissonance that has already emerged and which is growing in American and world society today. Many of these result, more or less, from conflicts between both the intentional products and unintentional fallout of modern science and technology, and the traditional cultural framework within which they were spawned.

At least since the publication of Rachel Carson's *Silent Spring*, the science of ecology has had a rapidly growing impact on human thought and behavior. Again and again, with increasing frequency, the ecologists have demonstrated irreconcilable incompatibility between various human activities and the ecosystems on which human survival and welfare depend. Ecology has taken two of the most fundamental premises of Occidental culture—the individual right of property and the political right of sovereignty—and blasted them at the root. In fact, ecology pulled the foundation out from under the whole elaborate superstructure of the Occidental notion of "human rights." Justice Holmes demonstrated the traditional concept when he said that the right of one man to swing his fist ends at the next man's nose. But ecology has made the functional distance between fists and noses vanishingly small, for in the complex web of the global ecosystem, as Hardin says, "We can never do merely one thing," and the flick of a single finger can cause a million nosebleeds half a world away.

The population bomb adds a demographic dilemma: does democracy make sense when human numbers themselves are a threat? Environmentalists are fond of pointing out that the United States, with 6 percent of the world's population, consumes about a third of the world's energy and roughly half of its nonrenewable resources. This seems, indeed, a colossal travesty of this country's mythology of "equality." What, then, is the alternative? A perfectly equal redistribution of the world's wealth, even if it were politically feasible, would only create the incentive for a "demographic sweepstakes" in which each nation, ethnic group, and even family would seek to maximize its rate of growth in order to attain a larger relative share of the pie. And this could only lead to a Malthusian catastrophe of astronomical proportions. But on what basis, if not equality, shall wealth and power be distributed? Such questions are being reflected in domestic as well as international issues. Many American towns, counties, and even whole states are now trying to halt their population growth and economic development in order to protect the quality of an uncongested way of life for their citizens, flying in the face not only of the overwhelming trend of American history but of a fundamental constitutional proscription of restraints on internal migration and trade. The answer to the basic question—Equality or what?—has barely been suggested, but the emergence of the question itself has contributed significantly to our critical state of dissonance.

The rapid development of technologies for various kinds of reproductive and genetic manipulation and for both the direct and indirect control of human behavior has seriously challenged conventional notions of human individuality and has rendered the model of what Skinner calls "autonomous man" obsolescent if not utterly obsolete. If we have not yet attained any of the popular dystopias—Orwell's *1984*, Huxley's *Brave New World*, Burgess'/Kubrick's *A*

Clockwork Orange—we have, in fact, already surpassed their level of science and either have or shortly will surpass their technologies. What role, concept, model of the individual, of the self, will replace the doomed autonomous man is a question that has been even tentatively answered by only a few. But it is a question which—yet unanswered—is more and more impinging on the consciousness of many, adding to current dissonance.

•

A few more concrete symptoms of the growing dissonance inherent in today's society are:

In San Francisco, a billion-dollar mass transit system called BART (Bay Area Rapid Transit) has gone into operation, a primary objective of the system being to alleviate the Bay area's traffic congestion. Public opinion surveys taken in the planning stages of the project indicated overwhelming public support for the *construction* of the system; bond issues for the project's financing were voted by a solid majority. But after its opening the system was underutilized and had only a minor impact on automobile traffic. Follow-up surveys showed why: people who had supported *construction* of the system generally did so with the expectation that *other people* would ride the trains and thereby make it easier for *them* to drive into the city.

A national survey sponsored by the National Commission on Population Growth and the American Future indicated that while 27 percent of the American people actually live in a "larger city or suburb," only 14 percent of the total population would *prefer* to. On the other hand, while only 12 percent of the people actually live in "open country," the survey indicated that more than a third, 34 percent, would *like* to. The apparent contradiction was clarified by another survey of Wisconsin residents, which asked the same questions but which also asked about people's preferred proximity to a large city. In this survey, a large proportion of those who would like to live in a more sparsely populated, rural area still want to be *"within commuting distance* of a metropolitan central city." While the Commission report recognized that the results of the Wisconsin survey did not necessarily reflect national attitudes, it noted: "If they do, it means that people want the best of both worlds—the serene and clean environment of rural areas and the opportunity and excitement of the metropolis."[4]

In some extensive opinion research reported in a book entitled *The Hopes and Fears of the American People,* A. Cantrill and C. Roll found that while the majority of Americans were *optimistic* about their personal futures, a majority were also *pessimistic* about the country's future (that is, about everyone else's future).[5]

These examples may seem rather mild, but they expose something that lies near the heart of our current state of ecological and social crisis: the dichotomy between individual motives and collective goals, or what Richard Falk calls the "paradox of aggregation." "Let's clean up the environment, as long as I don't have to pay for it." "Let's stop the population explosion, but don't try to interfere with my sex life." "I'm in favor of mass transit if it will make it easier for me to drive to work." "We should conserve electricity so I can run my air-conditioner all day without worrying about brownouts and blackouts." "I believe in integration as long as my kid doesn't get bussed." "Let's cut military spending, as long as it doesn't hurt my business." "Let's stop inflation, but first be sure that I get the raise I deserve." And so forth.

This paradox of aggregation is a cardinal symptom of the kind of insanity I spoke of in Chapter 7. It results from the failure of conventional consciousness to recognize the true boundaries of *mind.* Instead, loops of the feedback structure are arbitrarily lopped off and pathways of communication are artificially severed. Individual *mind* is rendered largely incapable of perceiving the connectedness between itself and the collective social mind and is oblivious to its role as part of the larger Mind of the global ecosystem.

•

The prospects are that the severity of the dissonance that is now afflicting the Occidental mind has not yet approached its peak, that it will increase rapidly in the future. As we approach the limits to growth, the epistemological errors of Occidental culture will be fed back ever more intensely on themselves, and the ultimate closure of the global Mind will follow.

As we have seen, the challenge posed by the finiteness of the

Earth and the connectedness of the complex global ecosystem is not predominantly physical or technological, but is far more an epistemological, a philosophical challenge. As the limits close in on us, they raise some profound philosophical questions which become increasingly difficult to evade, not just for the intelligentsia but for all. There are at least four questions that are basic.

to be bamboozled by the epistemological fallacies of modern economics. In the last decade these fallacies became increasingly apparent to a growing number of people who began to see that the most popular quantitative indicators of "economic welfare" were either irrelevant or downright antithetical to what generally came to be called the "quality of life." More and more people are coming to realize that:

1. Economic growth is not necessarily good. The traditional Occidental notion, among capitalists and communists alike, is that while the distribution of wealth and income might or might not be just, the monotonic growth of the gross national product (GNP) is an unalloyed good. But the widespread *feeling* of increasing impoverishment of the quality of life that runs counter to the conventional indices of economic welfare has cast considerable doubt on this proposition.

2. Unlimited economic growth is not, in fact, possible. This is the essential message of *The Limits to Growth,* but it is an issue that should have been settled conclusively by Columbus and Magellan. Nevertheless, a large segment of the public has finally begun to accept the fact that the earth is a sphere and has come to realize, at the same time, that the dominant school of "flat-earth economics" has not recognized this fact.

3. "Spillover effects" often outweigh economic "goods." It is evident that virtually every economy in the world today, capitalist or communist (with the possible exception of the Chinese), is generating economic "bads" faster than any economic "goods." The roots

of this fallacy of conventional economics lie in the old maxim, "the best things in life are free." The fact that they are treated as free results in the continual sacrifice of *non*economic welfare to the exigencies of economic growth and hence in the progressive erosion of the actual quality of life.

4. Discounting the future is "crazy." This is perhaps the most serious indictment of conventional economic wisdom. To the American Indian, who lived in an equilibrium society for thousands of years, the white man's practice of discounting the future in favor of immediate gains was shockingly evident. The Indian could see that "the men who did this were crazy." The cynical rebuttal of Western economics has always been, "What has posterity ever done for me?" Hearing no answer to its rhetorical question, the economic system has callously gone about its business of ripping off the future. If we discount the future even at the modest rate of 5 percent per year, posterity's economic vote, or dollar, is reduced by half every 14 years. After a hundred years, posterity's vote is only 1 1/2 cents on the dollar. At the double-digit rates of inflation that currently exist, the vote of our grandchildren, perhaps even our children, is reduced to insignificance.[7]

One of the manifestations of this is the fatuousness of most conventional economic cost/benefit analysis. For example, even if we took the projections of *Limits* as actual predictions, it would turn out that even the enormous catastrophes forecast for a hundred years hence, if discounted in reverse back to the present, would not cost enough in terms of current dollars to be worth the investment necessary to prevent them. Of course, if the people who will be alive then could have a voice now, they might contradict the conventional economic decision. But that is just the point: discounting reduces their vote to practically zero.

The ultimate fallacy underlying the dominant economic theories of today is one of *reification*. Somehow it was forgotten that "economic welfare" was only assumed to be a proxy for general human welfare. And somewhere along the way, the *means* for measuring economic welfare came to be treated as *ends* in themselves. GNP transcended agnostic mathematics, to become the focal point of a kind of religion, a demigod demanding assiduous worship and endless sacrifice. But the reified goals of modern economics are goals that are best served by technology rather than by human beings. The result is a trend that has accelerated since the inception of the industrial revolution: the coercion of human beings and the biosphere to adapt to the demands of machines. We are now approaching the ultimate reductio ad absurdum of this epistemological disaster: a lifeless world populated by computers and gadgets, serving no other function than their own manufacture and repair.

WHAT IS MORAL OR ETHICAL?

...mate blame for ecocrisis squarely at the feet of the most fundamental axioms of Occidental culture which, he says, derive directly from the tenets of Judeo-Christian theology. Specifically, he alludes to the biblical mandate for man's "dominion" over the earth, the Christian notion of progress, and the nineteenth-century coupling of science and technology whose philosophical foundation was laid earlier by Francis Bacon. In White's view, ecocrisis cannot be solved as a purely technological problem. Rather, his overall conclusion is that "we shall continue to have a worsening ecologic crisis until we reject the Christian axiom that nature has no reason for existence save to serve man."[8]

White's thesis has strongly influenced the developing environmental movement. It has been accepted by many as virtually a cornerstone of the emerging "ecological conscience." This is not to suggest, however, that White's views have escaped criticism, perhaps the most notable of which is a direct rebuttal by Lewis Moncrief.[9] Moncrief asserts that Judeo-Christian religion is *not* a necessary condition for an environmental crisis, and argues that White has recognized this. In his own examples, Moncrief says, White points out that "human intervention in the periodic flooding of the Nile River basin and the fire-drive method of hunting by prehistoric man have both wrought significant 'unnatural' changes in man's environment. The absence of Judeo-Christian influence in these cases is obvious."[10]

Moncrief's own view, on the other hand, is that the environmental crisis, in the United States at least, is actually the result of the combination of a number of cultural forces—democracy, technology, urbanization, capitalistic mission, and antagonism (or apathy) toward the natural environment. Granting that the Judeo-Christian tradition has probably influenced these forces, Moncrief, nevertheless, concludes that "to isolate religious tradition as a cultural component and to contend that it is the 'historical root of our ecological crisis' is a bold affirmation for which there is little historical or scientific support."[11]

But even Moncrief's critique does not contradict the view that basic moral/ethical premises have contributed to the cause of environmental crisis or have been significant obstacles to its solution. Moreover, Moncrief's criticism skirts one of the most crucial points of White's thesis, namely, that Baconian Christian philosophy laid the groundwork for the nineteenth-century marriage of science and technology which was the fountainhead of three or four of the five cultural factors to which Moncrief directly attributes the contemporary environmental crisis.

White emphasizes this point in dramatic terms, saying that the widespread acceptance of "the Baconian creed that scientific knowledge means technological power over nature" as a standard of behavior "may mark the greatest event in human history since the invention of agriculture, and perhaps in nonhuman terrestrial history as well."[12] This crux of White's thesis is vindicated by William Leiss in his dissertation on the origins and implications of the Occidental concept of mastery over nature.[13] But Leiss shows that it was the *decline* of Christian influence that unleashed the destructive potential of the epistemological errors implicit in Bacon's Christian philosophy. In Leiss's view, the "Baconian synthesis" envisaged moral and technological development moving forward *concomitantly* along parallel paths. Thus man's progressive return to his original "dominion over the Earth" would be matched by a concurrent return to his original innocence (that is, humility and submission to the rule of God). But the actual separation of these two paths of human development and the subsequent withering away of the mitigating influence of orthodox Christian morality unleashed an Occidental culture with a pervasive commitment to the domination of nature through scientific/technological progress, based on an implicitly anthropocentric and materialistic ethic. It is this "anthropocentric illusion" which Bateson sees at the very heart of the softworld conception of ecocrisis.

Another way of exposing the ecological bankruptcy of the dominant contemporary moral premises is to analyze them structurally rather than historically. This is the approach taken by Garrett Hardin in a treatise entitled "The Tragedy of the Commons," which perhaps has become even more of a classic of the environmental movement than White's essay. Hardin uses the term *tragedy* as it was defined by Whitehead: "The essence of dramatic tragedy is not unhappiness. It resides in the solemnity of the remorseless working of things."[14] The tragedy of the commons, then, is exemplified by the historical phenomenon of the destruction of commonly held pasturage through overgrazing. The tragedy lies in the fact that the implicit incentive structure of the commons remorselessly leads to its own

that believes in the freedom of the commons."[15] Hardin asserts that the fundamental problems of ecocrisis—pollution, depletion of natural resources, and especially overpopulation—are all direct results of the tragedy of the commons reproduced on a global scale. Hence, he argues, these problems have *no* "technical" solution and can only be ameliorated through political reforms.

Hardin further contends that, especially in the area of population control, the appeal to "conscience" (that is, the call for voluntary restraint) cannot work. It cannot work in the long run, he says, because the process of natural selection will itself progressively reduce the proportion of those with "conscience" to zero. And in the short run, the appeal to conscience will only serve to generate widespread anxiety by creating a classic Batesonian double bind. That is, the individual at whom the appeal to conscience is directed actually receives two contradictory messages. The explicit message is, "If you don't do as we ask, we will openly condemn you for not acting like a responsible citizen." But the contradictory, implicit or *meta*message is: "If you *do* behave as we ask, we will secretly condemn you for a simpleton who can be shamed into standing aside while the rest of us exploit the commons."[16]

Instead of counterproductive laissez-faire, Hardin urges a strict return to the principle of Rousseau's *Social Contract* ("mutual coercion, mutually agreed upon"). Recognizing that this approach raises the ancient issue of *Quis custodiet ipsos custodes* (Who will watch the watchers?), Hardin argues that appropriate feedbacks can improve the quality of administrative law and that its inevitable imperfections are still preferable to the remorseless tragedies inherent in the unregulated commons.

A rather pessimistic rejoinder to Hardin's essay comes from Beryl Crowe.[17] Crowe agrees with Hardin, that the fundamental problems of ecocrisis are not amenable to "technical" solutions. Like Hardin, he is "very suspicious of the success of either demands or pleas for fundamental extensions in morality." But Crowe, a political scientist, is also doubtful whether a political solution to these problems is possible. Crowe asserts that Hardin's political solution is actually based on three "myths": (1) that common values, or criteria, for judgment exist or could be created for making nonarbitrary choices among incommensurable utilities and disutilities; (2) that even with such criteria, coercion could be "mutually agreed upon" and that the application of coercion would be effective; and (3) that an administrative system armed with criteria for judgment and the power of coercion, could, or would, "protect the commons from further desecration."

Crowe argues that not only does a common value system not exist, but the trend in modern society seems to be in the direction of growing "tribalism" (that is, the fragmentation of society into a number of subcultures with largely antagonistic value systems). Second, even if a consensus on criteria for "optimum population," "quality of life," and so forth were possible, it is still unlikely that the means and application of coercion could be readily agreed on. Even if this could be done, Crowe points to the Vietnam War and to urban and campus riots to show that coercion would almost certainly not work. Finally, even if these obstacles could be overcome, Crowe notes that the history of administrative law in the United States reveals that the regulators inevitably become the captives of those being regulated, and that the *quis custodiet* problem is, therefore, far from trivial.

Many of Crowe's objections are ameliorated, if not disarmed, by Thomas Schelling's excellent explication of Richard Falk's "paradox of aggregation," of which Hardin's tragedy of the commons was but a single variation, in an essay entitled "The Ecology of Micromotives."[18] Schelling provides an impressive analysis of the collective effects of individual human behavior. The gist of his analysis is that collective social behavior is more often than not at variance with the individual "micromotives" that comprise it. Schelling gives several illustrations of the human meaning of synergy and the "counterintuitive" behavior of complex systems.

Schelling cites the common phenomenon of an accident in the northbound lane of an expressway precipitating a traffic jam in the southbound lane as drivers slow down to take a quick look at what's going on on the other side of the road. Soon cars are backed up, the drivers waiting 10 minutes for a 10-second glance at an accident that may already have been cleared away. Every driver who gets to the front of the line has paid his 10 minutes and insists on getting his 10-second peek even if there is nothing to see. If the drivers could communicate to each other, they might decide to forego their 10-

would simply stop and remove the mattress, it would benefit every-one—everyone, that is, except himself. After crawling along in the hot sun for an hour or so, each driver who finally reaches the mattress decides that he has paid his dues and has earned the right to floor the accelerator and get moving again. Here again, if the people in the jam could only communicate with each other, they could chip in enough money to pay someone to remove the mattress. But they can't do that, and once each of them has finally reached the mattress, it is no longer worth their while to remove it for the mattress is then someone else's problem.

The first example above illustrates the problem of getting every-one in a community to refrain from doing something, for the good of all; the second illustrates the problem of getting someone to do something for the good of everyone else. In both cases, each in-dividual's motivation produces a collective effect no one really wants. Schelling's analysis exposes the dichotomy between micromotives and collective goals that is central to the current state of ecocrisis. Superficially, this may sound like plain, old-fashioned hypocrisy. But as Schelling makes clear, most such apparent hypocrisy is merely the result of people's legitimate fear of being taken advantage of. When people are able to communicate and thereby act in concert, they are often willing to make individual sacrifices for the collective good. In the absence, or inadequacy, of collective organization, though, no one wants to be a sucker for the next guy.

The general solution to this problem is unquestionably some-thing like Rousseau's *Social Contract*, perhaps in the more sophisticated version of John Rawls' *Theory of Justice*.[19] In any event, Schelling's analysis shows that Crowe's critique of Hardin's call for "mutual coercion, mutually agreed upon" interprets the latter too simplistically, and that the social contract includes various mechanisms for governing collective behavior. Among these are regulation, taxation, subsidy, and the market system. Schelling shows that each has strengths and weaknesses and that no single mechanism works effectively in all situations. In other words, there was revealed a functional relationship between the effectiveness of any means of social/individual control and the *context* in which it is applied. Schelling notes, contrary to the view of both Hardin and Crowe, that, all things considered, in many instances one of the best mechanisms for governing individual behavior for the collective good is altruism, or conscience. He argues that in many situations it is to everyone's benefit for some people to act as Good Samaritans even when most other people do not. For example, in the case of a power shortage, Schelling contends that those who turn off their air-conditioners and cut down on their use of power are not merely being exploited by the majority that doesn't, because they are still sharing in the collective gain of avoiding a total blackout.

Schelling does not interpret the inexorable need for "mutual coercion" to solve the various paradoxes of aggregation in a totalitarian sense, nor does he share Crowe's pessimism over the feasibility of political/moral solutions. Schelling's view is: "If there is sand in the Sahara where once cattle grazed, it is not because the problem of overgrazing was unsolvable, but because it was unsolved."[20]

In short, it has become clear that, in both historical and structural terms, ecocrisis has exposed conventional moral/ethical standards of human behavior as being either ineffectual or counterproductive and hence, obsolete. While a picture of what some of the alternatives might be is emerging, the effect of this revelation on current dissonance is extreme.

WHAT IS "NORMAL"?

Every society has implicit or explicit standards of "normalcy" according to which its members may be divided into the normal and the abnormal, the adjusted and the deviant, the well and the sick, and so on. Of special importance in contemporary society are the normative parameters of *intelligence* and *sanity*. It is symptomatic of the pervasive dissonance today that the conventional standards of intelligence and sanity—even the very *relevancy* of these standards, as well as the respectability of *normalcy* itself—are under attack and are the subject of unprecedented controversy.

Intelligence has recently become the center of a growing storm of debate over the relative significance of genetic (and by implication, racial) differences in IQ. Recent work by Jensen, Herrnstein, Eysenck, and others tends to stress the significance of the genetic as

white children higher IQ scores than any other group of children."[21] Kagan argues that *intelligence* is nothing more nor less than an arbitrary mechanism for the unequal distribution of power in American society. This controversy not only casts doubt on the popular instruments for measuring IQ, but it raises profound questions about the meaning and significance of *intelligence* as a normative concept.

If the foundations of conventional normalcy are being shaken by questions about the meaning of intelligence, they are being demolished by a widespread and growing indictment of the established notions of sanity, the latter being advanced by the spreading awareness that the dominant Occidental culture is itself "crazy." A leading prophet of this is psychiatrist Ronald Laing: "A revolution is currently going on in relation to sanity and madness, both inside and outside psychiatry. The clinical point of view is giving way before a point of view that is both existential and social."[22] Laing's objective is to blast the equation of *deviance* with *pathology*, the pervasive epistemological error of establishment psychotherapy. Essentially, he is rooting out and attacking the massive reification of the dominant psychodynamic schools. Relentlessly he shows that, unlike the relative objectivity of most medical diagnosis, psychiatric diagnosis of such alleged pathologies as neurosis, psychosis, and schizophrenia, predominantly reflects a social-political value judgment. For example, of schizophrenia, Laing writes: "There is no such condition as schizophrenia . . . the label is a social fact and the social fact is a *political event.*"[23]

Laing's basic thesis has been widely substantiated by a number of other researchers and therapists. Some research supporting his views has been reported by D.L. Rosenhan in an article entitled, "On Being Sane in Insane Places." Rosenhan arranged for eight collaborators to be admitted to 12 psychiatric facilities by feigning a single symptom—hallucinations. The specific hallucinations he had his colleagues simulate were of a kind that had never before been reported in the scientific literature. Aside from that, the pseudopatients presented "no further alterations of person, history, or circumstances" and behaved as normally as possible. The results of this imaginative experiment were: "Eleven of the pseudopatients were diagnosed manic-depressive. All were discharged 'in remission.' *None was found sane.*"[24]

In discussing this research, Rosenhan, like Laing and others, exposes the pervasive reification of psychodynamic practice, observing: "Whenever the ratio of what is known to what needs to be known approaches zero, we tend to invent 'knowledge' and assume that we understand more than we actually do. We seem unable to acknowledge that we simply don't know." In this regard, contrary to the common practice of most psychotherapy, Rosenhan concludes from his own research that "we cannot distinguish insanity from sanity."[25]

In considering the implications of this, Rosenhan rhetorically wonders how many people are sane but in psychiatric institutions; how many have been needlessly stripped of privileges and rights; how many have feigned insanity in order to avoid criminal prosecution, and conversely, how many preferred to stand trial rather than face indeterminate confinement in a psychiatric hospital; how many have been stigmatized by erroneous diagnoses; and finally, how many patients might be sane outside the psychiatric institution but seem insane within that bizarre setting.

Altogether, Rosenhan finds such questions "not merely depressing, but frightening."[26] Little wonder, then, that the growing attacks on established concepts of "normalcy" are aggravating to the general state of dissonance.

Laing is fond of pointing out that 400 years ago in England, the Establishment of the time labelled some people "witches" and had them burned at the stake. This was, of course, done with the benevolent intent of spiritual therapy. In the official parlance of the exorcists, the incinerated witch was said to have been "relaxed." From our current perspective, it seems that any doubt about the relative sanity of the sixteenth-century inquisitors and witches ought to favor the witches. Yet today, while the fire has been replaced by the tranquilizer and electric shock, the process of "relaxation" of those who deviate from the established standards of normalcy goes on, and, whether in the Soviet Union or the United States, the underlying judgment is no less relativistic, no less "political."

We live in a world that is divided into two (or more) countervailing cultures. The diagnosis of *insanity* in one may be taken as a certification of merit in the other, for to be judged crazy in the

What is "reality"? Every person—indeed, every mental system from an amoeba to American Motors—has an answer to this question, an implicit model by which it orders its perceptions of self-in-environment. No one, neither the philosopher nor the file clerk, the logician nor the longshoreman, can evade this question nor the dissonance that usually results from trying to answer it. The challenge to the conventional Occidental model of reality creates the consummate double bind. Those of us who are more or less steeped in this dominant culture are, if our vision is at all honest, being forced to choose between maintaining our "self" images in the context of a reality that is increasingly being proved unworkable and fallacious or abandoning our obsolete selves in favor of a workable reality in which our selves are as yet undefined and may be frighteningly undefinable. The double bind emanates from this: *I* cannot choose, since *I* implies the continued existence of my conventional *self;* but if *I* abandon my *self* in order to choose, the choice no longer needs to be made, and, in fact, there is no one left to do the choosing.

We live in a culture that has had a tradition of perceiving reality in dichotomous, or polar, terms. But modern physics has bankrupted the dualistic epistemology of Occidental culture. The most fundamental dichotomy of classical science—that of "matter" and "energy"—was vitiated by relativity theory, which rendered matter and energy mutually transmutable versions of the same basic "stuff." Is light composed of particles or waves? The modern physicist knows that the answer depends on the context in which the question appears and the purpose for which it is asked. Today's science comes more and more to view reality as containing *intrinsic ambiguity,* reflecting not any inconsistency in nature but rather, in our mechanisms of perception. Consider the drawing in Figure 4. Are we looking *down* at a flight of stairs from *above* or are we looking *up* at a flight of stairs from *beneath?* Which image is "real"? Or is there really a staircase at all? These questions are impossible to answer conclusively; they are of the kind the logician calls *complex.* Asking *which* staircase you see begs the question of whether there is an image of a staircase at all. But asking *whether* there is a staircase begs the question of whether you can discriminate between a *real* and an *apparent* image of a staircase. Of course you can't, which is precisely why ontology is a fruitless exercise.

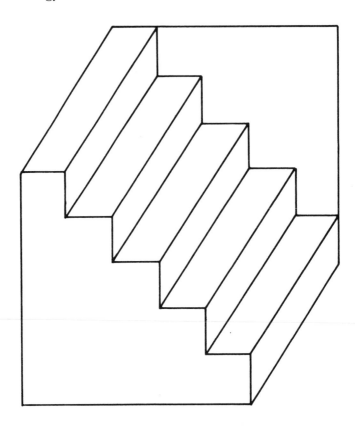

FIGURE 4. WHAT IS "REAL"?

One perception of the picture may "work" better than another in terms of some criteria other than perception itself. For example, the picture might be part of a psychological test you must pass in order to get a certain job, and the tester may have a predilection for seeing the looking-down-from-above staircase. In this case, that percept may work better than any other, in *this* context and for the purpose of *passing the test.* If the test is part of an army induction physical and you want to *fail,* the looking-up-from-beneath staircase might be the reality that works best. Such a process of trial and error,

private/public
individualism/collectivism
freedom/control
sanity/insanity
liberalism/conservatism
capitalism/socialism
segregation/integration
war/peace
conscious/unconscious
guilt/innocence
construction/destruction
reality/perception
work/leisure
centralization/decentralization
mind/body
structuralism/reductionism
competition/cooperation
life/death

In the modern world all of these distinctions are becoming more or less grayed, and those who cling to them find themselves more and more out of joint with a perplexing oxymoronic reality.

There is probably no more impressive and illuminating demonstration of the limitations of prevailing Occidental epistemology and the potentialities of alternative "ways of knowledge" than in the work of Carlos Castaneda. Andrew Weil cites a particular episode from *The Teachings of Don Juan* that is especially revealing.[27] While the account of Castaneda's experience with the *Datura* root and the subsequent dialogue with Don Juan is lengthy, I think it is worth recounting here:

> I followed his directions. The paste was cold and had a particularly strong odor. When I had finished applying it I straightened up. The smell from the mixture entered my nostrils. It was suffocating me. The pungent odor was actually choking me. It was like a gas of some sort. I tried to breathe through my mouth and tried to talk to Don Juan, but I couldn't.
>
> Don Juan kept staring at me. I took a step toward him. My legs were rubbery and long, extremely long. I took another step. My knee joints felt springy, like a vault pole; they shook and vibrated and contracted elastically. I moved forward. The motion of my body was slow and shaky; it was more like a tremor forward and up. I looked down and saw Don Juan sitting below me, way below me. The momentum carried me forward one more step, which was even more elastic and longer than the preceding one. And from there I soared. I remember coming down once; then I pushed up with both my feet, sprang backward, and glided on my back. I saw the dark sky above me, and the clouds going by me. I jerked my body so I could look down. I saw the dark mass of the mountains.
>
> . . . . .
>
> The same day, Friday, July 5, late in the afternoon, Don Juan asked me to narrate the details of my experience. As carefully as I could, I related the whole episode.
>
> . . . . .
>
> There was a question I wanted to ask him. I knew he was going to evade it, so I waited for him to mention the subject; I waited all day. Finally, before I left that evening, I had to ask him, "Did I really fly, Don Juan?"
>
> "That is what you told me. Didn't you?"
>
> "I know, Don Juan. I mean, did my body fly? Did I take off like a bird?"
>
> "You always ask me questions I cannot answer. You flew. That is what the second portion of the devil's weed is for. As you take more of it, you will learn how to fly perfectly. It is not a simple matter. A man *flies* with the help of the second portion of the devil's weed. That is all I can

tell you. What you want to know makes no sense. Birds fly like birds and a man who has taken the devil's weed flies as such."

"As birds do?"

"No, he flies as a man who has taken the weed."

"Then I didn't really fly, Don Juan. I flew in my imagination, in my mind alone. Where was my body?"

Suppose, for the sake of argument, one of my fellow students had been here with me when I took the devil's weed. Would he have been able to see me flying?"

"There you go again with your questions about what would happen if. . . . It is useless to talk that way. If your friend, or anybody else, takes the second portion of the weed all he can do is fly. Now, if he had simply watched you, he might have seen you flying, or he might not. That depends on the man."

"But what I mean, Don Juan, is that if you and I look at a bird and see it fly, we agree that it is flying. But if two of my friends had seen me flying as I did last night, would they have agreed that I was flying?"

"Well, they might have. You agree that birds fly because you have seen them flying. Flying is a common thing with birds. But you will not agree on other things birds do, because you have never seen birds doing them. If your friends knew about men flying with the devil's weed, then they would agree."

"Let's put it another way, Don Juan. What I meant to say is that if I had tied myself to a rock with a heavy chain I would have flown just the same, because my body had nothing to do with my flying."

Don Juan looked at me increduously. "If you tie yourself to a rock," he said, "I'm afraid you will have to fly holding the rock with its heavy chain."[28]

Castaneda, a trained "social scientist," cannot, at this stage in the evolution of his "consciousness," see that the paradox he is trying so assiduously to resolve arises from the inherent fallacies of his own Occidental epistemology. He is vainly trying to "solve" his flying experience as a hardworld "problem," when, in fact, it is purely a softworld phenomenon in which perspective is not a problem at all. Castaneda's problem arises not from the experience itself but from his *questions* about it. Don Juan can no more tell Castaneda whether he really flew than he can tell us whether the picture in Figure 4 is really a staircase seen from above. At this point, Castaneda is not prepared to accept, much less generate, the proposition that his experience is real because he experienced it; it is a real experience; that is as real as it can get.

The appropriate (and implicit) answer to Castaneda's question, "Did I really fly?", is "Why do you want to know?"[29] In other words, Castaneda's question cannot be answered until its objectives are defined. Obviously Don Juan knows this, but Castaneda doesn't, thus their dialogue is mutually frustrating. The difficulty might have been resolved had Castaneda asked: "Does this experience [alternate reality] *work?*" To which the reply would be: *"Work in what way?"* [Why do you want to know?] Well, Castaneda might wonder whether the devil's weed might be used as a new technology for delivering air mail, in which case Don Juan would probably say no, it doesn't work for that. In fact, Don Juan does try to answer this question, since it's the only question he *can* answer, when he says that with the devil's weed, a "brujo", can travel a thousand miles to "see what is going on" or can "deliver a blow to his enemies."

The answer to the question, "What is real?" is "Why do you want to know?"; and the answer to the question "What is reality?" is "Reality is what works."

•

What is the "good life"? What is "moral"? What is "normal"? What is "real"? These are the kinds of questions ecocrisis is imposing on us. They are frightening questions; for some, they may be overwhelming. Little wonder, then, that the most prevalent response is to try to evade or escape them. But the symptoms of the crisis are so pervasive that ignorance has become virtually impossible and apathy itself has become strenuous. As Robert Hunter observes:

> In the dense informational environment of mass society, true ignorance of the dimensions of the problems we face

can only be achieved through the purposeful exclusion of facts which keep intruding at every turn. Apathy itself is purposeful. It is really avoidance, a "positive" act. Rather than risk having their equilibrium overwhelmed, great numbers of people chose existentially to look the other way: to escape into the banality of television serials or movies or sports activities. This deliberate, even though perhaps

the epistemological stress becomes unbearable, our only remaining escape is to "rise above" the dilemma itself, to go *out* of our mind. This is the essence of Bateson's double-bind theory of schizophrenia. Inevitably, the insanity Occidental culture inflicts on the global Mind is fed back through the cybernetic network into human consciousness and drives our individual minds mad too.

REVOLUTION

The result of this massive epistemological dissonance, this vast and pervasive double bind, is a kind of global schizophrenia. The global Mind is undergoing a great schism, and the manifestation of this in human terms is fast coming to be recognized as a "revolution in consciousness." It was Charles Reich's *The Greening of America* that first popularized the vision of a "consciousness revolution," but the same basic view has appeared in the work of Robert Hunter, Andrew Weil, Carlos Castaneda, John Lilly, William Irwin Thompson, Ronald Laing, Alan Watts, Baba Ram Dass, and Gregory Bateson.[31] While there are common threads that run through the theses of these writers, there are also great variations and even inconsistencies. No one of them has yet convincingly defined the *consciousness revolution* in terms of what is happening, how, and why. This is hardly surprising, considering the recentness and suddenness of the revolution, its profound implications which have barely yet been grasped, much less explicated, and its challenge to verbal expression itself.

While the consciousness revolution is of the greatest importance, I must admit that I cannot explain it conclusively, neither within the scope of this book nor otherwise. But because it is relevant to our discussion, I would like to offer some speculations about it, based on what I have gleaned from the works of the other authors, as well as on personal experiences of "altered states of consciousness."

The first question that must be raised in any discussion of the consciousness revolution is, what do we mean by *consciousness?* I do not have any single answer to this question. The word *consciousness* means different things to different people and in different contexts. *Consciousness* meant something different to Sigmund Freud than it does to Timothy Leary, and it probably means something different to Maharishi Mahesh Yogi than it does to Leary, although the magnitude of any of these distinctions is almost impossible to gauge, since we are dealing with subjective and as yet unquantifiable phenomena. The dictionary is hardly helpful, making only circular allusions to "awareness." More poetic descriptions of *consciousness*—"the window of the mind," "the mind's eye," even the "TV screen of awareness"—are hardly more illuminating. Perhaps the best we can say, then, is that *consciousness* is "experience," that one's consciousness is what one experiences. If our current notion of the meaning of consciousness is vague, it is probably because those who are now most inclined to talk about it are those whose own consciousnesses have been expanded or otherwise modified through experiences that may be associated with drugs, meditation, yoga, psychotherapy, or some kind of "schizophrenogenic" stress.

I believe there is an equation—even perhaps an identity—between the notion of *consciousness* and the concept of *reality* as I have used it above. Thus the subtitle of Castaneda's first book is *A Yaqui Way of Knowledge* (that is, epistemology, or *consciousness*), and the second is *A Separate Reality.* Other authors talk of "ordinary consciousness" and "ordinary reality" or "altered consciousness" and "alternative realities," more or less interchangeably.

This brings us to the notion of a kind of baseline of consciousness, or reality. Andrew Weil calls this "ordinary" reality, while John Lilly calls it "consensus" reality, or, in terms of consciousness, the "planetside trip." These, of course, are distinguished from other "trips," "altered states of consciousnesses," "satoris," and so forth. In some respects, this "ordinary" reality is the same as what we have been calling the *hardworld.*

Sometimes the altered states of consciousness, which are distinguished from the ordinary state of consciousness, or reality, are spoken of as being part of, located "in," or simply constituting the "subconscious" or "unconscious". In other contexts we hear of "higher consciousness," "consciousness-raising," and so on. This gets confusing. Are these other states of consciousness higher or lower than the ordinary? Can they, indeed, be ranked on a continuum at all, or are they described by a number of different, independent dimensions? I do not know of anyone who knows the answers to

model, or paradigm, of the two halves of the brain. The left hemisphere of the brain controls the right side of the body, and vice versa; or rather, this would be the case were it not for a bridge of brain tissue called the *corpus callosum* which links the two halves. As Ornstein says, from animal and human experiments, where this connection between the two sides of the brain is severed, we have learned that the two halves of the brain are not identical but rather that they function in distinctly different ways. The left side of the brain appears to be associated with an analytical, linear, verbal kind of consciousness, the right side with a holistic, spatial, nonverbal consciousness. Ornstein associates the left side of the brain with Occidental culture in general and with western psychology (which has traditionally considered the left side the *dominant,* or *superior,* side of the brain) in particular. Alternatively, he associates the right side of the brain with the Orient and particularly with the "esoteric" psychology (for example, Zen and Yoga) of the East. The notion of some sort of tension or even dichotomy between language and verbal modes of thinking, on one hand, and other, more holistic, modes, on the other, is not new. It is reflected in earlier work by such people as Dorothy Lee, Benjamin Whorf, and Marshall McLuhan. Many great thinkers are known to have anguished about the conflict between language and thought. Albert Einstein was perennially frustrated over his inability to translate his intuitive conceptualizations of physical systems into a satisfactory verbal form. Ornstein, though, has done some useful work by formalizing this notion, organizing and providing its scientific basis, and projecting its implications. Even so, he admits that the work needed for an adequate understanding of human consciousness has barely begun.

I believe that when we eventually undertake the kind of extensive and intensive research effort that will be required to scientifically comprehend the complex phenomena of *consciousness*, these phenomena/experiences may, probably at a fairly crude level, be ranked along some kind of a continuum from *paraconscious* through *conscious* to *metaconscious*. I would guess that some of the states of consciousness associated with ESP might fall at the metaconscious end, while a strong alpha-state might perhaps fall at the paraconscious end of the spectrum. But I further suspect that as our investigations of alternative realities proceed, our model of consciousness will improve and become more elaborate. Probably a number of independent dimensions of consciousness will be distinguished, and while some of these will be *continuous*, others will be *discrete*. To clarify this concept, let me use the analogy of a TV monitor to represent the "screen of consciousness." The typical TV monitor, as a message source, has basically three independent dimensions which may be altered to produce a variety of different states (we will discount the audio and consider only the video). The first dimension is that of intensity, or brightness; the second is contrast. Both dimensions are continuous and may take on a virtually infinite number of values between their boundaries. The third dimension, however, is that of the channel. This is clearly a discrete dimension, there being only a countable number of values or states possible within it. Similarly, various states of consciousness, like the marijuana "high," may vary continuously over a range, from totally "straight" to totally "stoned." Others may seem to be divided into discrete, hierarchical levels, as in Lilly's hierarchy of "satoris."

One fascinating question is whether there might be in the softworld of consciousness an analog of the Einsteinian relativity of the hardworld. That is, might there not be some quantity or perhaps quality that remains constant under the transformation from one state of consciousness to another, just as in the physical universe, the speed of light remains constant under the transformation from one frame of reference to another? My own hunch is that some such invariant, or invariants, will be found, but I have practically no support for this. Much more exploration of alternative realities will have to be done before we can know for sure.

•

Admitting that we haven't really defined *consciousness* conclusively, let us, nevertheless, consider the next question, which the notion of a consciousness revolution necessarily raises: What is revolting against what? What is the difference between the "old" and the "new" consciousness? Charles Reich originally called the new consciousness "Con III" and divided the old into "Con I" and "Con II." Robert Hunter, who sees no real value in the latter distinction, asserts that they are both merely minor variations of the old consciousness which, borrowing from Herbert Marcuse, he sometimes calls the

2.   Attachment to the senses and thus to external reality.

3.   Attention focused on outward forms rather than inner contents, leading to materialism.

4.   Perception of differences rather than similarities.

5.   Negative thinking, pessimism, and despair.

"Stonesville," on the other hand, has these general characteristics:

1.   Reliance on intuition, as well as intellection.
2.   Acceptance of the ambivalent nature of things.
3.   Experience of infinity in its positive aspect.

The old consciousness, being what we are familiar with, may not warrant further explication, but the new consciousness requires a bit more description. There is no limit to how detailed a description of the new consciousness could be, and Reich and Hunter have written books on the subject. I think Hunter gives a good synoptic description, which represents the general view of the new consciousness fairly well:

By nature, the new holistic consciousness is basically an *ecological* consciousness. The less it is constrained by the narrow operational mode, the more it is capable of responding to the kind of "over-view" provided by ecology. The ecological consciousness, by itself, must lead us inevitably to a holistic philosophy, back to the pre-Socratic notion of every-thing being in a state of flux. This awareness is as alien to Western thought as Zen. Ecology involves, finally, the rec-ognition of whole systems, instead of incomplete subsys-tems. It teaches us to recognize gestalts, to understand syn-ergy, to appreciate the extent to which we are only one facet of an environment. Already it has opened the path leading to a theology of the earth, thus short-circuiting Christianity and pointing the way back toward the kind of unfragmented, harmonious mental space understood per-fectly by the ancient Chinese and—more intuitively—by primitive peoples the world over. Ecological consciousness, in short, is the common denominator of the real revolution which is just now beginning inside the gates of the comforta-ble concentration camp fashioned by technique. It is the root whose growth will make the difference, in the future, between freedom and unfreedom, stagnation and flower-ing.[35]

The dominant consciousness is therefore being challenged by a new ecological consciousness. The prevailing reality is in the process of being replaced with a new reality. Of course, the dominant model of reality has been challenged and changed more than once in hu-man history.[36] But with the exception of the birth of the scientific method, what may be *unique* about the current revolution is that it may not be simply a change in the *content* of the model of reality but a change in the *concept* of the model, a change in the very process of modeling reality itself. For example, Forrester's work in system dynamics challenges not only the *ontology* of contemporary eco-nomics but its *epistemology* (that is, not just what the economic establishment claims to "know" but *how* it claims to know it).

If, as was implied in Chapter 6, the modeling process is based on the self-validating refractory *premises* of Learning II, then what is now occurring seems to be a change in those premises; hence it is evidence of Learning III. The current consciousness revolution may differ from previous revolutions in the dominant reality by a quan-tum jump of logical type.

As indicated in Chapter 7, evolution is implicitly a learning pro-cess, but the new evolution may be an entirely new phase. Just as the equalization of matter and energy released vast new stores of energy, the equalization of cultural and genetic evolution may have created similarly dramatic changes. Matter itself has now become the most powerful source of energy. Human ideas are now becoming the most powerful force in genetic evolution. The teleonomic apparatus of the cell has now been plugged into a global cybernetic network and the perennial boundary between soma and germ may soon be breached (that is, the DNA code may soon be "dictated").

The actual "consciousness revolution" of today is not, in my view, merely a cognitive shift from Con I/II to Con III, from

way," as opposed to Don Juan's "one way," but rather, that the trouble is "one-wayness" itself.

The rising stress of widespread dissonance results not just from uncertainty about the content of reality but from the fruitlessness of even trying to define it conclusively, rather than accepting that reality itself changes according to context, that it is "what works." In pursuing comprehension of an absolute reality, people today are driving themselves "crazy," like Castaneda trying to determine if he "really" flew or the Zen student attacking his "koan,"[37] like "a mosquito biting on an iron bar." Whether the result is disorientation or enlightenment depends largely on how it is subjectively interpreted and how the experience is used. Thus the growing tendency to go crazy in an insane world is simultaneously the most pathological symptom of ecocrisis and the most dramatic promise for its cure.

CHAPTER 9

THE ECOLOGICAL

velopment posed by ecocrisis is so pervasive and prodigious that it is now evident that the cure for this pathology demands a profound and far-reaching transformation, not only of human society but of human consciousness as well. The changes which are implied if human and even planetary evolution is not to reach a sudden dead end may appear so radical to some that the term *utopian* may be derogatorily applied to them, with the implication being that such changes depart too extremely from the status quo to be workable. This may well be so; the fate of homo sapiens and of the terrestrial biosphere may already be sealed beyond reprieve. Yet it may not be so. There may be as much cause for optimism as for despair. What *is* clear is that if there is to be any future for man on this planet, that future must be dramatically different from the present unstable state. Regardless of what the "flat-earth economists" may say to the contrary, the world of the not-too-distant future is going to be some kind of an equilibrium state. The only questions that remain are whether man will be a part of it, and if so, what kind of human society the state of global equilibrium implies. Specifically, if only out of curiosity, we should want to know what the optimal, sustainable state for our posterity might be.

The word *utopia*, literally translated from the Greek, means "no place." A utopia is therefore a model of a society that *does not exist.* It is a common mistake to assume that a utopian novel or treatise is proposing a model of society that actually ought to be; the *u* in *utopia* is often treated like the Greek *eu*, meaning "good." Thus some modern novels which intentionally depict not the world of our dreams but that of our nightmares are often called *dystopias,* using the Greek suffix *dys,* meaning "bad." Many of the so-called utopian writers did not present idealized societies as models or plans that ought to be implemented; rather, they used utopia as a vehicle for criticizing the status quo. In this sense, both utopian and dystopian literature are cast from the same mold. But many utopias have been proposed as serious programs for creating the good life. In the nineteenth century many such plans for ideal human societies were put into operation. Indeed, the experimental commune is an entity that persists today.

Yet *utopia* and *utopian* are terms that have acquired the connotation of something impractical, naive, and quixotic. No doubt this is largely due to the obvious unworkability of many utopian schemes and the eventual failure of all the nineteenth-century utopian communities. But this attitude, on the whole, does injustice to the value of utopian thinking, which was the precursor of modern systems analysis and computer simulation. As a conceptual device for "testing out" various alternatives for the structure of human society, utopian thinking has had a significant impact on the structures society has actually realized. It would probably not be much of an exaggeration to say that the American and French revolutions and the modern revolutions in Russia and China constitute utopian experiments not unlike those of New Harmony or Oneida, though on a vaster scale.

Our previous examination of the nature of ecocrisis leads us to consider some kind of model or utopia that would represent the general solution to the macroproblem which ecocrisis poses. This utopia differs from its predecessors in that it must be expressly an *ecological* utopia; so we will refer to it as "ecotopia." (Admittedly, this does more violence to the etymology of *utopia* by joining the Greek words for "home" and "place," but the term serves the purposes of this discussion.) This is a significant departure from earlier utopias which are uniformly anthropocentric, always dealing with optimal criteria for man in society, rather than man in environment. Ecotopia is not truly a utopia, for we are not concerned here with "no place" but, on the contrary, with a particular place: the Earth, or more precisely, the global ecosystem. We are not concerned so much with a world that either ought or ought not to be, but with the optimal world that *can* exist within the constraints of the global ecosystem, and still contain man.

Because such a project raises a host of questions, our sketch of ecotopia must be skeletal. We will consider the basic criteria by which the viability of a potential ecotopia must be judged. Establishing these criteria, we will briefly review some modern utopian ideas, especially those of B. F. Skinner, to see what they can contribute to the final model. Finally, we will look at some of the minimal characteristics which seem to be required for an adequate ecotopia.

CRITERIA FOR AN OPTIMAL STATE

stipulate here that the appropriate rank-order among the criteria of survival, welfare, and development is just that in which they have been mentioned (survival first, welfare second, and development third). The rationale for this rank-order may already be obvious, but before defending it, let me first define these terms more clearly.

SURVIVAL

The concept of *survival* itself needs no explicit definition here, but it is important to note that the general criterion of survival begs an additional question of priorities: Where conflicts arise, who or what is to survive? This question implies another rank-order as its answer. The one that seems most rational is the following:

1. Biosphere (life)
2. Autotrophs (green plants)
3. All other species including Homo sapiens
4. Race/culture
5. Community
6. Family
7. Individual

The rationale for this ranking is simple. Every order in this hierarchy is presumed to contain all of the lower orders as subsets. Therefore it would be impossible to sacrifice any higher order to the survival of a lower order. This is a simple ethical proposition which, I admit, does not cover many of the conflicts that arise within subsets of each order of the hierarchy. Nevertheless, it is useful at an aggregate level as part of the general criteria for ecotopia. While this ranking may seem trivial, its simple logic is absent from the implicit values of Occidental culture, as evidenced, for example, by the elaborate preparations to exterminate the entire biosphere for the sake of "national defense."

WELFARE

The problem of quantitatively measuring the "quality of life" seems to be so full of pitfalls that some have despaired of ever making headway in this area.[1] On the other hand, currently employed economic indicators such as the GNP seem to be so perverse and contrary to our subjective perceptions of the quality of life that almost any change would seem likely to be an improvement. Even the modest change from GNP to some kind of rough measure of Net National Welfare would probably lead to dramatic changes in social and economic policy. In the long run, much research remains to be done to develop truly useful indicators of social, economic, and ecological welfare. While no singular breakthroughs in this area appear imminent or even ultimately likely, there seems little reason to doubt that progressive refinement and improvement in the measurement of the quality of life is possible; clearly it is urgently required.

It seems to me that the ultimate direction the development of some comprehensive indicator of the quality of life will take has been forecast by Athelstan Spilhaus. Spilhaus has suggested that a good index of the quality of life—qualitatively and perhaps ultimately quantitatively, as well—is the number of choices or alternatives a society or culture provides its individual members.[2] This index not only is harmonious with most of McHarg's subjective notions about the meaning of entropy, but, if it is appropriately defined, it can be made virtually isomorphic with the entropy or the information content of a social/ecological system. In this regard it is necessary that our comprehensive index of the quality of life be thought of less like the subjective notion of "freedom of choice" and more like the physical/mathematical concept of "degrees of freedom." This would mean that our index of the quality of life as *number of choices* or *degrees of freedom* would have to be defined not from the point of view of a real person but rather from a perspective similar to that of

J. Rawls' "representative person" in the "original position."[3] It may even be useful to expand the concept of the "representative person" to include not just any human being but any living organism in the biosphere.

DEVELOPMENT

to the existing trend. However, *development,* as defined here, is an essential criterion for an ecotopia. No other notion of *development* would be consistent with such a state. The cardinal measure of development, therefore, will be the change in entropy, or what is the same thing, the change in information content of the global ecosystem.

In defense of this set of criteria for an optimal state, let me, first of all, recognize that several other criteria could be and in fact have been suggested (for example, "freedom of choice," "justice," and "self-actualization"). Without discussing these other criteria, I will merely say that every other criterion of which I am aware is either corollary to or inconsistent with the criteria of survival, welfare, and development. Thus, for example, the concept of *justice,* especially as developed by Rawls, I see as a derivative of the concepts of survival, welfare, and development. On the other hand, the notion of an absolute "right to life," as it is construed by some groups, I see as contrary to these criteria.

More important perhaps than these criteria is the rank-order in which I have cast them. No doubt there are some who would disagree with this ranking and probably some who would despair of assigning priorities to fundamental "needs" at all. For the latter group there can be no satisfaction; the rule of logic demands priorities among the criteria of optimization. As for the rank-order I have indicated, I defend it with the same argument given for my hierarchy of survival. That is, each order in the hierarchy is so defined that it will include its subordinates. Thus *survival* is prerequisite to *welfare,* and *welfare* is prerequisite to *development.* Again, this ordering may seem trivial, but it is still a departure from the existing priorities of the dominant Occidental culture. Even as respected a scholar as Daniel Callahan can suggest that "freedom of choice" ought to be given priority over "security-survival."[4] Such a position, while emotionally appealing, is logically indefensible for, as Hardin or Skinner would undoubtedly observe, it is in the nature of the process of natural selection that a culture which assigns a higher priority to freedom than to survival will inevitably be displaced by one whose priorities are the reverse.

As is, no doubt, obvious, there exists considerable overlap between the criteria of survival, welfare, and development. Survival is prerequisite for welfare, but the conditions for maximizing welfare are also important for continued survival. Thus as a system's negentropy is increased, and along with it, the system's general complexity and stability, its adaptability to new contingencies of survival is also augmented. Similarly, welfare is prerequisite for development, but the conditions required for development are an important part of current welfare; that is, the research and learning necessary for further development are activities that enhance the current quality of life independently of their outcome.

These criteria are closely related to each other and cannot be easily separated at the broadest level of generalization. But when applied to specific issues or alternatives, the priority hierarchy is germane. Thus, for example, the question of whether fast-breeder reactors (FBRs) should be promulgated as a major energy source can be analyzed within this framework. According to these criteria, FBRs are contraindicated. Whatever their potential value to short-range welfare, they pose too great a threat to both survival and development to be justified. (Survival because of the immediate hazards of either an accident or intentional use of nuclear materials as a bomb or contaminant; development because of the irreversibility of both physical contamination and the opening of a political Pandora's box.)

Survival, welfare, and development also reflect the range of time perspective. Survival is immediate but also perpetual; it is something that must be constantly guarded, both in the immediate present and continuously into the future. Welfare is essentially short-term (a generation or less, that range of time within which feedback can still affect current actors). Development is long-term.

Basically, welfare is equivalent to the maximization of negentropy of a system within current (short-term) constraints. This is functionally equivalent to the use of existing free-energy sources and heat sinks with maximum efficiency; that is, the maximization of welfare is in the elimination of waste or noise. Development lies in the relaxation of existing constraints on the state of the art of maximizing welfare as a product of research and learning.

Finally, an additional condition which I will hold to be essential to any ecotopia—a condition that is not itself a criterion of optimization and which is, in fact, independent of these criteria—is that the criteria of optimization be manifested in the *consciousness* of the

every instance, classical utopias are microcosmic, isolated from the outside world, and largely self-structured. However authentic they may be as societies, they are almost totally unreal as ecosystems.

Nor do the modern dystopias have much to offer. Invaluable as the modern dystopian novels have been as criticism of contemporary social trends, they do not depict systems that could be stable within the constraints of the global ecosystem. In this regard, these modern dystopias fall into the same pitfall as the classical utopian schemes: they are not ecologically viable societies. This is true even of Huxley's *Brave New World* which ostensibly represents a projected response to two of Richard Falk's four dimensions of planetary danger, the war system and the population problem. But Huxley's dystopia is not only not adjusted to the constraints of environmental decay and resource depletion, it is actually based on the logical extension—perhaps the ultimate reductio ad absurdum—of the ethos of economic "growth-mania." Orwell's *1984* used the utopian genre as a literary vehicle for criticizing the rise of Stalinism and particularly his own country's toleration of it. Burgess' and Kubrick's *A Clockwork Orange* is merely a logical projection of current violence and an illogical attack on behaviorism. This is not to say that the kinds of societies depicted by these authors could not come to exist (to some extent, they already do) but rather that they could not *endure* within the constraints of the global ecosystem any longer than any existing society. In fact, they would probably be even more unstable and hence more ephemeral. These societies fail not only according to the criteria of development and welfare but the primary criterion of survival: in the long run they are not capable of it. These novels fail even as dystopias, for the tragedy—in the Whiteheadian sense—of a true dystopia lies in the very notion of its *permanence*. The sense of terror in *Brave New World, 1984,* and *A Clockwork Orange* derives not from the unpleasantness of the societies they depict but from the implication that these societies are remorselessly unchangable. But this implication is probably dubious on social and psychological grounds, and it is downright fallacious from the ecological viewpoint.

With two vast world wars, the advent of the Bomb and the cold war, and the insidious debacle of Vietnam, the twentieth century has been a dismal epoch in human history and thus has not encouraged much utopian thinking. H. G. Wells, Robert Heinlein, and Arthur C. Clarke are leading contributors in this area, but of these, only Wells offered full-fledged utopian schemes. Wells' ideas are generally too technocratic and Occidental and too little ecological to be relevant to a model for ecotopia, but he did make at least two important contributions. First, he virtually invented the idea of futurism: designing and planning a culture for future development rather than preservation of the past. Second, and probably more important, he was among the first to recognize that a modern utopia would have to be *global*. Much of the utopian thinking of Heinlein and Clarke also falls into the pitfalls of technocracy and ecological irrelevancy, but they also have made a crucial contribution. With Heinlein's *Stranger in a Strange Land* and Clarke's *Childhood's End*, we have two of the first major visions of utopian *consciousness*.

Skinner's *Walden Two* is by far the most significant utopia of the twentieth century. While *Walden Two* is not an adequate ecotopia, it nevertheless constitutes a good first approximation and has both strengths and weaknesses that are worth noting. The strengths of *Walden Two* as an ecotopian model are:

The basic design of *Walden Two* is evolutionary and adaptive, with a "program" that is more heuristic than algorithmic. In general, *Walden Two* is explicitly designed to change and evolve, to avoid ossification and the strict adherence to a status quo. Skinner envisages the optimal state not as any final solution but as an ongoing process of experimentation with a well-defined direction but no attainable goal.

The means of control in *Walden Two* are based on positive rather than negative reinforcement, reward rather than punishment.

While the governance of the society is in the hands of what appears to be an elite, Skinner deals with the "Quis custodiet" problem by creating a feedback structure that insures control of the controllers. Negative feedback is effected partly by requiring the controllers, like everyone else, to perform their share of labor and partly by having a sufficiently high rate of turnover in the ruling class that no one can accumulate any reward from the abuse of power. It

available a significant choice of roles and life-styles.

But *Walden Two* has some serious weaknesses which disqualify it as a satisfactory ecotopia:

There is the typical failure of utopian designs to deal with ecological constraints. The basic man-environment relationship is still the traditional Occidental one of dominance and exploitation. The problem of population growth is recognized, but Frazier, the fictional designer of *Walden Two*, anticipates Hardin and asserts that the population of a "responsible" culture must grow in order to become dominant: "It's no solution of the Malthusian problem to lower the birth rate of those who understand it. On the contrary, we need to expand the culture which recognizes the need for birth control."[5]

The latter makes sense only in the context of Frazier's enclave approach to social change. This social model is based on an analogy to the biological principle of *competitive exclusion*. For example, if there are two species of beetles living in a sack of flour, the more successful competitor of the two will eventually eliminate the other. Similarly, Frazier believes that his designed culture has such a competitive advantage over the "external" culture that it will simply grow until it takes over completely. But this enclave model is predicated on the belief that the dominant culture will not react to Frazier's subculture as a threat and seek to subvert or destroy it while it is still weak:

"I'm not at all easy, though, about your relation to the existing government," said Castle. "What sort of deal can you make with it?"

"All we ask is to be let alone," said Frazier quietly.

"But will you be let alone?", said Castle.[6]

Frazier believed, in 1948, that they would. Whether they would then is questionable, but it is absolutely certain that they would not be today. A *Walden Two* of today that managed to achieve the success of Frazier's community would be infiltrated by FBI agents and drug pushers, investigated by Congressional committees, demonstrated against by the YAF and the PLP (and maybe even the PTA), reported on by TV newsmen, exploited by advertisers ("Smoke new *Walden Two* little cigars, the ones with the utopian flavor!"), and flocked to by tourists. Ultimately it would be either zoned out of existence by the local board of selectmen, taken over by the Mafia, or franchised by Colonel Sanders. In short, Frazier's "enclave" model of social change could not work in the Cybernetic Age.

Skinner recognizes the evolutionary need for diversity but holds that planned diversity, guided by scientific experimentation, is superior to accidental diversity. While this may be true, it fails to account for the possible need for diversity in the planning model itself. In *Walden Two* there is a good deal of planned diversity among the individuals who comprise the society, but little group and no cultural diversity. While virtually anything in the society is potentially liable to change through experimentation, including the fundamental constitution or code by which the society is governed, the basic epistemological premises are sacrosanct. At one point, Castle attacks Frazier:

"You have ruled out points of view which may be more productive. You are implying that T. E. Frazier, looking at the world from the middle of the twentieth century, understands the best course for mankind forever."

"Yes, I suppose I do."[7]

With regard to this latter point, the chief shortcoming of Frazier's (Skinner's) confidence in the viability of a behavioristically designed society is that it fails to account for some of the basic principles of modern game and decision theory. Under conditions of uncertainty, a "player" may make a decision according to, at the extremes, either a pessimistic or an optimistic strategy. A pessimistic player will adopt a *minimax* strategy, seeking to minimize his maximum possible loss, while an optimistic player will adopt a *minimin* strategy, seeking to minimize his minimum possible loss. (Corresponding to these are the *maximin* strategy for maximizing the minimum gain, and the *maximax* strategy for maximizing the maximum gain.) It is axiomatic, however, that the strategy of play chosen has *no* influence

is a minimax strategy, and the latter a minimin.

Skinner underrates the problem of risk and uncertainty in the game of survival. He seems to imply that the survivability of a species or culture can be ranked on a single continuum. He doesn't adequately account for the fact that the ecosystem within which natural selection occurs is neither fixed nor even dynamically deterministic, but is to a large extent stochastic.

Is it necessarily true that the culture most committed to survival is the one most likely to survive? No. But this is what Skinner seems to be saying in *Beyond Freedom and Dignity*. Actually, one cannot know what the best strategy for survival is except post hoc. Robert Boguslaw shows that those most favored to survive under one set of rules may not be favored when the rules change.[8] Under "natural" conditions the swiftest wolves will be those that catch the most deer and thus those that have the best chance of survival. But if hunters come and use the deer as bait for the wolves, the swift wolves will be those that come into the hunters' sights first, and the contingencies of survival will then favor slow wolves.

Also, a major fallacy which commonly crops up in discussions of evolutionary change is the notion of "survival of the fittest" (a phrase which originally derives not from Darwin but from Spencer). The fact that the most unfit do not survive is *not* equivalent to saying that only the most fit do survive. Many genetic and cultural "ideas" survive for a long time not because they are necessarily fit but simply because they are not fatally unfit. Peacocks have colorful plumage mainly because peahens like it, not because fancy feathers contributed anything significant to the peacock's physical survival. The teleonomic apparatus of natural selection works in many strange ways its wonders to perform. Survival per se indicates little or nothing about the direction of evolution at any *point* in time. It is only historically that trends can be detected, but these predict virtually nothing about future development.

Evolution, as Monod tells us, is the result not merely of initial conditions but of *emerging contingencies* which are largely stochastic and which can be neither predicted nor derived from first principles. While Skinner-cum-Frazier's *Walden Two* is more flexible and adaptive than most existing societies, it may still not be flexible enough to meet the long-term contingencies of survival and development. *Walden Two* has a blind spot, its strict adherence to Frazier's Learning II premises. Since these premises tend to be self-validating, a society that provides no mechanism for challenging these premises is liable to the kind of ossification that can ultimately render it obsolete and maladaptive in the face of new contingencies of survival. Skinner's original design for *Walden Two* failed to provide such a mechanism, and 25 years of subsequent refinement of his ideas have not corrected this deficiency. His utopia is still frozen at the level of Learning II; but as we saw in the last chapter, the contingencies of ecocrisis demand an ecotopia that cultivates Learning III and possibly even Learning IV.

•

This criticism of Skinner's work should not be taken as discounting the enormous value of his contribution to ecotopian design. Skinner's work has, to a large extent, been unfairly maligned by those who in many instances have misunderstood some of the fundamental behaviorist principles on which his ideas are grounded. Therefore a brief digression on behaviorism seems warranted here.

It is important to discriminate between the reification of psychodynamic theories and the circularity of certain behaviorist concepts. The definition of many psychodynamic entities commits the fallacy of reification because the thing named (for example, *ego*) is treated as something autonomous from the "symptoms" that identified it in the first place. Thus it is fallaciously implied that *ego* exists even when the behavior which is evidence of it is not demonstrated. This is what Bandura calls "zoognick" theory.

At first glance it may appear that the definition of *reinforcement* commits the same error. *Reinforcement* is defined as any stimulus (stimuli) that is consequent to a response and which has the effect of that response becoming more probable following the same initial stimulus. Thus *there is no absolute reinforcer.* A *reinforcer* is anything that has the effect of being reinforcing, and this effect is context-dependent and subject-dependent. It is therefore a *circular* definition; a reinforcer is anything that reinforces. But this is exactly why it is not an example of reification. Reinforcement is the *name* of an observable phenomenon which is presumed to exist only to the

reinforcers (money, food, sex). They assert that autonomous man will be perverse and reject such pleasures simply to free himself of control, agreeing with the essential argument of Dostoevski's *Underground Man:*

> And why are you so firmly, so triumphantly, convinced that only the normal and the positive—in other words, only what is conducive to welfare—is for the advantage of man? Is not reason in error as regards advantage? Does not man, perhaps, love something besides well-being? Perhaps he is just as fond of suffering? Perhaps suffering is just as great a benefit to him as well-being? Man is sometimes extraordinarily, passionately, in love with suffering, and that is a fact. . . .[9]

But there is no contradiction between the existence of such masochistic behavior and the concept of positive reinforcement. The behaviorist has taken full account of the apothegm, "One man's meat is another man's poison." Skinner and every other competent behavior scientist knows that the person who "gets off" on suffering is no less liable to operant conditioning than the epicure. This is one important reason why Skinner's vision of a controlled society is not the Procrustean bed his critics fear. No behaviorist would seriously believe that the broadcast application of generalized reinforcers to a large population could have more than the most general kind of influence on the average behavior of the individuals who comprise that population. More precise control would require more variegated reinforcement, and exact control of every individual would essentially imply that each person would get his own reward. The picture seems far more democratic than totalitarian.

There is also strong evidence of synergetic interaction in conditioning. A Swedish instructional film on classical conditioning of human subjects illustrates this. In the experiments presented in the film, a number of human subjects with known high degrees of hypnotic susceptibility were hypnotized and then classically conditioned to respond to various colored lights with different kinds of emotional behavior. A red light became a conditioned stimulus for anger, a blue for sadness, green for passion, and so on. Naturally some subjects were more expressive than others in their reactions, but all tended to react similarly to similar emotional stimuli. What was interesting in these experiments was that when subjects were exposed to conflicting or inconsistent stimuli *simultaneously,* they came up with unpredictable, highly individual responses. For example, flashed with the stimuli for *love* and *anger* simultaneously, one subject was apparently nonplussed, while another reacted with a form of behavior that would be called "psychotic" by some.

In the real world, people are continually exposed to many reinforcement contingencies simultaneously, many of which are inconsistent with each other. Most of these conflicts are inconsequential and ephemeral. When they become more serious and enduring, the result may be something like Festinger's "cognitive dissonance." When the conflicts become even more profound and permanent, Bateson's "double bind" is generated. In any case, the resulting behavior cannot always be understood in the framework of simple conditioning, even though we have every reason to believe that it must be consistent with the principles of behavior theory just as it must be consistent with the principles of quantum mechanics. Here again, as in other cases, it is the usefulness of a model that is germane: reality is what works.

In short, then, while the fundamental principles of behaviorism are almost certainly valid, the inability of behavior theory to predict or derive specific patterns of behavior can be rationalized in the same way that Monod rationalizes the limits of evolution theory. Any particular pattern of behavior is free to exist, but it is not required to do so. While complex behavior is consistent with behaviorist principles, it cannot generally be deduced from them or predicted by them.

The fact that, in the behaviorist view, we are all controlled by our environment—plus what Skinner calls our "genetic endowment"—does not prove nor imply that one person can exercise complete and arbitrary control over another or others, since generally it will be impossible to control the total environment and genetic endowment of even one individual, much less a group or a population. Indeed, Bateson questions whether the model of *unilateral* control

about promoting his own ideas. He wants people to abandon the model of autonomous man and adopt the behaviorist, mechanical model for the good of society as a whole. But it is an empirical fact that many people find his model *aversive* and the autonomous model rewarding. Under these circumstances, Skinner realizes that people are not likely to do what he suggests. His current solution to this dilemma is to focus on the advantages, the positive reinforcers, which behavioral technology would offer to society *as a whole*. But the evidence suggests that macrolevel reinforcement is not very effective at the microlevel. Further, nearly all of the reinforcers Skinner promises are long-term, not immediate. How can he seriously hope to convert people to his way of thinking?

I believe that the way to do this would be to show how operant conditioning principles and the cybernetic model can be more reinforcing *for the individual, now*. The cybernetic model can, in many ways, improve people's lives and their relationships with others (and with their environment) in ways that the old autonomous model cannot. People who realize that they are not fated to *be* what they intrinsically *are*, that they can, to a large extent, form their existences creatively, are—in my view at least—more truly liberated. Therefore, the initial emphasis must be on *self*-control (keeping in mind that Learning III makes the concept of *self* plastic and to some extent, irrelevant) before behaviorism can be successfully applied for widespread social change.

THE ESSENTIAL ECOTOPIA

A complete description of ecotopia is beyond the scope of our current state of knowledge. The social, technological, and scientific questions that would have to be answered by a comprehensive model of ecotopia have barely been posed, much less responded to. Nevertheless, it is now possible to envisage some of the most essential characteristics of an adequate ecotopia. These characteristics can be discussed within the framework of the fundamental criteria of survival, welfare, and development.

SURVIVAL CHARACTERISTICS

The minimal survival characteristics of ecotopia are (1) the establishment of a "stationary state," or "state of global equilibrium," and (2) the obviation and ultimate dismantling of the war system.

Advocacy of the stationary state is, of course, not entirely new. More than a century ago, Malthus and Ricardo observed the inexorable conflict between scarcity and growth, and John Stuart Mill argued forcefully for the stationary state:

> It must always have been seen, more or less distinctly, by political economists, that the increase in wealth is not boundless: that at the end of what they term the progressive state lies the stationary state, that all progress in wealth is but a postponement of this, and that each step in advance is an approach to it.
>
> I cannot . . . regard the stationary state of capital and wealth with the unaffected aversion so generally manifested towards it by political economists of the old school. I am inclined to believe that it would be, on the whole, a very considerable improvement on our present condition. I confess I am not charmed with the ideal of life held out by those who think that the normal state of human beings is that of struggling to get on; that the trampling, crushing, elbowing, and treading on each other's heels which forms the existing type of social life, are the most desirable lot of human kind.[11]

It has had its adherents from that time to this, yet these have till now been viewed as an apostate minority in the ranks of economists. But the work of Forrester, Meadows, and their colleagues has convincingly put the lie to the smug assurances of economic pundits who have consistently blinded themselves to the scourge of "progress," refusing to see what others viewed as the obvious—that unbridled growth is the philosophy of the cancer cell.

Some detailed conditions for a state of global equilibrium given by Meadows and others were given in Chapter 4. They can be boiled down to two essential constraints: zero growth in the stock of capital

ploited in such a way as to keep them truly renewable; therefore erosion, depletion, and pollution of such resources will have to be minimized. Energy use will have to be shifted away from such non-renewable and limited sources as coal, oil, and natural gas and toward such renewable or virtually unlimited sources as wind, tide, and especially solar power. Thermonuclear sources of energy may come to play a larger role, but these *must* be of the fusion type—if the requisite technology can ultimately be developed. The ecological and social/political hazards associated with "fast-breeder" fission reactors seem to me to preclude their existence.

The dismantling of the war system is an inexorable requirement for long-range planetary survival. In particular, the technology of mass destruction, nuclear and biochemical weapons, must be phased out of existence and strict regulatory mechanisms implemented to prevent its recurrence. Yet it is not only the technology of the war system but its psychology—its implicit breakdown-inducing influence—that makes it not only a direct threat to planetary survival but an intolerable obstacle to the establishment of the stationary state. We have already heard strident voices exclaiming that population control is a euphemism for genocide and that a no-growth economy would oppress the poor.[12] Obviously birth control could be used for genocide and zero economic growth could be used to create a caste system. But any policy pursued to an extreme or used for evil ends can be an instrument of tyranny. Taxes can be used to soak the rich or burden the poor. "Welfare" can liberate people from the scourge of poverty or it can enslave them. The same herbicide that can be used to kill weeds on an American farm can be used to destroy crops in a Vietnamese village. The "right to a quality education" can be a weapon against racism or an excuse for it. We have to recognize that unrestricted population growth can and will have just as devastating an effect on many of the world's peoples as the most pernicious program of genocide imaginable, also that economic growth today is actually widening the gulf between the rich and the poor, not narrowing it.

It is evident that the stationary state, to be one of truly *stable* equilibrium, would require a vastly more equitable distribution of wealth and power among all the people of the world than exists today. It is virtually inconceivable that a stable society could be created in which the two-thirds of the world's population that is currently impoverished and largely disenfranchised would be kept in a state of perpetual inferiority. Therefore the establishment of the stationary state and the obviation of the war system—and of the competitive/exploitive kinds of social and political relationships that are central to that system—are seen as inseparable and inevitable requirements for planetary survival.

WELFARE CHARACTERISTICS

These conditions of survival, while simple to state, are basic and have profound implications for the nature of human welfare (or more generally, ecological welfare) in ecotopia. To begin with, the political implications of the state of global equilibrium are ultimately far more radical than any of the existing political ideologies, whether Marxist or capitalist. In ecotopia the old anthropocentric politics of both the right and the left become obsolete, because the state of global equilibrium requires an expansion of the conception of *human rights* to embrace the entire global ecosystem.

Perhaps because the challenge of attaining global equilibrium seems so imposing, there are many who have precipitously jumped to the conclusion that the establishment of the stationary state would necessitate the abnegation of human liberty. These critics conjure up visions of *1984*, Big Brotherism, and people reduced to soulless automatons. But as we noted earlier, these dystopian visions are not viable ecotopias, because they are incapable of long-run survival. Such nightmarish visions are more likely to be realized as a result of continued exponential growth than by its elimination.

Certainly, in ecotopia some of our alleged human rights would have to be modified or abandoned, namely, the "right" to *breed* and the "right" to *greed*. We never really have had such rights in the first place. There have been all sorts of declarations, resolutions, and documents establishing people's rights to have all the children they please, to accumulate all the material goodies of the modern age, or, as the Bible put it, to be fruitful and multiply and have dominion over the earth. This is patent nonsense. The teleonomic apparatus of the global ecosystem does not give a tinker's damn for our constitutions,

of freedom" open to the "representative person." The measure of welfare in ecotopia is essentially proportional to the negative entropy or information content of the global system. In general, the welfare of the individual members of ecotopia will be directly related to the richness of the diversity of the society as a whole.

The practical implications of this ecological concept of welfare are clearly myriad, but at least two seem to warrant some discussion here. First, beyond the basic redistribution of wealth and power, which seems requisite for survival, the exigencies of ecological welfare seem to demand an even more complex distributive structure. Ecotopia will have to move beyond the meretricious system of "equality of opportunity" of capitalism and even beyond the idealistic and never realized communist notion of strict "equality," to something more like the multidimensional social mobility suggested in *Walden Two* and somewhat realized already in the People's Republic of China. In ecotopia I would envisage that at the very least the equivalency between social and economic status would be obliterated. Moreover, I would expect that individuals would perform a number of different social and economic roles, either simultaneously as in *Walden Two* or in contemporary China, or through the course of a lifetime, as is to some extent happening today in the United States. Certainly the notion of "upward mobility," as it is currently understood, would be obviated. Rather, the accumulated "wealth" of a lifetime would be represented less by *things* and more by *knowledge* and *experience*, by the aggregation of wisdom and love.

Second, this implies a radical redefinition of the role and meaning of *work,* both for the individual and for society. In an economy that is materially nongrowing and where individual mobility is no longer defined in purely materialistic terms, the rationale for work will be quite different from that of the Protestant ethic. It seems likely that the observed trend toward a "postindustrial economy," dominated largely by the education and service sector, would reach its logical conclusion in ecotopia, where the lion's share of economic activity would fall in this category. Buckminster Fuller anticipates that in a "spaceship economy" the major work will be the augmentation of "know-how." The conventional division between *education* and *work* would probably be eliminated in ecotopia, and the model of "recurrent," or "lifetime," education would likely become the rule. At the same time the value of meaningful physical labor may be restored by the decline in mass production and the resurgence of artisanship.

DEVELOPMENT CHARACTERISTICS

Clearly the characteristics of development and welfare of ecotopia must be closely related, since our notion of development is essentially tied to the long-term augmentation of ecological welfare. In this regard, the false impression is being promoted by some critics of the stationary state that *stationary* is perforce synonymous with *stagnant.* But as I have just indicated, the absence of material growth would not only *not* mean the end of spiritual, intellectual, and cultural growth, but, indeed, the latter would tend to be liberated and enhanced in a world with enough time, space, and resources to nourish this kind of development. John Stuart Mill observed:

It is scarcely necessary to remark that a stationary condition of capital and population implies no stationary state of human improvement. There would be as much scope as ever for all kinds of mental culture, and moral and social progress; as much and more likelihood of it being improved, when minds cease to be engrossed by the art of getting on. Even the industrial arts might be as earnestly and as successfully cultivated, with this sole difference, that instead of serving no purpose but the increase of wealth, industrial improvements would produce their legitimate effect, that of abridging labor.[13]

Our major criterion of development is the evolution of ideas, or the progressive transformation of the global ecosystem in the direction of increasing negentropy. Technically, this means increasing the information content of the system as a whole, but what are the implications of this?

We noted in Chapter 7 that McHarg's subjective interpretation of entropy was inexact and unreliable. Nevertheless, it does provide

has no single or simple answer.

Integration/differentiation and centralization/decentralization are terms that are not readily commensurable with entropy/negentropy. A society that is developing in the direction of negative entropy may be subjectively thought of as either moving toward greater integration or greater differentiation, and both views may be substantiated. At the extremes, a trend in either of these subjective directions from any reasonably ambiguous state would probably represent an increase in entropy. A highly integrated and centralized (that is, monolithic) state would be one of relatively high entropy, but so would a highly differentiated, highly decentralized (that is, anarchic) state. In either case the information content—the amount of information required to describe the structure—of such a simplified state would be less than that of a more complex, diverse society. Where the differences between alternative states are less extreme, it is the information content that provides the acid test.

The major characteristics of ecotopia, so far as development is concerned, are not so much superficial aspects of the society itself, but are rather those of the control and learning structures which comprise the total teleonomic apparatus.

It can be said, as Skinner does, that the direction of evolution (which we have labeled here as *development*) is just that which tends toward a more elaborate and effective structure of control.[14] To wit, Skinner asserts that the negentropic result of both genetic and cultural evolution is to "make organisms more sensitive to the consequences of their action."[15] In other words, the global ecosystem develops more and better (more efficient, more stable) feedback loops. But as Garrett Hardin points out, the general cybernetic concept of control, translated into social terms, is just what philosopher Charles Frankel calls "responsibility": "A decision is responsible when the man or group that makes it has to answer for it to those who are directly or indirectly affected by it."[16]

In *Walden Two* such responsibility was achieved by the mechanism described above. In postcultural-revolution China, responsibility seems to be insured in part by periodically sending the members of the higher echelons of the political and economic structure back to the fields, the mines, or the factories to experience first hand the results of their actions, to get feedback from those who are most directly affected. In recent years in the United States, there has been a growing movement for greater accountability in consumer, environmental, and political affairs, but fundamental system changes have not yet occurred to redress the preponderant lack of responsibility. The fundamental control system of ecotopia should therefore be, in Frankel's sense, *responsible* and should develop in the direction of ever greater responsibility.

Beyond this, we may inquire what form the control system of ecotopia might take. Boguslaw has identified four distinctive approaches to the design of such systems:

The formalist approach
The heuristic approach
The operating unit approach
The ad hoc approach[17]

The formalist approach is essentially algorithmic. It seeks to design a system to operate according to a fixed, strict set of rules, the performance of such a system thereby being largely hard-programmed. The heuristic approach, on the other hand, is based more on strategic, or aesthetic, rules of thumb, which are far less inviolable guidelines for system performance.[18] The operating-unit approach seeks to optimize the performance characteristics of the system's components, leaving the performance of the system, as a whole, relatively unrestricted. The ad hoc approach is, in a sense, the "null" system design, being based on the immediate response to current contingencies.

Any actual system is likely to combine aspects of any or all of these approaches. Specifically, the control system of ecotopia might be based on any such combination. I believe, however, that the control system of ecotopia, at least to meet the criterion of development, would probably be based more on the heuristic and operating-unit approaches than on the formalist and ad hoc approaches. Too great a reliance on the latter (which, in fact, is characteristic of most current social systems) seems to preclude the degree of flexibility and hence adaptability that would be required for the continued development of the ecotopian system.

malist and ad hoc approaches to ecotopian design.

THE ECOLOGICAL CONSCIOUSNESS

It is essential to ecotopia that the fundamental features just described be manifested in the consciousness of such a society. This means that a new ecological consciousness ultimately will have to develop, especially among those who exercise the greatest control (that is, those who function at the nexus of critical loops of the feedback structure). People will have to adopt new ways of thinking and knowing, and this means learning new ways of learning, which, of course, is the essence of a Learning III culture.

Perhaps one of the best descriptions of a holistic, ecological mode of thinking is provided by Robert Heinlein's contemporary classic, science-fiction novel, *Stranger in a Strange Land.* Valentine Michael Smith, the book's hero, is a human whose singular fate was to be raised from infancy by Martians. Smith's body may be human, but his mind is distinctly Martian, vastly exceeding the power of even the most extraordinary terrestrial mind. The initial and most important lesson that he teaches his human comrades is the art of "grokking." *Grok* is a Martian word that can best be understood—or grokked—by induction (by reading the book). Essentially, it means to comprehend something completely, holistically, "in all its fullness," with the additional connotation to love, cherish, and praise.

The *grokking* mode of thought seems to be emerging from modern computer technology, especially in the fields of systems analysis in general and Forrester's system dynamics methodology in particular. One finds more and more people in these fields talking about "thinking in systems" in a manner strongly reminiscent of Heinlein's grokking. Forrester has observed that complex systems are predominantly "counterintuitive" in their behavior; hence, they are most comprehensively analyzed and understood with the aid of a high-speed computer. But many of Forrester's colleagues and students have found that experience with system dynamics enables them to *grok* the behavior of complex systems to a large extent without the machine's assistance, hence the rise of *thinking in systems.*

Ecological consciousness, then, is the grokking-level awareness of the global ecosystem, of its synergetic behavior, of its complexity, of its connectedness, and of the place and role of man within its multidimensional web. Since the global ecosystem includes all biomes and all biocenoses, as well as all anthropocentrically defined "man-made" (as if autonomous from "natural") systems as subsystems, ecological consciousness is a holistic vision of ongoing worldwide life processes in synergetic combination. It is polyconsciousness as opposed to monoconsciousness. It is, in short, the proper recognition of the role and performance of the individual mind within the context of the comprehensive global Mind. In the development of ecological consciousness, the emphasis is on process and form, on cybernetic structure, on unifying principles that govern dynamic behavior, rather than on categorical pigeonholing, naming of parts, simplistic pairing of cause and effect. To put it metaphorically, the emphasis is on the rules of the game and the strategy of the play, rather than on the score of the game and the names of the players.

A crucial subsystem within the overall framework of consciousness is a sort of heuristic program for ethical behavior. There are certain broad principles and rules of conduct which are assumed to shape, if not actually control, the behavior of any society. Written or unwritten values, ethics, or morals are fairly ubiquitous notions of what a society ought to do, if not what it actually does. Taken in toto, these things comprise what we commonly call *conscience.*

The dividing line between conscience and consciousness is vague. Regardless of one's philosophy, it is evident that the viability of any system of ethics—in sum, any social conscience—must be grounded in the conception of reality as reflected in consciousness. Men who owned slaves could write that "all men are created equal, endowed by their Creator with certain inalienable rights." This was no moral dilemma for those whose consciousness classified slaves as property and not as men. Conscience constitutes a set of guidelines for behavior, but a set of guidelines that is applied only in certain circumstances which are defined by a model of reality (that is, by consciousness). Therefore, distortions and loopholes in our consciousness create morally neutral territory in the real world, moral free-fire zones where individual and collective human behavior is freed from any ethical constraint and is governed solely by the dictates of expe-

unattenuated ecological crisis. A consciousness that is fundamentally exploitive and abusive toward what it perceives as *nature* must inexorably be exploitive and abusive toward man as well. As William Leiss puts it: *"mastery over nature inevitably turns into mastery over men* and the intensification of social conflict."[19]

The ecological conscience is not far different from our established collection of moral/ethical guides to human behavior. The major difference is that the ecological conscience, via the ecological consciousness, enlarges the relevant universe (that is, the functional context) of established moral/ethical principles to embrace the entire biosphere. It would probably not be necessary, therefore, to found a completely new, ecological religion in order to promulgate the ecological conscience. It would likely be enough if our existing theology or philosophy could adapt to a more viable model of reality (to a new ecological consciousness).

As we saw earlier, the view that the ultimate roots of ecocrisis lie in our fundamental consciousness has already become popular among environmentalists. Following the implications of Lynn White's thesis, however, this recognition often breaks down into a dialectic between western versus eastern modes of thought. The former is given most of the blame for our current predicament, while the latter is advanced as the key to salvation. Thus many have been led to embrace those Oriental disciplines which seem most alien to Occidental thought—Zen, The Tao, Vedanta, and Yoga—as *the* ecological mode of thinking.

This view of western thought as antiecological and eastern

thought as ecological has some objective basis, yet ultimately it is too simplistic to be very useful. It is true that many of the causes of our ecological crisis can be traced to dysfunctional aspects of western thought, but many of those aspects can be found in traditions other than the Judeo-Christian one. As Crowe observes, our current ecological crisis is not the first one in human history. Man has precipitated ecological crises throughout his history and on every continent. Civilization of any kind, East or West, being necessarily based on agriculture, has always resulted in severe and often fatal ecological stress. Only tribal peoples, living predominantly as hunters and gathers, have remained largely in harmony with the ecological system on which their survival has depended; and even to this statement there are exceptions.

As we have seen, the western mode of thought clearly has many "dysecological" aspects to it. It is anthropocentric and anthropomorphic, setting man apart from and dominant over nature, viewing man as God-like or perhaps more significantly, God as man-like. The emphasis on materialism and teleology, on the conquest of nature, on the Protestant ethic, and so on, has had an ecologically deleterious effect. But there are positive aspects as well. There is the emphasis on science, on art, and on creativity in general; an admiration for nature, a respect for reason, and an impulse toward intellectual advancement.

Of course, from an ecological point of view, the eastern mode of thinking has much to recommend it. Where the western mode of thinking is anthropocentric, linear, discrete, and simplistic, the eastern mode is cosmic, nonlinear, continuous, and complex, which makes it far more congruent with the exigencies of the global Mind. But the eastern mode also tends to fatalism, passivity, anti-technicalism, and anti-intellectualism, which are not very helpful attributes for dealing with many of the problems that make up today's ecocrisis.

Ecotopia demands a dominant consciousness, a consensus reality which will work optimally within the constraints of the global ecosystem according to the criteria of survival, welfare, and development. While we as yet have only an inchoate notion of what such an ecological consciousness will be like, it does represent a mode of thinking which synthesizes desirable aspects of both eastern and western, as well as other more "primitive" modes of thinking.

THE NEED FOR RESEARCH

These characteristics of Ecotopia seem to be necessary, but they are not sufficient. A vastly greater amount of information is needed to paint a reasonably complete picture of a viable state of global equilibrium. The task of generating this information has barely begun. The necessary theory and research in equilibrium economics,

BALANCING PRIORITIES IN RESEARCH

In recent years there has been a growing emphasis on support-ing applied research at the expense of basic scientific research. The Nixon administration, for example, tried to create a "war on cancer" by transferring government support funds away from many areas of basic medical and biological research and toward research which is applied to the treatment of cancer. Most scientists have condemned this tactic as pernicious. The crucial role of learning and knowledge in the creation and maintenance of an equilibrium society—both as a means for facilitating equilibrium and as an end in itself as a major component of the quality of life—requires that the attempt to trade off applied research for basic research, or vice versa, be abandoned and that support for basic research of all kinds be increased signifi-cantly.

NEW APPROACHES TO TECHNOLOGICAL RESEARCH

While a fairly large amount of money has been directed toward solving complex, physical-systems problems through the develop-ment of increasingly sophisticated, but costly "hard" technologies, very little money is being given to "soft" technological research projects which are consistent with equilibrium, that is, which provide answers to complex, physical-systems problems without increasing the consumption of energy or nonrenewable resources and without generating social and ecological costs that outweigh their benefits.

More specifically, I detect a number of critical needs that are not currently being met in applied research:

Intermediate Technology
There is a great need for more research and development of what E. F. Schumacher calls "intermediate" kinds of technology.[20] This is essential to reducing the environmental impact of technology in the overdeveloped countries and improving the quality of life in the less-developed countries at minimal environmental, social, and resource cost.

Energy
Currently there is far too much support being given to the development of nuclear fission, fast breeder reactors and far too little to research and development of other energy alternatives. In my view, nuclear fission power plants pose such an enormous ecological and social threat that not only should their further development be abandoned, but their very existence should be proscribed. There is a critical need for much more research and development of solar energy, possible fusion energy, and energy-conservation techniques.

Materials
We need to know much more about how to substitute renewable for nonrenewable resources. A great deal of research and development is needed on techniques for efficient and effective recycling.

Communications
Peter Goldmark is doing important research on the use of cable TV (actually broadband cable networks, or BCNs) to facilitate decentralization of human settlements.[21] His research underscores the magnitude of our ignorance about the "environmental impact" of communications/education technology. More research in this critical area is needed.

Modeling and Other Policy Tools
Computer models and simulations are tools for policy research which have come into widespread use only in recent years. Outside of the military and the space program, most of the models and simulations that have been employed have not proven very useful. Forrester's system-dynamics methodology offers a powerful new tool for policy-

makers which deserves further development. Other, more powerful tools for policy analysts and managers need to be developed, to enable these people to deal more effectively with the problems of highly complex systems.

EMPHASIS ON HOLISTIC RESEARCH

social, psychological, economic, and political aspects of the problem of energy use and distribution.

The emphasis in future research efforts related to the problems of growth and equilibrium must be shifted away from the technological and physical and toward a more balanced consideration of the human and total systemic factors. In particular, there is a great need for more study of the relationship of social, psychological, economic, and political factors to technical, structural, environmental, and physical factors. For example, we know little about the likely social, psychological, and political aspects of an economy based wholly on solar energy technology, except that they would almost certainly be radically different from those of our existing industrial society.

SOCIAL-SYSTEMS TRANSFORMATION RESEARCH

More research should be conducted not only on the consequences of growth and equilibrium for social systems, but on the means of bringing about the transformation from growth to equilibrium in social systems. This research task will be particularly challenging, for we possess only rudimentary models of change in small social systems (small groups and organizations) and even fewer viable models of transformation in large social systems (nations and international organizations).

Also one of the primary problems encountered in the field of planning change is that adequate attention (money, people, and time) is rarely devoted to the evaluation of change efforts (whether planned or unplanned). While evaluation of social systems is difficult, often biased, and sometimes even counterproductive, it is essential that systems transformations be evaluated in order to minimize the "reinvention of the social systems wheel." Further, only if we gain more experience at doing evaluations in real, complex systems can we hope to improve on the current evaluation procedures.

In planning for social transformation on a global scale, it becomes essential to consider the major differences and inequalities among world cultures and societies. It is now clear that, given population, environmental, and resource constraints, the poor nations of the Third World will never attain the current level of industrialization of the overdeveloped countries of the West. If future improvements in quality of life are to be attained in these countries, it will be necessary to *leapfrog* from a preindustrial to a postindustrial society. Since most conventional efforts at development in these countries have been directed at the impossible and undesirable goal of western/American industrial affluence, there is little experience or knowledge to indicate how this leapfrogging can best be accomplished.

The problem now appears to have two parts. Many Third World countries which are endowed with the vital material or energy resources needed by the overdeveloped countries may follow the OPEC model and achieve an intermediate redistribution of wealth through nationalization and the formation of cartels. However, as the oil-producing states have now discovered, planning for the postdepletion era of economies based heavily on a single, nonrenewable resource will prove an extremely thorny problem. For those less-developed countries not endowed with exportable reserves of critical resources (now coming to be called the Fourth World), the problem of creating an equilibrium society without the boost of intermediate affluence may prove even more difficult and perhaps even insurmountable without major assistance from outside.

While to some extent the transformation to an equilibrium society might seem easier for many less-developed countries than for the overdeveloped countries (many traditional cultures being fairly well attuned to the needs of equilibrium), the high vulnerability of the populations of these countries to the predations of famine, epidemics, and other disasters (for example, Bangladesh and the Sahel) makes the tolerable margin of error in planning for leapfroging comparatively smaller than that for the transformation of industrial societies. What is clear is that the problems of transformation to equilibrium are both quantitatively and qualitatively different for the over-developed and less-developed countries and that an equal or even greater research effort is required to solve these problems for the latter than for the former.

10

ECOLOGICAL

—of the views of many contemporary thinkers who have considered what the alternatives to our current industrial society might be. The characteristics of this model have been selected on the basis of my understanding of what the essential requirements for a "state of global equilibrium" implies for world society. A significant aspect of this model is that it is in many ways similar if not identical to the model of a "postindustrial society" forecast by Daniel Bell and others, who, for the most part, reject the notion of limits to growth.[1] Is there any important contradiction, then, between the positions of those who speak of a *postindustrial society* and and those who advocate an *equilibrium society?* I believe there is and that this contradiction is based on the distinction that can be made between the concepts of *transition* and *transformation,* that is, the difference between "moving across" and "changing form."[2]

While futurists of the Bell school may envision a future society which, in many ways, is similar to my model of an equilibrium society, they anticipate the emergence of such a society as the result of the smooth—and inevitable—convergence of existing trends of growth and development. Thus they view the problem of change from our current industrial-based society to the projected postindustrial society as mainly a matter of coping with an incremental and steady, though rapid and possibly "shocking," *transition* from where we are to where we are fated to be.

The view of the future of the Forrester/Meadows school is quite different. Their projections of existing trends indicate the likelihood of overshoot and collapse of the world's social/ecological systems unless major changes are made in the structure of those systems and in the policies that govern their dynamic behavior. In this view, then, a stable and sustainable society can be attained only through the conscious and radical *transformation* of the existing world system.

The difference between these two schools is, therefore, crucial, because it represents the difference between a passive and an active prospect of and approach to the future. Indeed, the contrast is so great that it can be viewed as being on the level of a Kuhnian paradigm conflict.[3]

The "beyond limits" school is concerned with two things: the design of real alternatives to growth, and the process of actually achieving a state of global equilibrium. In Chapter 9 I offered a sketchy and tentative model of an ecotopia, or equilibrium society. My major point in presenting this model is to demonstrate that a stable, sustainable world society will require the radical transformation of existing social and ecological systems. The crucial question which this model raises is: how could such a transformation be achieved within the limited time that seems to be available?

Many of my fellow stationary-state advocates who have considered this question generally seem to respond that "education" is the answer. Yet the predominant view of what the process of education is or should be is so narrowly constricted that the argument that education is the key to global equilibrium seems ingenuous and unconvincing. Many of my colleagues believe that if only the *facts* about the ecological crisis that confronts us today could be widely disseminated and understood, most men, being rational, would join us in pursuing global equilibrium. But the majority of men are not rational; in fact, nobody is predominantly rational in their behavior. For example, for some years now a vast educational campaign has been underway in the United States to acquaint people with the facts linking cigarette smoking with disease and death, even to the point of putting a warning on every pack, carton, and advertisement to remind them. There is probably not a smoker in America who does not know that smoking is likely to make him either sick or dead. Yet cigarette sales rise year after year. Obviously, education has not made smokers act *wisely*. In fact, it is hard to believe that mere education—at least, in many of the *conventional* connotations of the term—holds much promise of advancing our world toward the goal of equilibrium.

The softworld vision of ecocrisis makes it clear that the processes of control and learning are crucial to the establishment, maintenance, and evolution of global equilibrium. If we redefine *education* to fit this vision, it will follow that education does hold the key to planetary survival, welfare, and development.

THE RESPONSE OF EDUCATION TO ECOCRISIS

We should consider how the conventional system of education

count or disparage out-of-school, or nonformal, approaches, while those specializing in the latter may sympathize with Illich's deprecation of schooling and disdain any effort carried on within the educational establishment. The professionals who consider themselves communication specialists regularly eschew any identification with the field of education and sometimes look down their noses at any educator who has the temerity to venture onto their turf.

The parochialism of form is also reflected in the divisions of educational practice according to the chronological age of students, for example, early childhood, elementary, secondary, collegiate, adult. It is manifested again in the separation of vocational/technical from liberal arts institutions.

But the ultimate parochialism of form lies in the dominant notion of education generally as a narrowly defined, almost egocentric, system whose relationship with the larger social network is only dimly perceived and whose role within the total global ecosystem is either obscure or irrelevant.

The parochialism of content has perhaps an even more debilitating effect on efforts to promulgate an ecological consciousness. Today's education is structured according to disciplines, departments, and subjects instead of real-world problems. Students are taught a set of facts or theories grouped together only because they are derived from the same set of simplifying assumptions about reality or because they were developed from a common set of analytical procedures. Unfortunately, reality does not come neatly chopped up and packaged in disciplines or subjects. We would consider ludicrous a geographer who specialized only in those areas falling between two adjacent topographic lines on his maps. Topographic lines constitute the vocabulary of only a single grammar, or paradigm, of reality. To focus one's attention solely on the world that exists between eight hundred and nine hundred feet above sea level is to create an image of reality of extremely limited utility. Students with the misfortune to have taken this geographer's courses would find themselves unable to deal effectively with most of the navigational problems they would be likely to encounter out in the field. Unfortunately, the existing disciplines, departments, and subjects of conventional education have provided their students with visions of reality as useless as those of the hypothetical geographer, with the consequence that most graduates of the conventional system find themselves unable to deal effectively with the most critical problems afflicting our world.

The grossest manifestation of the parochialism of content is the overwhelming neglect by the conventional curriculum of the issues and problems that are most germane to planetary survival, welfare, and development. For the most part, conventional education has virtually ignored the existence of ecocrisis, much less contributed anything substantive toward its solution. But even in the small, problem-centered area of education, which presumes to deal with the problems of ecocrisis, there is a parochial fragmentation of content into almost countless subsets. At a general level there is the schism between "population education," on one hand, and "environmental education," on the other. Beyond this dichotomy there are more subdivisions. On the population side we have "population education," "family planning education," "sex education," and "family life education." On the environment side we have "environmental education," "ecology education," "outdoor education," "conservation education," "health education," and "urban studies."

The result of this parochialism is the phenomenon known on Madison Avenue as "clutter." Perhaps because of the financial stakes involved, the advertising executive is acutely aware of the information-eroding effect of the excessive multiplication of unrelated or contradictory messages. Outdoor advertisers have espoused the cause of reducing the number of billboards along highways, and advertising agencies have been pressing broadcasters to reduce the number of commercials broadcast per hour. But there has been far less sensitivity to this problem in the area of education, even though the real stakes, from a social and ecological point of view, are much higher.

Both in school and nonschool/mass media approaches to education, the clutter effect is severe. In schools at all levels, there is a greater tendency to add to the curriculum than to subtract from it. There is hardly a curriculum in existence that demonstrates rational design or priorities that are meaningfully related to current and long-term global needs. In the nonschool area the very proliferation and noncoordination of various agencies, organizations, and interest groups engaged in educational activities has created a cacophony of

mons which it is always to each separate organization's or group's interest to exploit, ignoring the ultimate limits on the public's time and attention and thereby reducing the effectiveness of everyone's communication.

Another aspect of the parochialism mentioned above is what might be called the "Paladin syndrome." Paladin was the name of a character played by Richard Boone in the old TV series, "Have Gun, Will Travel." Paladin was a hired gun who would serve any master who could pay for his services. The Paladin syndrome appears throughout the field of education but is particularly common in fragmented problem areas. Specialists, highly trained in a single, narrow discipline, move into an area such as "population education" because they view it as a field where the money and the action are. They tend to form cliques committed more to ideologies of technique than to the actual solution of problems. They define problems narrowly to fit the limitations of narrow disciplinary thinking. They construe solutions conservatively in order to satisfy the political constraints of the power structures from which they derive their support, prestige, and "success." Concomitantly, they tend to limit or preclude the participation of those whose training is more inter- or a-disciplinary, who conceive of problems more broadly in terms of complex systems, and whose paramount commitment is to solutions to problems rather than to parochial ideologies. These Paladins show little grass-roots or long-term commitment. When the action cools and the money dries up, they move on to other fields.

In spite of the popular call for the training of more generalists, the Paladin syndrome actually serves to limit the prospects for their useful employment and frustrates the sorely needed development of new kinds of professional training and expertise. Moreover, it is related to an important ethical issue. As Hardin states the fundamental law of ecology, "We can never do merely one thing." A corollary to this is that part of a good thing may be a bad thing. Thus, for example, while we have seen that the control of human population growth is an essential condition for human survival, welfare, and development, population control *alone*, in the absence of the other minimal conditions we have described for a viable ecotopia, could turn out to be a massive evil, serving as a diversion from or substitute for the other kinds of radical reforms required to maintain and improve the general quality of life. The Paladin syndrome is not only annoying and inefficient, it is to a large extent unethical.

In all fairness, it must be recognized that these problems of parochialism and Paladinism are not so much the fault of particular individuals as of the incentive structure of the existing educational establishment. Schools and research organizations structure the rewards of security, recognition, and advancement almost entirely on the basis of disciplinary specialization rather than interdisciplinary integration. Funding agencies, both governmental and private, predominantly direct their resources toward single—or at least simple—purpose projects which lend themselves to facile design and evaluation but not necessarily to useful results.

There is nothing wrong with population education, environmental education, health education—with problem-centered educational enterprises—per se. Nor is there anything wrong per se with specialists applying their skills to a series of different problems as demanded. What is wrong is the overall lack of a coherent framework within which these various narrow-focus activities can be synergetically coordinated and the lack of formal structure within which integrators can securely operate. These failures of the existing educational establishment are manifestations of what Donald Schon would call the current system's *dynamic conservatism,* the inherent tendency of an established social system to resist radical transformation.

Schon identifies two basic strategies of dynamic conservatism by which established systems seek to protect themselves from change: selective inattention (or what I prefer to call *willful ignorance*) and co-option.[4] The proponderant *lack* of response of the existing educational establishment to the exigencies of ecocrisis represents the first; the peripheral growth of parochial, problem-centered enterprises manned by individuals who continue to cultivate their credentials within the established structure represents the second.

THE PURPOSE AND PROCESS OF ECOLOGICAL EDUCATION

I prefer the term *ecological education*. *Ecological* because the goal is to resolve a situation of global, ecological crisis by the establishment and maintenance of global, ecological equilibrium. *Education* because, in spite of the often narrowly restricted connotations of the word, it derives from the Latin verb *educare,* which means "to lead forth," precisely what a mechanism for moving our society toward some kind of ecotopia must do. Ecological education, then, must be an effective mechanism for producing individual and social changes on a global basis to steer human society away from its current collision course with ecological catastrophe and toward a rendezvous with the stationary state. *It must be clearly understood, moreover, that when we speak of ecological education we are not merely discussing some esoteric subset of the general educational system—like adult education or sex education—but rather, of a new vision of the meaning of education in terms of both purposes and processes.*

The definition of ecological education carries with it an imperative that has generally been absent from traditional conceptions of education: to be purposeful. From now on, any activity to be subsumed under the rubric *education* should, by semantic rule, be required to be contributory to or at the very least consistent with the goals of planetary survival, welfare, and development. Anything that is inconsistent with or antithetical to these goals ought to be called something else, perhaps *mis-education* or *mystification.* Clearly much of what currently passes for education will fall under the latter category.

The two kinds of parochialism, the clutter effect, and the Paladin syndrome, characteristic of conventional educational responses to ecocrisis, hobble our efforts to develop a truly ecological pedagogy, an educational process that is ecological not only in subject matter but in its structure and dynamics as well. The content of ecological education must be as broad as the content of terrestrial life itself. It must be directed at all four dimensions of human development: intellectual, emotional, spiritual, and physical. It must also operate through all of the media that comprise the total learning environment, and must embrace the full spectrum of "behavior control" technology.

The requisites of ecological education demand that we open up our conception of the processes of education to include all phenomena that exhibit the cybernetic process we have called *learning*. The fundamental weakness of our traditional conception of education is that it is based on an erroneous model of learning. This is at least partly why Illich finds schooling to be not only irrelevant but antithetical to true learning. Pre-ecological education envisions learning as an essentially linear, open-ended process; information deemed relevant by the educational system is transmitted from the teacher to the student where it is to be processed and stored and later retrieved for the purpose of testing to see whether the information has been processed correctly and is still in storage. As the cybernetic scientist knows, this is not learning but merely information processing (the most rudimentary form of what we earlier have called *zero-learning*). This is not to say that learning does not take place within the system of schooling; but the learning that does occur is largely incidental Learning I. Those who do learn are merely monitored, graded, and classified by the system. Then at the end of the schooling process, they are channeled into various social and economic strata according to the amount of information they have processed and such learning as they have shown. The schooling system does little to cultivate learning and a great deal to stifle it by the system's overwhelming insistence on information processing as the fundamental model of system performance.

True learning is a nonlinear, closed-end, looped, or cyclical process. As we have seen, all learning above the zero level requires the essential process of trial and error. It is clear, then, where the antithesis between schooling and learning lies. Learning requires trials and errors, but schooling frustrates trials and punishes errors.

Because of the crucial role of feedback, learning is inherently cyclical. But in the conventional model, *education* is presented as a linear process. This is what we might call the *empty-head model of education:* knowledge flows one way—from an informed teacher or communicator into the empty heads of an ignorant class or audience. Of course, the experienced teacher or communicator usually develops at least partial recognition of the realities of give and take, but the structure of the educational system itself is predominantly based on the one-way, empty-head model. It may be possible to "talk back"

the cycle, and the result may not necessarily be benevolent. Like agriculture, education may lead to erosion, simplification, instability, and ultimate collapse, and the cause is generally the same: failure to recognize all (or even any) of the loops of the feedback structure of a complex system.

If the schooling system has been hostile or just indifferent to the "proto" level of learning at the levels of deutero-learning and beyond, the traditional system of education has been almost a complete failure. *Schooling* evaluates students according to their capacity for learning with the minimal number of trials and errors. It is not surprising, then, that IQ, which measures this capacity, is a strong predictor of academic success. But there is nothing sacrosanct or even especially valuable about this particular style of learning, except that it interferes minimally with the information-processing activity with which the schooling system fills most of its time, and that it also interferes minimally with the socioeconomic stratification process which the system serves so well. In any case, whether out of malice or indifference or sheer blindness, the schooling system does little or nothing to cultivate Learning II, the learning of the skills of learning. Yet it is not only at the level of Learning II but at that of Learning III and even to some extent of Learning IV, that the major work of ecological education needs to be done.

•

Ecological education is concerned with change, the change from our current unstable state to a sustainable state, change from lower to higher levels of ecological welfare, the change implied by negentropic development. But the kind of change, or innovation, with which ecological education is concerned is of such a fundamental nature that it entails a process of "diffusion of innovations" that is badly represented by the traditional center-to-periphery model, typified by the work of someone like Everett Rogers.[5]

As Donald Schon observes, innovations introduced into dynamically conservative social systems can be ranked according to the magnitude and depth of the disruption their acceptance is likely to cause. *Marginal* innovations are likely to undergo the kind of diffusion process described by Rogers; a process that entails communicating information from someone who knows about the invention to someone who does not. But for *basic* innovations, linked to system-wide changes, the diffusion process is more radical. It becomes a "battle for broad and complex transformation." The classical center-to-periphery model does not apply to such a process.[6]

Schon points out that in the case of the more "radical" kind of diffusion: (1) the innovation does not merely precede the diffusion, but to a large extent the two evolve together; (2) rather than merely fanning out from a single source, the innovation as a whole tends to arise from multiple sources of related and reinforcing innovations; and (3) the process consists less in the centrally managed dissemination of information than in the "reorientation" of existing sociotechnical systems.[7]

Schon says that a social system can be defined in terms of its structure, theory, and technology.[8] Marginal innovations are those which are more or less consistent with the prevailing structure, theory, and technology of the social system. Basic innovations entail major changes in either the structure, theory, or technology (or some combination of these) of the existing system, and because of the intimate connectedness of these three dimensions, imply or threaten to effect radical transformation of the system as a whole. Examples of marginal innovations in American society are: replacement of single-stage oil filters by two-stage ones; achievement of a number-one Nielsen rating by a new TV series; dropping of a "whites-only" policy by the Elks; replacing "junior high schools" with "intermediate schools." Examples of basic innovations are: replacement of the internal combustion engine in automobiles with a steam or electric engine; cable TV achieving dominance over broadcast TV; court-ordered bussing to integrate public schools across municipal or county boundaries; establishment of an "educational voucher" system.

Conventional education is generally not concerned with the kinds of radical transformation implied by the promulgation of basic innovations. On the contrary, conventional education not only practices its own self-serving dynamic conservatism but functions as a primary instrument of the dynamic conservatism of the society it is a part of. To the extent that the conventional system is innovative, the Rogers-type model may be applicable to its processes. But ecolog-

adoption of family-planning practices, including contraception and sterilization, with the intent of lowering fertility rates and thus the population growth rate. The control of fertility and the reduction of family size have been treated as marginal innovations; the efforts to achieve these objectives have followed a center-periphery model. The Indian government has made the achievement of these objectives a matter of policy and has sought to effect them through actions and resources directed outward through secondary control centers into local communities. Clinics offering contraceptives and sterilization have been established throughout the country. Information, exhortation, and tangible rewards have been used to promote adoption of fertility control. While these efforts have thus far been inadequate and of poor quality in many instances, the fact remains that what is still a fairly massive effort has produced virtually negligible results.

By contrast, in the United States fertility rates in the last several years have dropped to an all-time low without the adoption of a central policy or centrally managed process for diffusion of this innovation. Fertility reduction in the U.S. represents a radical transformation of the social system as a whole and has resulted from a nexus of technological, theoretical, and structural innovative trends, including: development in the technology of contraception, abortion, and sterilization; liberalization of restrictive laws; increase in the "opportunity cost" of children, including the employment of women, the costs of child-rearing, housing, and schooling; social, legal, and technological (for example, increasing automation of household technology) "liberation" of women; increase in the divorce rate; changes in sexual mores; and growing concern with problems associated with population growth.

If the differences between the United States and India seem too great to make the above comparison reasonable, one can turn to the case of the People's Republic of China, a country whose size and general situation are highly analogous to those of India, where fertility control has been achieved with much greater success by being tied to a comprehensive program for social transformation.

The point is that innovation such as control of human fertility, replacement of the automobile with mass transit, conserving and recycling nonrenewable resources, and redistributing wealth (the kinds of changes of crucial concern to ecological education) are basic, and not marginal, to existing social and ecological systems. Attempts to bring about such changes through center-periphery processes of diffusion of innovations are destined to be either unproductive or counterproductive. What kind of model, then, will work for the more radical kind of diffusion process that ecological education requires?

The answer is what Schon calls the "learning system." As he notes, in more radical responses to the failure of the center-periphery model, central no longer promotes a standard message but rather develops general policy themes on which the periphery creates its own variations. Central's role becomes facilitative rather than dictatorial. It serves to connect peripheral systems and helps them to transform themselves. "It goes 'meta' with respect to these discovered systems, prodding them to develop evaluative processes conducive to learning and linking them in learning networks."[9]

There are two important points to be noted about Schon's "learning system." First, the learning system as illustrated, for example, by the "movement," may sometimes evolve and endure without the action of any "central facilitator." Thus the learning-system model of ecological education permits us to consider the reduction of fertility in the United States described above as an example of effective ecological education even though no single central policy, plan, or administration was involved in its performance. This statement may at first seem facetious, but it is not. A return to the analogy of education to agriculture may again be appropriate. In agriculture some crops require intensive cultivation, while others essentially grow "wild" and merely wait to be harvested. From the educator's point of view, in those instances where effective learning systems are already operating in a manner commensurate with the purposes of ecological education, no further intervention may be required nor, indeed, warranted.

Second, the statement that the learning system is *meta* to peripheral or component systems reveals the essence of Schon's learning-system model. When Schon speaks of *learning systems,* he is referring not to Learning I but to Learning II. He says that the task which our current unstable state "makes imperative, for the person, for our institutions, for our society as a whole, is to *learn about learning.*"[10] The learning-system model is therefore a Learning II

nism of these higher levels, however, will operate essentially the same way as Schon's learning system, so the fundamental model remains the same.

What, then, is the mechanism by which the learning system carries out its role as a cultivator of learning? The answer is suggested by two major characteristics which Schon identifies as being typical of currently emerging learning systems (business systems, new kinds of governmental operations, dominant social movements): "a shift upward in the level of generality at which organizations define themselves, and a shift away from center-periphery to network modes of growth and diffusion."[11] Since the first represents, to a large extent, the internalization of the network mode within organizational structures, it is really the concept of the *network* with which the fundamental mechanism of the learning system is identified.

The network concept stresses the metaphor of the net, which in turn emphasizes a unique interconnectedness, where a set of elements or nodes are all joined to each other through one another rather than through a center.[12] So ecological education must go beyond the center-periphery pyramid or wheel structure of conventional educational systems. It must rely on the decentralized but integrated network as the basic mechanism for carrying out its function.

The contrast between the classical center-periphery model of diffusion of innovations and the more "radical" network model is illustrated in Table 2.[13] The dichotomy drawn in this table applies to the distinction between conventional education and ecological education systems.

TABLE 2. MODELS OF INNOVATION

Center-Periphery	*Network*
A product or technique forms the basic unit of innovation.	A functional system forms the basic unit of innovation.
Diffusion is dissemination from center to periphery.	Diffusion is transformation of systems.
Communication consists of reproduction of a relatively stable, standard message.	Communication consists of an evolving family of messages.
Scope of the system is limited by central resources/energy, and by "radial" delivery capacity.	Scope of the system is limited only by networking technology.
Feedback links only primary center to peripheral centers.	Feedback operates universally, linking all nodes of network.

In terms of purposes and processes, then, ecological education stands conventional education on its head. The conventional education envisages itself as a narrowly defined subsystem within the larger social system, and in many ways considers itself neither responsible to nor dependent on the "external" system. Its goals are largely self-defined and self-serving. To the extent that it does presume to serve the external world, the orientation of conventional education is toward the past, and its basic commitment is to the status quo. On the other hand, the system of ecological education is as comprehensive as the global Mind. It is the complete cybernetic network of the global ecosystem. Therefore it considers itself essentially one with the entire biosphere—mutually dependent, mutually responsible. Its purposes derive directly from the teleonomic characteristics of the global ecosystem. The orientation of ecological education is toward the future; its commitment is to learning of high order and hence evolution in the direction of negative entropy.

11

TRANSFORMATION

In discussing the radical transformation of existing society to some kind of equilibrium society, it makes sense to begin at the level of the institutions that constitute and manage society. By the term *institution* I mean the same thing Seymour Sarason refers to as a "setting"; that is, "Any situation in which a group of people come together for a purpose."[1] Thus an *institution* may be as small as a marriage or friendship between two people or as large as a nation-state or world government.

My argument is that the radical transformation of society requires an institutional infrastructure that is capable of facilitating and managing transformation and, subsequently, of maintaining the desirable aspects of such a transformation. This implies two things: first, changes within most conventional institutions, and second, creation of some new kinds of institutions. A list of conventional types of institutions is presented in Table 3. The synoptic model of an equilibrium society presented in Chapter 9 implies important changes in all of these institutions. But major societal transformation also requires the creation of some new institutions, of a kind dedicated to the facilitation of transformation itself. These new institutions will be of basically two types: *inter-institutions* and *meta-institutions*. Inter-institutions are what Kenneth Boulding has called "intersects."[2] They are institutions which fill the "cracks" between conventional types of institutions. Historic examples offered by Boulding are the Tennessee Valley Authority and the Port Authority of New York and New Jersey. Meta-institutions, on the other hand, span the boundaries between conventional institutions. To some extent they are of a

TABLE 3. CONVENTIONAL INSTITUTIONS

I. GOVERNMENT

A. Executive
B. Legislative
C. Judicial
D. Communications/Education
E. Planning and Policy Analysis
F. Tribune/Ombudsman

G. Military and Security
H. Prosecution and Defense
I. Emergency
J. Regulatory
K. Corrections
L. Political

II. RESEARCH

A. Basic
B. Applied

III. ECONOMIC

A. Productive
B. Service
C. Financial
D. Agricultural

E. Extractive
F. Storage (conservation)
G. Labor
H. Distributive

IV. CULTURAL

A. Religious
B. Aesthetic
C. Recreational

D. Philosophical/Intellectual
E. Historical

V. HEALTH

A. Preventive
B. Maintenance

C. Curative
D. Ameliorative

higher order of logical type than conventional institutions, in the sense that they are institutions-of-institutions. My model of the meta-institution is based largely on Schon's concept of the *network*. In general, it seems clear that the transformation institutions that will be required to change the world to some kind of equilibrium society will have to have many or all of the qualities of Schon's learning system.

Will the kinds of institutions required for a radical transformation of existing society be the same kinds of institutions required for the maintenance of an equilibrium society? Certainly it seems necessary to continue to have transformation institutions in a viable equilibrium society, in order to facilitate the adaptive change, hence creative evolution, of such a society. It may also be that, once an equilibrium state is attained, the infrastructure of transformation

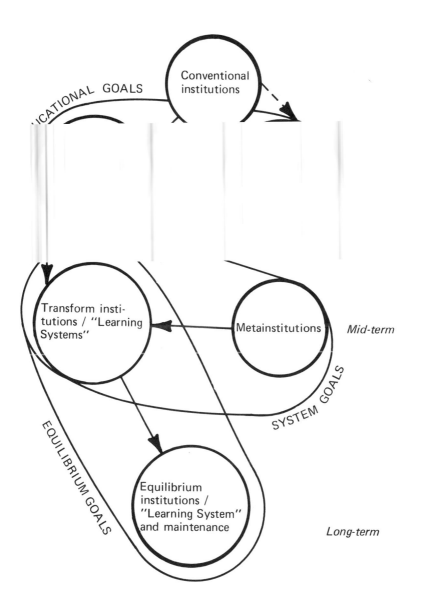

FIGURE 5. TRANSFORM SEQUENCE

211

institutions will have to be supplemented with an additional set of institutions designed to maintain the conditions of equilibrium. Just what these maintenance institutions will look like is as yet unclear. It is likely that they can be described only in relation to a fairly detailed model of a specific equilibrium society. What is clear is that before a viable equilibrium society can be established, it will be necessary to establish a creative transformation society comprised of institutions which are themselves transformational in nature.

In other words, the change from our current unstable state to a future stable and sustainable state cannot be made in a single great leap, but rather must be comprised of a number of intermediate steps. An initial schema for the sequence of these steps is offered in Figure 5. The long-term goal is to create an equilibrium society, which means at least to create a set of institutions something like Schon's learning system, and perhaps also a supplementary set of maintenance institutions. The midterm goal is to create a transformational system, which means creating an infrastructure of transformation institutions. Because these institutions are an essential feature not only of the transformational period but of the resulting state of equilibrium, their creation must be a major goal. To facilitate the creation and further transformation of the intermediate, transformational society, meta-institutions of various kinds will be needed. But who will design, create, manage, and change these new institutions? Clearly a new educational system will be needed in the short term to generate the know-how and competent manpower necessary for these tasks. The pattern of changing existing institutions and creating new kinds of institutions that is the intermediate global goal must be anticipated and realized in the educational world in the short term.

INSTITUTIONAL PARADIGMS: OLD VERSUS NEW

The transformational society and subsequent equilibrium society will require not merely cosmetic changes in existing types of institutions but a complete shift in the dominant institutional paradigm. An institutional paradigm can be discussed in terms of several constituent parameters, or characteristics, some of which are:

1. goals
2. technology/technique
3. life-support systems (flow)
4. physical structures (stock)

5. personnel
6. birth, growth, and death patterns

Table 4 provides an outline, comparing point by point the old institutional paradigm (hardworld) of our current society and the new institutional paradigm (softworld) which I believe will have to dominate the transformational and equilibrium societies. It should

There are few people today who do not recognize that the world is in a critical state, who are unaware of the crisis generated by exploding population, vanishing resources, environmental decay, and escalating violence. Recognition of the need for major changes in the governance of society is fairly widespread. Yet the individual who recognizes the need for change may respond in different ways to this need, not all of which are productive. Indeed, most of the attempts to solve the problems of conventional institutions and so-cial/ecological systems tend to be either unproductive or counter-productive. Therefore, the mere fact that people have in many cases recognized and responded to the need for change carries no guarantee that such responses will be constructive.

I have come up with four models of what seem to be the major responses of individuals, particularly those in positions of leadership, to the need for change. Model 1 is that of the monastic, brahmin, or what I simply call the "guru." The guru retreats from the world to lead a socially, spiritually, and/or ecologically idealized existence. Recognizing the corruption of the world, he pursues self-perfection. The only influence he cares to have on the world is the influence that will result from leading an exemplary existence. Model 2 is the jet-set reformer, the self-styled leader. He is exemplified by Orson Welles' *Citizen Kane*. The political and intellectual elite who fly around the world helping to solve the problems which their position, affluence or status enables them to escape or avoid, generally fall within this model.

Model 3 is the political revolutionary, typified and symbolized by

TABLE 4. INSTITUTIONAL TRANSFORMATION

OLD (Hardworld)	NEW (Softworld)
GOALS	
Growth/production	Dynamic equilibrium
Maximize production at minimal financial cost	Efficiency in use of human, energy, and material resources
React to stress, problems	Anticipate stress, problems
Avoid conflict	Embrace conflict
Benefit primary constituency: management/stockholder/owner/membership/voter bloc	Benefit entire social/ecological system
Institutional survival	Effective realization of goals
Defend against interference from environment (implies: secrecy; "public relations"; lobbying/manipulation; "dynamic conservatism"—i.e., willful ignorance and co-option)	Respond to needs/demands of environment (implies: openness; honesty; advocacy/ombudsmanship; systemwide learning)
TECHNOLOGY/TECHNIQUE	
Technological fatalism	Technological skepticism
Error-avoiding	Error-embracing[3]
Disjointed incrementalism	Synoptic planning[4]
Bureaucracy	Cybernetics
Hierarchy: central control	Decentralization: peripheral control
Center-periphery model	Network model
Routine functioning	Nonroutine functioning
Righthanded thinking	Left- and righthanded thinking
Uniformity by design	Diversity by design
Assumption of static behavior, linear cause and effect	Assumption of dynamic behavior, nonlinear cause and effect
Evaluation of outcomes/products ("results") is "objective," from a single perspective	Evaluation also of processes/relationships is qualitative, from multiple perspectives

214

Assumption of unlimited resources	Recognition of resource constraints
Attempted hegemony over flow sources	Noncontrol or shared control of flow sources
Dependence on constancy/growth of flow	Adaptability to changes of flow
Institution based on stock (tangible assets)	Institution based more on flow (intangible assets)
equals better)	
Form tailored to production	Form harmonious with personal growth, quality of life
Form indifferent to, obtrusive upon environment	Form responsive to, harmonious with environment
Edifice defines institutional identity	Processes and relationships joining its members defines institutional identity

PERSONNEL

"Organization man": loyalty to organization	"Boundary spanner": multiple constituencies, loyalties[5]
Status credentials	Functional credentials
Designated leadership based on status	Shifting leadership based on function
Organizational unit equals fixed, production group	Organizational unit equals "roving" task force
Operating unit equals individual employee	Operating unit equals functional skill community
Low tolerance of ambiguity/conflict	High tolerance of ambiguity/conflict
Conformity to organizational values	Concern for personal values
Emotion submerged	Emotion surfaced
Learning marginal	Learning basic

215

| Hierarchical governance; non-participation; feudalism | Nonhierarchical governance; participation; commonwealth |

BIRTH/GROWTH/DEATH

Linear concept of time: birth, death as initial and final	Cyclical concept of time: birth, death as arbitrary points of reference
Fate of organization determines fate of individual	Individual's fate independent of that of organization
Birth, death "accidental"	Birth, death controlled, planned for
Nonzero-sum game with other organizations (conflict resolution through growth)	Zero-sum game with other organizations (one's death equals another's birth)

the late Ché Guevara. To the revolutionary, positive transformation can be achieved only through the replacement of the established power structure by a new revolutionary power structure. Power cannot be won through reform; it must be seized, usually by violence.

Model 4 is the transformer, the person who is skilled at facilitating radical transformation in dynamically conservative systems. Ralph Nader and John Gardner are notable examples.

These four models can be further analyzed in terms of the various possible combinations of power and authority (see Figure 6).[6] The guru, Model 1, eschews both power and authority and seeks no greater influence on the course of change in the world than the vicarious influence of exemplary living. On the other hand, Model 2, the Citizen Kane type, tries to command both power and authority, an impossible undertaking which ultimately leads to the erosion and loss of both. Authority is based on integrity, credibility, and competency, but power corrupts. What it chiefly corrupts is integrity, credibility, and competency. Model 3, the revolutionary, lacks authority but tries to seize power. In fact, one might define *revolution* as the unauthorized taking of power. Of course, the revolutionary may try to put on the illusory trappings of authority provided by ideology before and during the revolution, in order to recruit public support. But the illusion of authority is often quickly eroded once a revolutionary seizes power and is confronted with the problems of running a society. Model 4, the transformer, is generally wary of power. He tries to exert a significant influence over the course of change and the governance of society through the strength of his authority. This is misunderstood by people who promote a Nader or a Gardner for President.

	POWER	NO POWER
AUTHORITY	Model 2 CITIZEN KANE	Model 4 TRANSFORMER

The transformer is the model of response to the need for fundamental change which I find the most promising and attractive. Its superiority to the guru and Citizen Kane models is fairly clear. Both roles are essentially masturbatory in nature; neither espouses (nor can achieve) radical transformation. The inferiority of the revolutionary to the transformer is less obvious. Both espouse radical transformation, but the deficiency of the revolutionary lies in the fact that he does not know how to practice it. The lesson of historical evidence is that most political revolutions fail to achieve fundamental transformation of the societies in which they occur. In the words of the French philosopher, "the more things change, the more they remain the same."

The only political revolution in history of which this seems not to be true is the American, yet that is because the American Revolution was not a revolution *for* change but a rebellion against a monarch who was threatening to subvert the political and economic status quo of the American colonies. The Revolution was fought not to create liberty but to preserve it. The American Revolution required no radical transformation of American society, and it apparently succeeded. The French Revolution, which required a radical transformation of its society to achieve the same political and economic goals, failed. Unlike the Communist Manifesto, the American Declaration of Independence is an *apology,* not a mandate, for revolution.

The common failure of the revolutionary can be attributed to his lack of understanding of the causes and consequences of basic change, which results in his inability to create and manage it effectively. This is illustrated by Seymour Sarason in his *The Creation of Settings*. Sarason refers to an "amazingly revealing" speech made by Fidel Castro in 1970 in which the Cuban leader admits that his revolution has failed.[7] "What Castro is telling us . . . is that in the endeavor to create a new setting he wrongly assumed that agreement on basic values and goals, possessing the strongest motivation to succeed, and finally achieving power were the necessary and sufficient conditions for achieving stated objectives."[8] Castro concedes that there exists neither adequate *material* nor, perhaps more important, *human* resources in Cuba to meet the goals established for the revolution by its leaders. Thus the powerful motivation to succeed and overcome obstacles leads to the "burn out" of the revolutionaries. The fault of this failure, Castro admits, lies with him and the other leaders of the revolution who "could and should have known this from the beginning."[9]

Sarason further notes that in his late, private writings, Lenin sensed the same danger of failure of the Russian revolution and for the same reasons Castro mentioned.[10] Even the Chinese cultural revolution failed to completely achieve the radical social transformation it espoused. In their book, *Change*, Watzlawick, Weakland, and Fisch observe: "One of the changes effected by the Red Guards during the early stages of the Chinese Cultural Revolution was the destruction of all public signs (of streets, shops, buildings, etc.) which contained any reference to the reactionary, 'bourgeois' past, and their replacement by revolutionary names." A more radical break with the past could hardly be imagined. Yet, as Watzlawick and his colleagues point out, "in the wider context of Chinese culture, this break is fully in keeping with that basic rule which Confucius called the *rectification of names*. . . ." In other words, the Red Guards not only failed to change a central feature of traditional Chinese culture, they "actually re-emphasized it."[11]

In spite of zealous sincerity and dogged determination, most revolutionaries fail to bring about radical transformations. They fail because almost invariably they view the problem of societal change from a hardworld perspective. The common revolutionary vision is narrow-minded, dogmatic, shortsighted, violent, and, above all, simplistic. In Castro's words, "We could best be classified as ignorant. . . . Most of the time we make the mistake of minimizing the difficulties, of minimizing the complexity of the problems."[12]

The distinction between the revolutionary and the transformer can be illustrated by an ancient fable of Aesop. According to the tale, the sun and the north wind were having an argument over who was the more powerful of the two. Tiring of the debate, the sun spied a traveler walking down a road and challenged the north wind to a contest. "Whichever of us can remove the traveler's cloak shall be the stronger of the two," said the sun. The north wind, accepting the challenge, attempted to blow the traveler's cloak off. To his consternation, the north wind found that the harder he blew, the more

powerful instrument of change than direct force.

TRANSFORMER ROLES

The transformer must be capable of carrying out a variety of different new kinds of roles which are implied by the new institutional paradigm described above. A number of these roles are described briefly in Table 5.[13] There are probably other, unique roles that are implied by the new institutional paradigm, but this list includes several that I consider significant.

Except for the "brakeman," and the last four, the roles listed in this table are inter- or meta-institutional. These roles all entail spanning the boundaries dividing institutions and are crucial to the network, or learning-system, model of transformation. The "brakeman" is intra-institutional. The last four roles mentioned in the table are critical transformer roles which do not fall within the institutional paradigm and which are in a significant sense, "noninstitutional." I have followed Sarason in defining *institutions* as situations in which people come together for a purpose. One characteristic of the last four roles in the table is that they do not necessarily require their practitioners to join with others. A second characteristic, which is perhaps more significant, is that they are roles which in an institutional sense are without purpose, or at least whose purpose is on a different level than that of an institution.

The observer, the futurist, and the historian have as their

TABLE 5. TRANSFORMER ROLES

Broker: acts as matchmaker, referral agent, developer of personal networks, connector for the purpose of transactions (e.g., buyer/seller).

Facilitator: works to integrate people/groups with common interests; fosters the development of networks, acting under varying circumstances as consultant, expediter, guide, trainer, change agent, convener, and conflict manager.

Systems expediter: serves to expedite transactions and resolve conflicts between individual and system, acting as ombudsman, middleman, advocate, and red-tape cutter.

Network manager: operates formal/official networks, insuring the flow of resources and information; acts as gatekeeper, convener, energizer, maintainer, expediter.

"Underground" manager: operates informal/underground networks; functions like the network manager but additionally may have to maintain anonymity, a low profile.

Maneuverer: operates on a project basis, creating ad hoc networks to get the job done; often has to act as persuader and manipulator.

Network builder: acts as catalyst for the creation of formal or informal networks, connecting the nodes and building the infrastructure.

Gadfly: the provocateur who surfaces and focuses attention on hypocritical, irresponsible, or even illegal behavior/conditions.

Whistle-blower: provides feedback from institution to environment which circumvents official channels of authority/censorship (e.g., Daniel Ellsberg).

Brakeman: works to maintain stability under conditions of change, acting as moderator or "flywheel."

Conflict manager: works against social/institutional breakdown, acting as peacemaker, arbiter, negotiator.

Evaluator: develops and applies instruments of evaluation or assessment, acting as tester or judge; effectiveness depends on his independence and on getting evaluative information to feed back to points of action.

Observer: provides feedback on what is happening from a disinterested perspective, acting as news analyst, diagnostician, short-term historian; like evaluator, his effectiveness depends on his independence.

Futurist: generates alternative futures and projects them into the present; assesses the possibilities of, probabilities of, conditional rela-

most general purpose the generation of metaphor—the creation of ideas. These roles have ancient roots. The role of the observer has often been played by the clown (for example, Will Rogers). The role of the futurist is as old as the shaman, the astrologer, and the prophet. The role of the historian has often been performed by the poet. Without these rich sources of metaphors, ideas, and insights to draw on, all other transformation roles would quickly become impotent.

The transitions assistant is slightly different. His is a kind of interface role between the institutional and the noninstitutional. People or institutions in transition, to some extent at least, have lost their sense of reality, value, and competency. An important part of the transition assistant's role is to help restore this sense to those who have become disoriented, by making available to them the resources of the metaphor-generators.

The significant fact about the roles in Table 6 is that, by and large, there is currently no formal training provided for performance in these roles. There has been little identification of the skills required to perform these roles effectively; in fact, there is probably little formal recognition that many of these roles even exist within the conventional institutional paradigm.

It may be that the best transformers are born and not made. But we need to make many more competent transformers than currently seem to exist. If anything like a democratic society is to endure, if the inevitable transformation from a state of ecological crisis to a state of global equilibrium is to take place peacefully and constructively, we must try to create the kind of education that can allow every citizen to become a competent transformer. Learning is the key to a positive transformation; an adequate ecological education is therefore a prerequisite to a hopeful future.

12

AN ADEQUATE

In this chapter I suggest some key characteristics which I believe an adequate ecological education should have. The model suggested here is by no means comprehensive or final. Not everything mentioned here may be necessary; nor, on the other hand, may it all be sufficient. My intention is merely to sketch the broad outlines of the beginning of ecological education.

CURRICULUM CHARACTERISTICS

A number of education programs now in existence attempt to do part of what I believe is needed for an adequate ecological education —for example, programs in environmental studies, urban studies, studies of the future, systems science, and system dynamics. But I know of no programs that do all that is probably necessary. An adequate ecological education should be:

1. *Multilevel.* It must function at all three major levels of learning—Learning I, Learning II, and Learning III.
2. *Interdisciplinary.* It must span the boundaries between conventional disciplinary and professional fields. Sometimes this is called transdisciplinary, a-disciplinary, or nondisciplinary. I distinguish this from *multidisciplinary* which often refers to a cafeteria approach which does not truly remove disciplinary barriers.[1]
3. *Problem-centered.* It must focus on and be responsive to the critical problems of the real world. It must consciously attack the

threats to planetary survival, the constraints on human and ecological welfare, and the barriers to further planetary evolution and development.

4. *Future-oriented.* Rather than concentrating on the past and serving the status quo, it must be forward-looking and concerned with the imagination, design, and realization of alternative, sustainable futures.

5. *Global.* This means it must not be parochial, chauvinistic, or provincial in its perspective. Rather, its perspective must be *at least* planetary and probably also interplanetary and cosmic.

6. *Humanistic.* It must be concerned with the maximum realization, exploration, and expansion of what is commonly known as "human potential." This includes not merely the development of cognitive and affective skills but also the development of the kind of physical competency associated with the control of physiological states through meditation, yoga, biofeedback, and conditioning, as well as the kind of spiritual competency associated with psychic phenomena, altered states of consciousness, and mystical and religious experience.[2]

I believe these six characteristics are essential to an adequate educational response to our current ecological crisis. By this standard, virtually no educational program in existence today can be considered adequate to the times in which we live.

THE STUDENTS

Who are the students of ecological education? Ultimately everyone. In fact, to be even more general: all of the human and systemic minds which together constitute the global Mind. But ecological education becoming the standard paradigm of world education is a long-term goal. In the short term the objective is to create increasing numbers of effective transformers, individuals competent to lead the global transformation from ecocrisis to equilibrium. This means that for the near future, some groups of potential students of ecological education will be more important than others.

Among those who have recognized the challenge posed by ecocrisis, there is already widespread agreement that education holds the key to the transformation to the state of equilibrium. Much of the response so far, though, has been directed toward innovations in elementary and secondary schools. While such efforts are welcome, the priority effort in ecological education in the near term must be made in *postsecondary education*.[3] The overriding reason for this is the belief that we may have only one generation or less in which to make substantial progress toward establishing global equilibrium. If this is so, it is essential to have an immediate impact on the premises, values, consciousness, and skills of those who are either already in or about to enter positions of leadership in the institutions that govern

to decline after 1980, but much depends on whether and to what extent the proportion of high school graduates either continuing on to higher education or "dropping back in" will grow. Many futurists today feel that enrollments in postsecondary education of all kinds will grow for another 30 years or more, although full-time enrollment in four-year colleges and universities will probably decline.

This means that an investment primarily in innovation in elementary and secondary education is certain to have diminishing returns, not only in terms of absolute numbers educated but perhaps even more importantly in terms of "generational dominance." The baby-boom generation is going to have a lot more power in this society for at least the next 30 years than is the baby-bust generation, just as they exercised a dominant influence in recent history, compared to the Depression generation. If we want to get this society out of the jaws of crisis, we had better get the baby-boom generation attuned to the needs of the equilibrium state, and intensive efforts in postsecondary education are going to be essential.

Fortunately, the time is ripe for significant innovation in higher education. Some think that higher education is entrenched and resistant to change. Departments are the seats of power; this balkan structure makes change embattled and slow. Undoubtedly this has been true in the past and still persists to a considerable extent; yet I think we have now entered a unique epoch when the prospects for major innovation in higher education are promising if the opportunity which now exists is properly exploited. Institutions of higher education in the U.S. today are in a state of enormous stress if not crisis, and the pressure for change is great. Financial problems are the chief, but not the only, source of this pressure. Colleges find themselves competing for students who are demanding to get more for the time and money they invest. This creates the pressure for new, more attractive, and more relevant programs. The department is no longer the bastion of security for faculty it used to be. The Ph.D. glut is creating strong pressures to limit or do away with the tenure system. New influxes of research money are likely to be far more problem-centered than before, demanding greater capabilities for interdisciplinary work. Further, postsecondary education is rapidly expanding beyond the bounds of collegiate education. All of this seems to make both the need and the possibility for rapid and exciting innovation in higher education prodigious.

Aside from my contention that the baby-bust generation is likely to be perennially impotent in comparison with the older, more populous baby-boom generation, the time factor also mitigates against the prospects for radical or even significant change through elementary and secondary education. There are two time factors to consider: the *lag* time and the *relaxation* time. The lag time is the time that elapses between input and resulting output. In this case, it is the time that will pass between the implementation of curriculum innovations and the potential impact of those innovations on the social, economic, political, and other institutions that govern our society. The relaxation time is merely the time it takes for most of the effects of the curriculum to wear off. An innovative input into high schools will have a lag time for output in terms of effective impact on governing institutions of from 10 to 30 years or more. The relaxation time for most school subjects is as high as 90 percent in one year.[4]

In general, then, the lag times for innovations introduced through elementary and secondary school are much greater than their relaxation times. We can call this the *civics syndrome.* Long ago, people who were disturbed by demagoguery and corruption responded by introducing civics courses into junior high schools. Probably Egil Krogh, Jeb Stuart Magruder, John Ehrlichman, H.R. Haldeman, and even Richard Nixon took civics courses in junior high school. The solubrious impact of this curriculum innovation has not been overwhelming. The key lessons seem to be forgotten long before the time comes when they are most needed. It is better to teach those things that need to be learned for positive social transformation to those who are about to or have already entered the power structure (including the general adult citizenry) that governs society.

Granting that I would like the paradigm of ecological education to permeate all forms of education at every level, transforming the goals and processes of education in a fundamental way should be easier to do from the top down than from the bottom up. Changes in the performance criteria of graduate and professional education are more likely to precipitate matching changes in undergraduate education than the other way around. In hierarchical systems, control is exercised from the top down. What graduate and professional

fading. Even ROTC is coming back. Flamboyant idealism seems to be yielding to a resurgent pragmatism.

The same kind of dominance applies to the subordinate steps of the educational hierarchy. This top-down direction of innovation also applies to the development of instructional materials. It makes more sense to develop the most sophisticated and advanced materials—for example, for something like system dynamics—first, then simplify and consolidate these for lower levels and more general audiences, rather than the other way around. This has certainly been the general trend in science education.

Beyond these reasons for concentrating the early development of ecological education at the postsecondary level, I have a nagging feeling that elementary and secondary schooling is a mechanism of co-option, an instrument of the dynamic conservatism of the reigning social system. I am not talking here about the role of the schools in inculcating the status quo upon the young. On the contrary, I am talking about the schools as a target of liberal zeal.

Throughout my career in elementary and secondary school, adults were always referring to us kids as the "leaders of the future." The implication was that school was the crucible in which the saviors of the world would be formed, that through schooling, the current adult population was attempting to prepare us kids to solve, at some time *in the future,* the problems they had failed to solve. I emphasize *in the future* because that seems to be the linchpin of the salvation-through-schooling mystique to which I have only recently begun to be sensitive.

In the five years that I have been working on the ecological theory of education contained in this book, I have had contact and worked with many educators and others in the areas of environmental education, population education, and futures studies—areas of education attempting to respond to some of the critical problems of ecocrisis. The overwhelming majority of these people have been focusing their efforts on the education of children. I used to think that this was just a coincidental manifestation of the common tendency of people in our society to equate education with schooling and children. It is only recently that I have begun to suspect that the infatuation of liberal reformers with the education of children is more insidious.

What I have come to feel is that the salvation-through-schooling mystique represents a conservative mechanism for deflecting and disarming the forces of radical transformation. This mystique is, in effect, a Faustian bargain between the mechanisms of dynamic conservatism in our society and many of the proponents (especially middle-class) of change. The deal is virtually never articulated, but in words it would go something like this: We, the conservative forces of society, will not allow you, the liberal forces, to introduce any basic innovation into the existing social system. Any attempt on your part to introduce basic change directly will be met by forceful, perhaps even violent, opposition. In order to assuage your frustration, though, we will permit you to work for basic change *at some time in the future* through the education of children.

Why are the forces of dynamic conservatism willing to make such a deal? Simply because, from their viewpoint, it is to their advantage. There are two reasons. First, as mentioned in Chapter 8, the existing growth-based economic order, both capitalist and communist ("state capitalist"), *discounts* the future at such a high rate that no event more than five years in the future has any significant current value. From the conservative viewpoint, the future economic welfare of our children and grandchildren is worthless *in the present,* so why should their education be of any importance? Second, the conservative forces know what the civics syndrome demonstrates, that schooling is almost completely impotent in creating basic changes in the social order. The conservative mechanisms recognize that schooling's leaders of the future are mythical. The leaders of the future, like those of the present, are not created by schools but by the reward-punishment-selection structures of existing social, political, and economic institutions which select for positions of leadership those with the maximum commitment and ability to preserve the status quo, or failing that, those with minimal commitment and ability to create basic change. The schools often collaborate in this filtering process, but they have little or no power to oppose it.

Why do many proponents of basic change accept this deal? I suppose that they do so generally because of the sheer fatigue of the inevitably uphill struggle for fundamental change and, in some cases, fear of the sanctions which the mechanisms of dynamic conservatism

The argument that adults are incapable of learning and change is contradicted by a large and growing body of educational and psychological research and experience. We are learning that adolescence is a process that extends throughout adult life and that adults go through many crises and changes in the course of their lives which are as significant as those of the childhood and teenage years. The success of many existing forms of psychotherapy demonstrates that adults are capable of dramatic learning and fundamental change. Granting that the product of Learning II is resistant to change, it is not immutable. The increasing number and popularity of both traditional (Zen, Yoga) and newer (gestalt, psychosynthesis, synectics, scientology, EST, and mind dynamics) esoteric techniques for the expansion of consciousness and development of human potential indicate not only that adults can learn but that they are highly motivated (in many cases more so than children) to do so, given the proper resources and circumstances.

The belief that elementary and secondary schools are a more fruitful target for fundamental innovation than higher education institutions is equally erroneous. True, in some gross, quantitative sense, more innovation seems to occur at the elementary/secondary level than at the postsecondary level. That is because adult society, for the most part, does not care what happens in schools as long as a few basic requirements are met. These are: (1) incarcerate children for several hours a day, keeping them off the streets and in the neighborhood; (2) teach them a few instrumental skills; (3) don't expose them to anything containing sex or profanity; (4) don't increase our taxes. Within these broad bounds, parents and taxpayers don't care what happens in the schools. Ambitious teachers and administrators, though, earn a lot of professional points by appearing to be innovative, with the result that a lot superficial innovation does take place in schools, usually paid for by agencies outside of the school district, notably the federal government. But nearly all of these alleged innovations are marginal. The schools resist radical transformation as sedulously as any other dynamically conservative institution. Basic innovations—those that require a fundamental change of the goals or processes of schooling—almost never occur, and when they do, they tend to be short-lived.

The fact is, whatever meaningful innovation has occurred in American education in recent years has occurred mostly at the postsecondary level. One reason for this is that the college instructor enjoys far greater autonomy in the design of his own curriculum than does the school teacher. The greater power of the faculty as a whole at the college level may make the introduction of systemwide curriculum change more difficult, but individual faculty members can be almost as innovative in their own teaching as they please. Second, the more mature student at the postsecondary level is more capable of appreciating innovation and adapting to it. Also, because higher education institutions increasingly have to compete for students, there is an incentive for the creation of a unique institutional identity, while the great variety of goals, media, methods, and settings among postsecondary education institutions makes uniqueness more difficult to achieve.

Because I argue that ecological education at the postsecondary level should initially receive top priority for immediate development, this is not meant to suggest that we can or should ignore the education of children.

In one sense, young children of today *are* of relatively low priority in terms of the goals of ecological education. That is, given the exponential rates of change of most of the key variables comprising our current ecocrisis, and the long time lags inherent in the dynamics of the global social/ecological system, it is evident that unless some radical changes occur in the system within the next 5 to 15 years, an ecological catastrophe of rather drastic proportions becomes inevitable. The major changes and decisions will have to be made by today's adults and young adults if disaster is to be avoided. Today's kids and infants will inherit the outcome, but for the most part they will have little influence on it. On the other hand, assuming that at least a first approximation of ecotopia can be established within another generation, the crucial task of maintaining and developing such a state will befall today's children; hence, their preparation becomes greatly significant.

I have already underscored the failure of schooling and of conventional education to respond adequately to the challenges posed by ecocrisis. However, in recent years there has been rapidly growing interest and activity in the area of what has come to be called *early childhood education*, focusing on the years from birth to five

teacher. I have detected a similar opinion in the works of a number of contemporary writers, for example, Illich, Reich, and McLuhan. William Torbert provides additional support for this view in his book on experiential learning. Torbert observes that "children are forever reading their own meanings, fantasies, and bodies into what they see. They have yet to develop the experience, discipline, and language to recognize which aspects of this interpenetration are common to all persons, which are unique to them, and which reflect specific space-time configurations." But rather than helping them, parents and schools conspire to deprive them of the experience, discipline, and language that could make complexity meaningful. Instead, they extinguish the child's naturally evolving softworld vision of his own existence in favor of the imposed simplicity of what I call the *hard-world perspective* or what Torbert and some others call the *mystery-mastery process*. The result of the schooling experience, Torbert says, is that "children lose touch with a complex, profound, and immediate stratum of experience as they are educated into the mystery-mastery process."[5]

While I am no expert in this field, from what I have learned and observed, the overwhelming impression is that most contemporary efforts in early childhood education—at least as it is practiced in the United States—are augmenting conventional education's tendency to exterminate the very mental processes that ecological education must cultivate. The major emphasis in these efforts, whether implicit or explicit, is on preparing kids to be "successful" in school. The underlying assumptions appear to be that success in school is somehow analogic to success in the real world, that the criteria for success in school will not significantly change over time, and that the criteria for success in the real world will not change significantly over time.

But these assumptions are false. That is: (1) the school is one of the most dynamically conservative of all social institutions, and it is well insulated from and out of phase with the dynamics of the larger social/ecological system in which it is set; (2) the massive dissonance and epistemological stress of the contemporary world is creating enormous pressure for the radical transformation of conventional education, and even if the system yields only grudgingly, it seems certain that the school of 10 to 15 years hence will be a significantly different place from what it is today; and (3) the current global state is one of such unstable and exponential change that it is virtually guaranteed that, for better or worse, today's children will be adults in a world that is radically different from that of today.

What is most hopeful about the emerging concern with early childhood education is the recognition that the early years are a stage of human development too important to be neglected or left to the whims of unenlightened parenthood. If efforts in this area are to be successful, they must be freed of their infatuation with the prerequisites of schooling and become reconciled instead to the purpose and process of ecological education. Specifically, we should be preparing children for life in a world that is at the very least more like a viable ecotopia than what we have now, placing our bets on the most palatable future, if not the most probable one. Even if the worst possibilities of ecocrisis come to pass, the qualities required for planetary survival, welfare, and development should still be those of greatest currency in the aftermath of an ecological catastrophe. Whether as stewards of a renovated world system or as rebuilders of a shattered one, the children of today and tomorrow warrant consideration as students of prime importance to ecological education.

It is thus that parents become an important "target group" for ecological education, aside from whatever other roles they fill as adults. Extensive research has pretty well established that the family is the most powerful influencer of human development, followed by the peer group, the mass media, and the school (at least this is so in American and most other western cultures). It seems likely that, while greater socialization of child-rearing (through day care, Head Start, and so forth) may diminish its importance somewhat, parenting will be the major force in the development of children for some time to come. Still another great failure of conventional education is therefore evident. Currently there is virtually no worthwhile training for parenthood being provided. Such training is needed; it must focus not only on the requisite skills for effective child-rearing but also on such related categories of human behavior as loving, sexuality, "pairing" (being married or living with someone), and pregnancy and birth. Of course, ecological education demands that, beyond becoming skillful in these domains of behavior,

and then further development of a viable ecotopia, or state of global equilibrium. Operationally, this is equivalent to the cultivation of ecological consciousness and the creation of a growing cadre of competent transformers. This broad goal implies a large number of subordinate learning objectives which can be discussed in terms of the several levels of Bateson's learning hierarchy. Thus we can identify Learning I, or management objectives; Learning II, or learning-to-learn objectives; and Learning III, or selfhood objectives.[6]

In what follows, I will discuss some of the objectives, or lessons, of the ecological curriculum at each of the three major levels of learning, briefly mentioning a few subjects at each level which relate to these objectives. I will say little about specific methods for teaching these things except to note here that while the experience and materials for most potential components of an adequate ecological education already exist, the skills and materials required to put these pieces together in a comprehensive and conceptually sound whole ecological curriculum are so far nonexistent.

Clearly a large number of different curricula could be developed to serve the objectives discussed here, satisfying the essential criteria of an adequate ecological education given at the beginning of this chapter. I have found no curriculum currently in use that does so. The following discussion is an attempt to suggest what an adequate ecological curriculum might be like, though it is neither complete nor even necessarily satisfactory. I offer it mainly to illustrate what considerations might go into designing curricula for an adequate ecological education.

LEARNING I: MANAGEMENT

In general, Learning I objectives would be concerned (by definition) with achieving *proto-learning,* which is equivalent to adaptive transformation of existing control (including information-processing) systems. Examples of Learning I objectives of concern to ecological education are: reducing litter; increasing recycling of materials; increasing conservation of critical resources, decreasing human fertility through the adoption of family planning; preventing, ameliorating, or eliminating various diseases or health hazards; reducing or eliminating specific forms of violence, such as rape, murder, and biochemical warfare. In view of the vast scope and complexity of ecocrisis, the possible number of such objectives for ecological education is virtually unlimited. In general, such objectives entail adaptive changes in existing systems of control which, in human terms at least, imply transformations in the constituent knowledge, attitudes, and practices that make up particular patterns of behavior. Thus Learning I is directly related to the management of social and ecological systems.

Learning I lessons might be built around comprehensive patterns of behavior—for example, "adopting family planning"—or they might focus on constituents of such patterns as "understanding alternative techniques of birth control and how to use family-planning services"; "having feelings and expressing attitudes favorable to family planning"; "practicing a technique for birth control."[7] Learning I lessons can (in fact, must) also be framed in nonhuman, collective, or systemic terms. For example, a government that adapts to a growing demand for family-planning services by learning to establish, maintain, and improve government-supported clinics would be demonstrating the systemic mental equivalent of the individual Learning I lesson, "adopting family planning." That is, like an individual person, a government can learn to "plan its family," a corporation can learn to "stop littering," and a labor union can learn to "take care of its health."

The lessons mentioned so far are, in a sense, rather hardworld in their content. Another lesson, or set of lessons, that are more softworld—although they are at the same level of learning—concerns adaptations in the control of communication, or "information processing." Information processing has become a complex skill in a contemporary world which provides an information-rich environment using diverse and often sophisticated technology. Learning the skills required for effective communication and information processing—for example, literacy in print and other aural and visual media, skill in verbal and nonverbal interpersonal communication, knowing how to acquire information as from libraries or government agencies, knowing how to use communication and information-processing technology (telephone, television, copying machine, computer, camera, tape recorder)—involves important Learning I lessons. Again, such lessons are important not only for the individual but for the

agement curriculum, are community building, technology forecasting and assessment, communication, stationary-state economics, organizational behavior and development, ecology, planning, and design.

LEARNING II: LEARNING-TO-LEARN

The objectives of Learning II are learning, or cultivating, the skills of various forms of Learning I; learning to transform Learning I systems; and learning patterns of what Bateson calls "punctuating experience," which is equivalent to acquiring so-called character or personality traits. A specific Learning II objective related to the cultivation of ecological consciousness and the training of transformers is learning the art of *grokking,* or thinking in systems.

Some of the subjects that might be included in a curriculum for learning-to-learn are: cybernetics, including the study of learning processes; creativity (for example, synectics); systems science, including system dynamics; and futuristics. Other subjects or approaches might be included; for example, I see the study of the art of *magic* as a potentially powerful and exciting means for learning about learning. However, the major focus of the Learning II curriculum, especially for the training of transformers, must be on the broad process of *problem-solving.* Any mental system that is at all *stochastic*—that is, essentially whose gestalt of organism-in-environment experiences unanticipated changes or disturbances which exceed, stress, or even just threaten existing control functions—is continually confronted with problems, whenever such unanticipated events occur.[8] Confronted with such problems, a mental system will attempt to *adapt,* invoking the essential trial-and-error process of Learning I. Furthermore, a more sophisticated mental system, in order to improve its chances of adaptation and hence survival, will endeavor to learn-to-learn, escalating its efforts to the level of Learning II. Thus the process of problem-solving generally overlaps both Learning I and II, but acquires its greatest power at the level of Learning II.

The first and perhaps most important thing to say about problem-solving is that traditional approaches based on fundamental precepts of "scientific method" established by Galileo and Descartes—however useful they may be in certain contexts—for the most part do not work when applied to the great majority of real-world problems. As Forrester observes, the attempt to find simple, linear, analytical, or statistical solutions to problems set in nonlinear, complex systems more often than not produces counter intuitive results. Conventional scientific or social scientific methods applied to problem-solving in complex systems yield results that are either ineffectual or counterproductive. And, says Forrester, the overwhelming majority of real-world problems of interest and importance involve systems that are too nonlinear and complex to yield analytical solutions, hence the rationale for the development of system dynamics, a methodology for simulating the dynamic behavior of complex systems, analyzing problems, and testing potential solutions.

It is primarily at the initial stage of analysis that conventional or traditional approaches to problem-solving fail. Thus Schon observes: "Contrary to mythology, we are largely unable to 'know' in situations of social change, if the criteria of knowledge are those of the rational/experimental model."[9] Schon shows that the fundamental assumptions underlying the rational/experimental approach to what he calls "public learning" or what I call (in Chapter 4) "helping/governing science" are generally fallacious when applied to the existing unstable social state. That is, it is generally not true that: (1) it is possible to know whether a problem exists or even what is just happening in a given situation; (2) diagnosis is possible; (3) hypotheses can be experimentally tested; (4) the results of experiments can be attributed to experimental actions; and (5) experimental results can meaningfully be extrapolated or generalized either from the present into the future or from a small-scale to a large-scale situation.[10]

Combine this criticism from Forrester and Schon with the popular notion—reflected in the works of Theodore Roszak, Marcuse,

Leiss, Hunter, and Torbert—that the ethos of conventional science is predominantly that of the domination of nature or the "mystery-mastery process," and the failure of "scientific" approaches to most problem-solving seems complete. Of course, rejection of the established methods of science and technology can be carried too far, leading to a dangerous underestimation of their utility. But the fact remains that the conventional approaches are largely inadequate or

might even call the "new science") to a large extent goes *meta* with respect to the established rational/experimental mode. Rather than dogmatically accepting proven models as given, the existential/systemic mode's major activity is the development of what Schon calls "projective models" whose cardinal test of validity is *usefulness*. This new approach reflects what I have suggested as the fundamental epistemological rule of ecological education: reality is what works.

As Torbert observes, the new science, while it may not always reject the axioms of the conventional science, must continually reexamine them and throw them open to question and change.[12] To thus open up the premises of an established method of proto-learning to potential modification clearly implies the existence of Learning II. Again we see why the problem-solving process overlaps both Learning I and II. But the escalation of the problem-solving process at the level of Learning II by the existential/systemic approach has an important ramification. The premises of Learning II are manifested in what are commonly recognized as character, or personality traits. This implies that, in the new science, the researcher-as-person becomes an inseparable part of the process of research itself. This is at odds with the conventional stereotype of scientific objectivity; that is, not Monod's "principle of objectivity," which continues to be essential to truly scientific learning, but rather the *image* of science and scientist as being neutral and value-free. As Torbert puts it, "science must be viewed, from the systems perspective, as itself a valued action-project chosen by the scientist and dependent for its accuracy upon his development of contact with consciousness and his resultant sensitivity to his own and others' structuring of the world."[13]

In the existential/systemic mode of problem-solving or research, the consciousness of the problem-solver or researcher becomes vital. The success of his efforts at problem-solving or discovery in the real world will depend on the degree of his attainment of ecological consciousness.

The differences in the rational/experimental and the existential/systemic approaches to problem-solving probably pervade all of the phases of the problem-solving process, but they are noticeable mainly in the general stage of *analysis*. The two modes may not even agree on what is a *problem*. For example, it was the better part of a decade before Rachel Carson's recognition of DDT as a problem came to be shared by most of the scientific establishment. Similarly, it took a Ralph Nader to get the automobile industry to treat safety as a problem. On the other hand, Andrew Weil looked at the problem of "drug abuse" from an existential/systemic perspective and concluded that the real problem was the treatment of drug use as a problem, just as Ronald Laing concluded that the major problem with schizophrenia was the practice of treating people manifesting this form of behavior as "sick."

The two modes also differ in the way they go about gathering information and the kinds of information each considers valid or relevant. This is illustrated by the work of Carlos Castaneda. In the course of his first three books, Castaneda progressively shifts and expands from the rational/experimental to the existential/systemic mode of discovery.[14] Whereas in the first book he is trying to dissect and examine Don Juan like a specimen under a microscope, by the third book he has abandoned and committed himself to becoming the shaman's apprentice and is accepting his experience whole.

The difference in analysis between the two modes, as far as results go, is demonstrated by the unorthodoxy of the results of system-dynamics analysis of real-world problems, as compared to those of conventional approaches. Thus, when Jay Forrester studied "industrial dynamics," he found management chronically pursuing policies that were destined only to exacerbate the very problems they were supposed to solve. Similarly, when Forrester examined "urban dynamics," he found that politically popular programs of urban renewal promised only to perpetuate decay. It is, in fact, the very counterintuitiveness of complex systems that makes system dynamics in particular and the existential/systemic approach generally necessary for effective problem-solving. In other words, the rational/experimental mode fails by being too strictly hardworld, while the existential/systemic mode of problem-solving acquires its greater validity by expansion into the softworld.

Many lessons may be involved in developing an individual's skill in the general process of problem-solving, but the most essential one, which must be mentioned here, is the practice of *questioning.* To fully understand complex systems such as corporations, cities, soci-

many ways of the problem-solving process and even of ecological consciousness generally, is likely to be easier among children than today's adults. The key to cultivating a child's capacity to grok, or think in systems, is to reinforce the habit of persistent and critical questioning. Among most adults, however, this habit has been so thoroughly extinguished by the incentive structures of the prevailing educational, business, political, social, research, and other systems that considerable effort and practice (and even courage) will be needed to restore it.

Kids always want to know why things are the way they seem to be. However, this habit is often extinguished by the lack of reinforcement from impatient adults who usually try to terminate what appears to be an endless stream of questioning. The fact that such streams are often virtually endless is evidence that kids demand much more holistic models of the systems that concern them than the adult world is willing to provide or even in many instances, tolerate. Because "civilized" society (*especially* western society) is predominantly based on hardworld thinking, it usually treats softworld thinking as threatening or subversive, as, in fact, it often is (for example, the emperor's new clothes).

This lesson provides a good example of how the ecological curriculum may be irrelevant to or even at variance with the requisites of preparing kids for school, the overwhelming concern of most conventional approaches to early childhood education. Anyone who is familiar with American education would recognize that the habit of persistent question-asking is one that has neutral or even negative valence within our traditional system of schooling. It is a trivial observation that the crowded classroom stifles most opportunities for student-initiated interrogation. But this is only a superficial manifestation of how the dynamic conservatism of conventional education is at odds with uninhibited questioning. The conventional system of education is, more than anything else, a meritocracy, and it rightly perceives too much questioning by the uninitiated as a threat to its credentials, hence, its power. The same is true of the other meritocracies—business and government—which the educational establishment courts and serves. The end result of this pervasive and systematic discouragement of critical questioning can be symbolized in one word: Watergate.

Frankly, teaching kids to doubt and to ask critical questions is likely to make schooling an even more painful experience for many of them than it otherwise might have been. Cultivating the habit of questioning among adults is likely to make the stress of our existing state of dissonance even more severe. But it is precisely from such conflict and stress that the impulse for change and development arises. Thus may emerge not only more open classrooms but more open businesses, more open government, and in general a more open society.

LEARNING III: SELFHOOD

As noted in the discussion of the learning hierarchy in Chapter 6, Learning III throws open the largely unexamined premises of Learning II to question and change. It is at the level of Learning III that significant expansion and transformation of consciousness occurs. The crucial objective of Learning III is not just the redefinition of the *self* but, beyond that, the attainment of a conception of *selfhood* that is fluid and transmutable.

Our conception of *self,* Bateson says, is the result of the premises acquired through Learning II. "To the degree that a man achieves Learning III . . . his 'self' will take on a sort of irrelevance. The concept of 'self' will no longer function as a nodal argument in the punctuation of experience."[15]

Why is Learning III important? This is not easy to explain in the abstract, so let me try to approach it anecdotally. When I was teaching physics in high school, there was a black girl in one of my classes who was an average or better student. The fact that she was doing well in my course was gratifying to me; the number of blacks and females in my classes was small compared to the population of the school as a whole—a reflection, I felt, of a stereotype of blacks and females not being competent in hard sciences, of which physics was reputed to be the hardest. It was my regular practice to have students put individual homework problems on the blackboard and explain their solution to the rest of the class. This relieved me of the burden of correcting homework and also gave students an opportu-

years of experience in a system of education that had taught kids little else than to fear failure. So this girl's general discomfort in this kind of situation wasn't all that unusual. But her behavior followed a consistent pattern which revealed something that was, to me, both frightening and infuriating. After finally coaxing her to come up to the board, open her book, read the problem to the class, and pick up the chalk (all the while protesting that she was "not good at math"), these episodes proceeded something like this:

> Teacher: "Now, what's the first step in solving this problem?"
> Student: "I don't know, Mr. Perelman, I'm not good at math."
> Teacher: "Well, just write something on the board."
> Student: "But it will be wrong; I'm not good at math."
> Teacher: "I don't care if it's wrong, just write anything."
> (Student writes the first step in the solution.)
> Teacher: "Well that looks OK. What's the next step?"
> Student: "I don't know. I'm not good at math."
> Teacher: "Write something anyway."
> Student: "I don't know what to write. I'm not good at math."
> Teacher: "Write anything. Just write something."
> (Student writes the second step in the solution.)
> Teacher: "That's correct."
> Student: "But I'm not good at math."

And so on, step by step, until she had written the entire solution to the problem correctly, without an error or correction. When she finished, I would tell her that she had done an excellent job, and she would repeat again that she was "not good at math." After about two months, she dropped the course.

This experience was both frightening and infuriating. It was frightening when I realized how thoroughly insulted this girl's self-image of being "not good at math" was from all evidence to the contrary. It was infuriating because this girl had been imprisoned in a constraining image of her self that had been fabricated by the very system that was supposed to educate her, that is, the school, in collaboration with her family and friends. Here was racism and sexism in action, and it revealed the painfully frustrating nature of complex systemic behavior: a human being had been "wasted," yet no one individual could be blamed.

Since this experience I have become more and more aware of how both I and people I have encountered—some of whom were very close to me—have been imprisoned and wasted by the strait-jackets of self-images acquired through prior Learning II. To some extent I have learned through experience and study to liberate my self from the bondage of habit; others I know have gone further. But many people I have known, and some I have loved, continue to lead tragic existences, their capacities for learning and growth wasted in cages fashioned from bad ideas.

The premises of Learning II, as Bateson has observed, tend to be self-validating and hence resistant to change. The richness of experience provides an abundance of diverse data that can be selectively used to reinforce virtually any point of view. Thus a cynical person can always find ample justification for his cynicism; the person who is paranoid can always find a basis for his fears; the person who is insecure can always find threats to his security; someone who is aggressive can always find vindication for aggression. There are always criteria according to which virtually any reality will work. Since such criteria are taken as axiomatic to reality, they can never be tested against reality and either proven or disproven. But the premises of Learning II are even more insulated from change by the effects of *cognitive dissonance* and *reification*.

The effect of cognitive dissonance is to take the already self-validating images of self and make them into self-fulfilling prophecies. Thus a person who identifies her self with the image of "not good at math" will not only find validation for that image in every instance of mathematical error but will avoid or run away from a situation in which her actual behavior is consistently contradictory to that image.

Reification puts the seal on the premises of Learning II by taking these images of self, which are only ideas (actually just name tags of past patterns of behavior) and treating them as things, that is, character or personality *traits*. So someone who has perhaps failed at times in the past comes to be identified, by himself and others, as "a failure." A person who has made trouble becomes "a troublemaker." Someone who participates in homosexual behavior is "a homosex-

self is derived—from our here-and-now consciousness, experience, or existence. If self-validation, cognitive dissonance, and reification constitute the loopholes through which we escape from challenging the accumulated premises of Learning II, then Learning III requires plugging those loopholes. Thus *self* becomes plastic, or in some sense irrelevant, and alternative *selves* become possible. Learning III therefore opens us up to alternative modes of consciousness and hence may ultimately lead to what I have called a poly-consciousness.

There are any number of potential subjects that might be included in a Learning III curriculum. For example: the psychology of "altered states of consciousness" and "extrasensory perception"; "self"-control through biofeedback, meditation, hypnosis, and so on; the clarification and even engineering of values; art, especially as a form of meditation; survival training and experience of the sort provided by Outward Bound; epistemology; linguistics; and so forth. In particular, there are several learning methodologies currently in existence which, in one way or another, involve some Learning III. Yoga and Zen are traditional approaches, but they have been augmented by some newer techniques which synthesize both eastern and western approaches and which are evolving as quasi-commercial enterprises, for example, Esalen Institute, Synectics, Earhard Seminars Training (EST), Silva Mind Control, International Meditation Society (Transcendental Meditation, a.k.a. the "Science of Creative Intelligence"), and Arica Institute (using the techniques of Oscar Ichazo).

A caveat is in order. The transformation of the premises of Learning II, or of the *self*, which result from Learning III, may not always be desirable or useful. As Bateson notes, the "double bind" may lead to either enlightenment or disorientation. The difference may depend, in the parlance of the drug scene, on "the set and the setting." In any event, the fact that any of the techniques mentioned above may actually succeed in cultivating some kind of Learning III does not necessarily imply that such techniques are therefore appropriate for or even commensurate with the process of ecological education. Indeed, I suspect that some of these techniques may be highly antithetical to the purpose and process of ecological education and may actually produce transformations of *self* that result in even greater insulation from change and from further learning. There appears to be a reduction in wisdom and responsibility, hence a retreat from ecological consciousness. On the whole, much more independent research seems to me to be needed in this field, in order to determine what these various techniques actually do, how they work, and how they can be used to produce positive results.

PROCESS CHARACTERISTICS

So far our discussion has concentrated on curriculum, but we are also concerned with the *process* of an adequate ecological education. Here, I will identify several process components or characteristics that I think are especially important.

Micro- and macro-utility

An effective ecological education should have practical value at both the micro- and macro-levels. That is, it must be helpful both to the individual in dealing with critical personal problems and to society as a whole in dealing with critical collective problems. Many macro-level problems have their roots at the micro-level, and vice versa. For example, the macro-level problem of population growth has its roots in individual knowledge, attitudes, and behavior concerning reproduction. On the other hand, many apparently individual problems—from psychological depression to lung cancer—really have their cause and cure at the macro-, or societal, level. An educational process that serves only the individual or only the society, and ignores the other, is destined to fail.

Fun and play

The process of ecological education should be *fun,* and the process should, to a significant extent, be *playful.*[16] An educational process that can help us avoid a somber and scary future need not itself be somber and scary. On the contrary, a process that is somber and scary will turn people off and not engage the enthusiastic participation of the people it must engage to be effective. Also, only by being playful

The process must emphasize *alternatives.* In the transformation to equilibrium, the most critical need now is for settings in which growth alternatives can be both "tried out" and "tried on." It should be emphasized that when I speak of growth alternatives, I mean not only economic or technological alternatives but political alternatives, social alternatives, cultural alternatives, alternative values, and alternative realities. The salient characteristic of the kinds of new settings needed for the process of ecological education is that they create, provide, and evolve comprehensive social/ecological alternatives.

Harmony between social/physical structure and content

There is a critical relationship between social structure (that is, the structure of relationships among trustees, faculty, administrators, staff, and students) and physical structure (physical plant, energy system, and food service) of an educational setting on the one hand and the curriculum on the other. This is illustrated by the qualitative contrast in two innovative institutions: the College of the Atlantic and the University of Wisconsin at Green Bay. These are two institutions whose curricular philosophy is similar and whose curricula reflect the theme of human ecology. At COA a conscious effort has been made to create a physical and social community that is harmonious with the philosophy expressed in the curriculum. UWGB, on the other hand, is from a physical and social standpoint virtually indistinguishable from any other typical state university campus. The harmony between process and content at COA is impressive, especially in contrast to the tension between the setting and the curriculum at UWGB. COA is not an ideal example, nor is it a model that every other higher education institution can readily emulate. However, it demonstrates that the more harmonious the setting of ecological education can be made with the curriculum, the more effective the educational process will be.

Emphasis on experience

All of the different new kinds of educational institutions that are possible and are needed in general would emphasize the concept of an educational institution as an *experimental/experiential* setting. There is a need for settings where alternatives to existing growth-based systems are not only developed in theory but also where these alternatives can be experimented with and developed in practice and where real human beings can actually experience them to see how they "fit." As E. F. Schumacher puts it, the need is to make "viable alternatives visible."[18]

Beyond the need for including experience in the design of growth alternatives, effective education for competent transformers must include other major experiential components. Many different kinds of experience that might be included in the process of ecological education can be imagined, but at least three general types are worth mentioning here. First is the apprenticeship experience acquired by working in real-world settings (for example, public interest research groups, internships, and field work). Second is the learning experience acquired in simulated or sheltered settings (for example, alternative campuses, experimental communities, or smaller-scale settings like T-groups, games, and simulations). Third is the personal experience that can lead to the expansion of consciousness.

It is also important to emphasize that there is a difference between mere existential "happenings" and useful learning "experience." As the late Saul Alinsky once observed:

> Most people do not accumulate a body of experience. Most people go through life undergoing a series of happenings, which pass through their systems undigested. Happenings become experiences when they are digested, when they are reflected on, related to general patterns, and synthesized.[19]

Ecological education must provide its students with experiences that are designed and structured to provide maximum learning.

Interdisciplinary Discipline
Virtually no real-world problem of any significance can be analyzed or solved within the bounds of any one of the established academic disciplines. The problems of growth and equilibrium require interdisciplinary approaches in research and teaching. Indeed, recognition of the need for interdisciplinary studies has been so widespread that many interdisciplinary courses and programs have appeared on

dent's point of view, such programs have often been inefficient and largely ineffective. A crucial need, therefore, in the curricular responses to the problems of growth and equilibrium is the development of an interdisciplinary discipline.

New Roles for Disciplines and Professions
Some may feel that the thrust toward greater interdisciplinarity in postsecondary education means the eventual abolition of established disciplines and professions. I see most established disciplines and professions continuing to play an important role in the postsecondary education of the future but with the now rather rigid boundaries between disciplinary and professional turf becoming vastly more flexible and permeable to the interests and activities of faculty and students alike.

On one hand, many aspects of traditional disciplinary studies may take on new meaning and relevance in the context of ecological education. For example, as novice transformers learn the importance of reality images and value structures in the effective solution of real-world problems, their appreciation of and thirst for the wisdom to be offered by the arts, literature, and philosophy may be heightened to a level undreamed of in the traditional liberal arts college. On the other hand, the needs of a more ecological educational system will, no doubt, lead to significant qualitative changes in the nature of many disciplinary and professional studies. For example, the study of history may place greater emphasis on the role of the historian in providing more "instant history," or short-term feedback on major social/ecological trends, as well as adapting more to a concept of "alternative histories" analogous to the concept of "alternative futures." The study of history itself may come to be seen more as an exercise in the process of metaphor-generation than fact-determination.

Credentials

In the new institutional paradigm I described in Chapter 11, I called for more emphasis on credentialing and employment to be placed on functional competency, and less emphasis on status. In the short term, however, this paradigm is not yet dominant. It would be naive to disregard the relation of academic credentials to employment in conventional institutions. Many existing interdisciplinary problem-centered programs provide their students with educational experiences that are obviously relevant, but which do not necessarily provide them with credentials that permit them—and the heightened consciousness and skill they have acquired—to be introduced into the established institutions that govern our society. A major challenge in introducing innovations in postsecondary education is not only to create a generation of competent transformers but to see that they are employed.

Requirements

Some parts of the total curriculum should be required. It has become popular throughout much of our contemporary educational system to do away with requirements altogether, to leave students free to "do their own thing." This trend seems to be based partly on an erroneous presumption that people can anticipate the value of knowledge or experience they have not yet acquired. I think effective ecological education should have some requirements. In particular, I believe that there should be a required core curriculum central to all disciplinary and professional training in higher education. The essential requirement here should not be for the student to learn a particular set of *things,* but rather to *confront* a critical set of issues, problems, and experiences. It should be clearly understood that what I am proposing here is not to sell a particular position on the issues surrounding limits to growth or particular solutions to the problems of growth and equilibrium. What I propose is simply an educational process that will compel students to confront these issues and problems and which will, hopefully, provide them with tools and skills that will be useful in creating their own positions on these issues and in seeking their own solutions to these problems.

Cooperation

Consistent with the symbiosis implied by a negentropic value system, ecological education must be based on cooperation. Conventional education stresses competition, evaluating on the basis of comparisons of one student to another. Rather, evaluation in ecological education should be based on performance criteria, and evaluation mechanisms should be collaboratively developed or chosen by

have maximum autonomy in defining and planning projects and in defining the criteria of evaluation of success or failure of the projects. The role of the teacher should be that of group co-member, action guide, resource referral agent, and learning facilitator. Since there is a conflict between the teacher's role as a member of the group and the role of evaluator, in most cases the teacher should not evaluate the outcome of the project or at least should not be the sole evaluator. Rather, evaluation of the project's outcome should be done by an independent agent chosen collaboratively by the group.

Individuation

As a complement to group learning, there is a need for modularization and individuation of instruction, particularly in disciplines or other areas where there are knowledge bases or skill sets that are useful or essential to interdisciplinary problem-solving. For example, members of a group studying land-use problems in their local community may need supplementary training in statistics, demography, geology, and law. The currently typical structure of collegiate education, almost completely organized on the basis of semester, trimester, or quarter courses, will serve the needs of these students badly, if at all. What are needed are shorter instructional modules, for example, from one to four weeks, and programmed or computer-assisted self-instructional materials that can fill the student's individual needs for concise but coherent packages of knowledge.

Lifelong Education

Many educators have called for a change from our current predominantly child- and adolescent-centered education system to a system of lifelong or continuing education.[20] Harold Shane has argued persuasively for the promulgation of such a model, strongly basing his case on considerations having to do with limits to growth.[21] Many of the oracles of a postindustrial society also foresee the establishment of such a model. I feel that some kind of lifelong education is essential to the transformation to and maintenance of an equilibrium society. In the short term, my rationale is that the current adult and adolescent populations must play a leading role in the transformation to equilibrium. In the longer term, I foresee that education will be a central, if not the central, activity in an equilibrium society and that it will engage a major portion of the time and energies of people of all ages.

Engagement-Affirmative Action

There is little doubt that much of the response to date to the problems of growth and equilibrium has been led by predominantly white, male, middle-class people.[22] Affirmative action is needed to broaden the spectrum of participation in the process of transformation to an equilibrium society, to engage a representative proportion of women, minorities, Third World people, blue-collar workers, poor people, and other currently underrepresented groups in the leadership of transformation. Among other things, this means the creation of some postsecondary educational programs specially designed to engage these people in the transformation process.

Leapfrogging

As indicated earlier, the requirements of the less-developed countries in making the transformation to equilibrium are quantitatively and qualitatively different from these of the overdeveloped countries. Not only is there a crucial need for research on how the former can effectively and efficiently leapfrog from a pre- to a postindustrial society, but there is an equally urgent need for educational programs in these countries that can help them develop the kind of human capital that can guide and facilitate this different kind of transformation. We must develop programs for training competent transformers who are especially responsive to the needs of Third World societies. This need is only exacerbated by the fact that many of these countries inherited schooling systems from their colonial masters which are of dubious value in their native societies and which are grossly inadequate or inappropriate for the cultures on which they were forced. The trend toward naturalization of the educational systems—paralleling naturalization of the social, economic, and political systems—in many less-developed countries has already begun, but it needs to be accelerated if these countries are to be successful in developing their own approaches to an equilibrium society.

be *anticipated* in the educational sector. This is because I view the educational system as having an essential prerequisite and continuing role in fomenting transformation in the larger social/ecological system.

In Table 4 I have outlined the general institutional paradigm shift which I believe is implied by the transformation to an equilibrium society. Everything that was said in that table about the new paradigm for institutions in general applies to educational institutions in particular.

Besides this general institutional paradigm shift, there are also some changes implied by the discussion in the preceding sections that are uniquely relevant to educational institutions. These changes are mainly at the levels of goals and technology/technique. They are summarized in Table 6.

TABLE 6. EDUCATIONAL INSTITUTIONS PARADIGM SHIFT

OLD (hardworld)	NEW (softworld)

GOALS

Conservative	Transformational

The goals of the old educational institution tend to be conservative in the sense that they are oriented toward the past and to maintenance. By contrast, the goals of the new educational institution are far more future-focused and are more concerned with the adaptive transformation of society.

Relatively fixed model of the *educated person;* anthropocentric	Evolving model of the *educated person;* holistic

To the extent that educational institutions are product-oriented—that is, concerned with the production of educated persons—the old model of the educated person tends to be fairly rigid, based on values that are largely anthropocentric. The new model of the educated person is more flexible, evolving to meet the needs of transformation, and is based on values that are more holistic, in the sense of responding to not only social but ecological ideals.

Passive response to consumer demand	Interactive, collaborative response to consumer demand

To the extent that educational institutions are consumer-oriented—that is, concerned with providing educational services to meet the demands of students-as-consumers—the old model tends to respond to these demands in a passive way, operating on the implicit assumption that the student's demands are informed, nonarbitrary, rational, and of social/ecological value. The new model questions these assumptions, and attempts to synthesize both the product and consumer orientations by working interactively and collaboratively with students to formulate educational programs that are responsive to the needs of the student, the institution, and of the larger social/ecological system.

| The system focuses on Learning I | The system focuses on Learning II and III also. |

That is, the old system is almost exclusively concerned with learning as information processing. The new system is additionally concerned with learning to learn and with the expansion of consciousness.

| Research, teaching separate, often conflicting | Research, teaching in more complex integration |

One-way (empty-head model)   Interactive, facilitative, cyclical

In most of contemporary education the dominant model of learning is a one-way model in which knowledge is seen as flowing one way from an informed instructor to an uninformed student (the *empty head*). In the new model, learning is viewed as an interactive, cyclical process of trial and error, of giving and receiving feedback. The teacher's role is far more that of facilitator than of pundit.

| Authority-based | Experience-based |

Again, in the old, learning flows from sources of authority; in the new, learning flows from experience.

| Error-avoiding | Error-embracing |

The old discourages trials and punished errors. The new facilitates and encourages the process of trial and error.

| Negative Reinforcement | Positive Reinforcement |

The old methodology shapes behavior through the withholding of rewards or through punishment. The new shapes behavior through positive incentive structures.

Imposed timing/pacing	Self-timing/pacing

In the old instructional methodology the schedule or pace of learning is imposed by the institution and faculty. In the new, the student is far more in charge of determining the pace of his own learning.

Competitive	Cooperative

The ethos of the old is almost totally competitive, social Darwinist. The ethos of the new is cooperative, symbiotic.

Isolated learning	Group learning

Consistent with 6, in the new, group learning complements individual learning.

Comparative (competitive) evaluation	Criterion-referenced (performance-based) evaluation

In the old system, evaluation is symbolized by the "curve." The individual's performance is evaluated in comparison with that of his peers. In the new system, evaluation is referenced to performance criteria.

Imposed goal-setting and evaluation	Participatory goal-setting and evaluation

In the old, goals are set by authority; performances ere evaluated by authority. In the new, students participate in the establishment of learning goals and in choosing the criteria and methods of evaluation.

CHAPTER 13

CREATING ECOLOGICAL

where who are interested in and are actually doing research and teaching that fit some if not all of the characteristics of ecological education mentioned in Chapter 12. These individuals and institutions form an inchoate "beyond limits" network that is beginning to work toward the creation of an ecological education. But the development of an adequate ecological education will require more than just the interest of a large number of dedicated people and organizations. For ecological education to attain a level where it can make a significant contribution to the transformation from ecocrisis to equilibrium, several important needs related to its development will have to be met. This chapter describes the major needs, or ingredients, for the creation of an adequate ecological education.

UNDERSTANDING THE NATURE OF THE PROBLEM

I have found little evidence of informed understanding of the nature of the problem presented for education by the "beyond limits" school. Although interest is fairly high, it is thus far unaccompanied by a thorough conceptual grasp of the problem of transformation to equilibrium and its implications for postsecondary education. Many whom I have met or about whose work I have read, display a partial or nearly adequate concept of the problem which is useful, as far as it goes. But it does not go far enough. I have not found any educational program that satisfies all the criteria of an *adequate* ecological education. There are a number of programs in existence that are multilevel, interdisciplinary, problem-centered, future-oriented, global, or humanistic; a few even combine two or more of these characteristics. But none, to my knowledge, combines all. A few people I have encountered do share a conception of the educational problem posed by ecocrisis which is similar to mine. But because of professional, institutional, financial, or other constraints, or perhaps because of flawed or limited perspective, none has yet implemented the broadly ecological educational program called for here.

INSTRUCTIONAL MATERIALS/TECHNIQUES APPROPRIATE TO ECOLOGICAL EDUCATION

The essential ingredients of a well-developed ecological curriculum are: (a) appropriate instructional materials that have been developed through trial, evaluation, and revision; (b) appropriate instructional techniques, also tested and revised; and (c) people who are experienced and/or trained in the use of these materials and techniques. While these do not exist for ecological education as a whole, they do exist for most potential component areas, for example, systems science, planning, futuristics, environmental studies, communication, and consciousness-raising. On the other hand, since many of these component areas are themselves relatively young, their curricula are generally raw and frequently in need of further development and refinement. But the critical need is for further development of these curricula in some integrated manner which can lead to the evolution of a complete ecological curriculum. In addition, there is a pressing need in all of these component curriculum areas for *evaluation*. I have found little literature on evaluation of educational programs in most key component areas. However, enough curriculum experience and materials exist to make the creation of a prototype curriculum for ecological education feasible. The major needs (in this order) are: integration, application, evaluation, and dissemination.

FOUR KEY CONSTRAINTS

While attending the Advanced Study Institute on Social System Dynamics, at Dartmouth College in 1974, I had a number of conversations with many of the other participants—a group that included scientists, government and business planners, educators, and foundation staff, as well as college faculty and administrators—about the need for proliferating system dynamics teaching and research. In the course of these conversations, four key constraints on the spreading of system dynamics in higher education seemed to be mentioned continually. On later reflection, I concluded that these four constraints applied not only to the development of system dynamics but

fore ecological disaster strikes. Second, the expert individuals whose input will be required in a quality curriculum-development effort are very busy people who have little time to spare for such an endeavor. This seems to be a generally valid rule of thumb: people who do not fancy themselves as professional "educationists" will usually endorse the need for curriculum development but will rarely invest much of their own time and energy in the process unless there are powerful incentives (for example, money, tenure, sabbatical time) for doing so.

3. *Money.* There is virtually no money available for curriculum development in most of the component areas of ecological education, nor in ecological education as a whole.[1] In fact, funds for curriculum development in postsecondary education generally are scarce, especially for such major developmental efforts as that required to create an adequate ecological education.

4. *Content.* We have few, if any, answers to most of the urgent questions about growth and equilibrium. The answers that we do have, for the most part, are in the nature of processes rather than solutions. In other words, we have some ideas now about processes that may make people more effective in finding solutions to the many problems of ecological crisis, but we have no simple prescriptions or canonical solutions to teach our students. This fact is often frustrating and confusing to many of those anxiously seeking answers, especially people in business and government who have become accustomed to seeking and finding packaged solutions.

NEW MODELS OF EDUCATIONAL INSTITUTIONS

The creation of an adequate ecological education implies an immediate need for substantial change in the institutions of post-secondary education. This is not to say that great public universities, small private liberal arts colleges, community colleges, or other conventional educational institutions must or will cease to exist. But it does suggest a major qualitative change in the nature of these institutions and of postsecondary education as a whole. The overall need is for an educational system which is more consistent with the essential characteristics of an adequate ecological education, which is far more responsive to the pressing needs of its social/ecological environment, and which is far more actively and consciously engaged in the process of transformation to an equilibrium society.

This system change implies not only major adaptations of existing educational institutions but in many cases, the creation of whole new educational institutions. As suggested in Chapter 12, the practical need is for models of educational institutions as experimental/experiential settings that are harmonious with the goals and processes of ecological education. By *models* I mean both conceptual models (detailed ideas or plans for new educational settings) and empirical models (settings that have actually been created). Surprisingly, in my professional experience I have so far discovered few of either. While in recent years there have been a few instances of critically designed and meaningful innovation, much of the would-be innovation in higher education has been marginal, in many cases, little more than showmanship.[2]

The need for new educational institutions could be met in various ways. In some cases they might emerge as autonomous institutions as a result of the building of new institutions or the transformation of existing institutions. In other cases, they might develop as offshoots, or "alternative campuses," of conventional higher-education institutions. Some of these new institutions would serve as "community systems laboratories" where students, teachers, scholars, managers, public officials, and other citizens would come together for the purpose of experimenting with and experiencing alternative communities for satisfying human needs and aspirations, while remaining viable organisms within the constraints of the global ecosystem. In fact, in some cases, the "campus" would not even be localized but would be comprised of a decentralized network of settings and experiences.

INCENTIVES

The creation of new educational curricula and settings will not be successful unless there are adequate incentives for the principal actors involved—students, faculty, and educational administrators—to adopt the changes required. Many interdisciplinary and other innovative programs attempted on campus fail because they are irrele-

Student incentives

Some major incentives that would help attract students to innovative programs in ecological education are:

Sense of relevance. Programs should project a sense of relevance to the future and of service to society.

Work opportunities. Programs should provide meaningful work opportunities in conjunction with training, for example, internships, field projects, and public interest research groups.

Viable employment credentials. Programs should provide their graduates with credentials that have high face validity in the job market. Program directors should develop placement services to direct competent graduates to employment opportunities.

Scholarships/fellowships. Programs that can provide financial support for students are obviously going to be attractive.

High academic standards. Programs that confer prestige on their students and graduates will attract more and better students.

Faculty incentives

A Delphi survey conducted by the Western Interstate Commission for Higher Education indicated that faculty are generally perceived to be by far the greatest obstacle to innovation and change in higher education.[3] Following are some incentives that could help mobilize faculty support for innovative ecological education programs:

Profit/prestige. Programs will receive more enthusiastic faculty support if they provide participating faculty with opportunities for profitable and/or prestigious extramural activities: e.g., consulting, input to government, etc.

Opportunities for publication. The publish-or-perish syndrome in higher education has been perennially condemned, but whether it is a good thing or not, it continues to exist. A significant constraint on the development of nontraditional, interdisciplinary areas of higher education has been the relative scarcity of journals in these areas in which faculty could publish. For example, in the "futuristics" field, there are only a handful of major periodicals. The same is true in other component areas of ecological education and certainly ecological education as a field itself.

Access to funds. Funding agencies should require that programs or institutions seeking or receiving support demonstrate their commitment to developing and providing adequate ecological education.[4] Some higher education administrators might wish to fight for similar priorities in the allocation of their institutions' "hard-money" budgets.

Direct Support. Funding agencies should also seek out, encourage the development of, and provide direct support for innovative programs designed to provide an adequate ecological education. However, direct support of such teaching/research programs should always be tied to and contingent upon institutional commitment to long-term support and survival of the programs.

Administrator incentives

Some incentives that could help encourage administrative endorsement and support of innovative programs in ecological education are:

Cost-effectiveness. Programs demonstrably using the resources of the institution in a cost-effective manner will be more attractive to administrators.

Institutional attractiveness. Programs which demonstrably enhance the attractiveness and/or prestige of the institution will be more readily supported by administrators.

Faculty/student acceptance. To receive administration endorsement, programs in ecological education will have to demonstrate that they enjoy at least the acceptance and preferably the support and enthusiasm of faculty and students.

Beyond the need for these specific incentives is a general need for an effective demand for the products (research and manpower) of an innovative postsecondary education system. My impression is that demand for the research products and trained personnel that such ecological education would produce already exists and can be expected to grow. People directing ecological education programs which are almost adequate—Jay Forrester, Dennis Meadows, Edward Weidner, Arthur Harkins, and Harold Linstone—have indicated that their graduates are in demand and generally have little trouble getting jobs. If true, this is significant, given the unfavorable job market that graduates in traditional disciplines now face. My

substantial and, given just about anybody's image of the "most probable future," is almost certain to increase.

New Recognition of Educational Roles/Functions of Other Institutions

Closely associated with the need for new models of educational institutions is the need for greater recognition of the important educational roles and functions of other institutions which do not primarily think of themselves as educational. The educational role of the mass media is widely recognized, but there is actually little effort made to maximize the educational effectiveness of these media. The educational functions and responsibilities of other social institutions—labor unions, business firms, public interest groups, charitable and service organizations, the military, and government agencies—are only now beginning to be realized. The fact is, these latter kinds of institutions can be expected to play an increasingly important role in postsecondary education in the future, a trend that will be matched by a decline in the relative importance of conventional colleges and universities.

The participation of these other institutions in postsecondary education will be critical to the development of the new kinds of educational institutions discussed above. The requisite diversity of settings and experiences can only be achieved with the active engagement of these other social institutions. Conversely, the growing importance of the educational roles of institutions that are not primarily educational implies a need for more conscious and rigorous planning and management of the educational functions of these institutions. In general, I envisage both the need and the likelihood of a blurring of the boundaries between educational and noneducational institutions.

New Directions for Educational Management and Development
The rapid growth of higher education in the past two decades has been attended by an increasing interest in improving the management of educational institutions, in order to increase both the efficiency and effectiveness of educational enterprises. Not surprisingly, higher education has tended to try to adopt the scientific management practices of the modern business firm. Also, there has been a growing inclination in higher education to follow the example of many business firms in creating organizational development units within the organization and/or calling in professional consultants to assist in the tasks of managing innovation and increasing organizational effectiveness. Although these efforts are a promising beginning, knowledge and skills in higher education management and organizational development are limited in quality and tend to be localized within the institution of origin. In the noncollegiate sector, while proprietary (profit-making) institutions are, by their very nature, more business-like in their operation, on the whole, the available modern management and organizational-development resources are probably as limited as in the collegiate sector.

Yet as limited as existing management and organizational-development resources in higher education are, most of these are already obsolescent. The consequences of "limits to growth," both in the higher education system and in the social/ecological system as a whole, imply several years of turbulent change in the postsecondary education system. This era of rapid and dramatic change will pose problems of management and development in educational organizations whose solutions generally will not be found in historical precedent or the experience of the business world.

First, there is the now generally recognized fact that higher education, in the U.S. at least, has reached its own limits to growth. With the passing of the baby-boom generation into adulthood, enrollment in colleges and universities in the next several years can be expected to level off and even decline. For private institutions a depressed economy has diminished income from endowments, discouraged contributions, and dried up the flow of foundation grants —all reducing income while inflation has caused costs to skyrocket. Public institutions are only slightly better off, as taxpayers and legislators have become more budget-conscious while inflation again has taken its toll.

The short-term response to these conditions has included cost-cutting, retrenchment, and more active (sometimes cutthroat) competition among institutions to attract increasingly scarce dollars and students. These conditions are not a transient perturbation, however, but rather a secular trend which, even independently of the various

diversity, with deleterious consequences for the quality of post-secondary education as a whole.

A second major challenge for the development of educational management is suggested by the needs for unorthodox educational settings and the growing educational function of noneducational institutions. The creation of these new settings and new educational roles will lead to educational management problems to which conventional know-how will not be applicable.

These problems imply a need for some new directions in educational management and development. Existing management and organizational-development resources are inadequate to the task of change that lies ahead. This is a critical need which must be met if we are to exercise creative guidance over the future evolution of the postsecondary education system. Specifically, the need is for research on the dynamics of change in the postsecondary education system, combined with training and continuing education of managers and organizational-development professionals who can understand and facilitate the kinds of changes implied by "limits to growth" and the requirements of ecological education.[5]

New Educational Inter-Institutions

All of the needs for innovation in educational institutions described above imply, in turn, the need for new structures for inter-institutional cooperation in postsecondary education. In a system that has already attained its own limits to growth, debilitating competition and unnecessary duplication of effort become intolerable. Furthermore, many of the research, curriculum, and institutional needs of ecological education can be met in no other way than through inter-institutional cooperation. This suggests that if these needs are to be satisfied, the role of educational intersects and consortia will be important. Where these kinds of inter-institutions already exist, I see their role needing to be strengthened and where they do not, the need for their creation. The development of interdisciplinary research and curricula, student and faculty exchange, and "alternative campuses" are just a few areas where the contribution of educational inter-institutions would be valuable.

THE ESSENTIAL NEED: META-INSTITUTIONAL

In light of everything stated so far, I believe the most essential need is for the creation and development of one or more educational "meta-institutions," based on Schon's network concept and devoted to the creation of an adequate ecological education at the post-secondary level. Such a setting would work by facilitating and managing the activities of a network of individuals and institutions that belong to that community of interest I earlier identified as "beyond limits."

There is, to my knowledge, no organized setting which is (a) expressly concerned with the problem of transformation from a state of ecological crisis to a state of equilibrium, and (b) capable of facilitating the meaningful change and innovation in the postsecondary education system that ecological education would require. Without the catalytic assistance of such a meta-institution, the process of transformation in educational institutions—and by implication in other social institutions—will be slow in coming, erratic, and far more crisis-laden than it need be.

There are several reasons why the creation of such an educational meta-institution is both justified and needed. First, while an informal beyond-limits network is already in existence and does seem to be growing, the inchoate network needs some kind of central facilitator to become really productive.[6] Second, while the higher education system is in a state of inexorable change, this change must be directed properly if the postsecondary education system is to provide an adequate ecological education. That is, creation of an ecological education requires not merely cosmetic changes in higher education, but fundamental changes in curricular philosophy *and* institutional structure. The kind of change required is on the order of a Kuhnian "paradigm shift." While this change could happen spontaneously, it is far more likely to occur if a small but competent group is organized to actively promote it. Third, for change to occur, three kinds of activities must take place, but in an *integrated* manner. One is *networking* to bring all of the necessary ingredients of innovation into active communication. Another is *research* on curriculum design and the structure and dynamics of edu-

Like the gears and springs of a disassembled clock, the key ingredients for innovation are dispersed in a way that is not yet functional. Only when the parts are brought into active communication within some integrated system can meaningful movement occur. As I see it, then, the challenge facing us is to create a watchmaker who can put the pieces of the clock together and make it tick. I do not doubt that this can be done; but besides adequate funding, it will require dedication, skill, and creativity.

CHAPTER 14

IN CONCLUSION

or several volumes. I am not capable of it, nor do I know of anyone who is. Until recently most people were not even aware of the limits-to-growth problem. Indeed, many intelligent and sincere individuals persist in denying its existence. A handful of people and organizations have moved beyond the limits to growth and begun to think critically about the awesome problem of peaceful transformation to an equilibrium society, but their pioneer efforts have barely scratched the surface.

Spaceship Earth is sailing in dangerous waters, on a collision course with disaster. Many of the passengers and crew do not—perhaps will not—recognize the danger that lies ahead, and the captain steadfastly denies its existence. Still, some of those aboard see the crisis and are working to change the ship's course. But, not being experienced sailors, those who want to save the ship do not know exactly how to change the course. Even assuming that they could do this, none of them knows how to navigate the ship through the unexplored waters that they hope will lead to a safer and happier voyage for all. Even though time is running out, the immediate task for those who want to save Spaceship Earth is to learn how to learn how to navigate.

In this book I have tried to provide a conceptual framework for a new education to respond to the challenge of ecocrisis and to help us to learn how to learn the art of planetary navigation. In this final chapter I will restate the major immediate goals for those who want to become ecological educators. The following are four key goals for the near-term activities of ecological educators:

Not merely to further the "growth debate" but to go beyond limits. Merely promoting more debate about the limits to growth is too timid and unfruitful a goal for ecological educators to pursue, especially in view of the limited resources currently available for our work. Rather, we must bend our efforts toward the cultivation and further development of the beyond-limits network. This is a community of interest less concerned with the academic question of whether there are limits to growth than with the challenging task of designing and achieving possible equilibrium futures. Our goal must be to *elevate* the discourse on growth and equilibrium from the whether-limits level (Is the world round?) to the beyond-limits level (How shall we navigate?).

To educate people to be competent in finding solutions to the problems of growth and equilibrium rather than to sell a particular position on limits to growth. This point cannot be emphasized strongly enough. It is possible, and often necessary, to attack the critical and complex problems of growth and equilibrium at the beyond-limits level without being compelled first to genuflect at the altar of Rome (the Club of).

Because the seriousness of our overall goal is at no less a level than planetary survival, a highly dogmatic, even canonical, approach to educational transformation might seem justified. That is, because the human predicament is apparently so urgent, it might seem necessary that we indoctrinate our students with a prescribed and catholic set of ideas, feelings, and patterns of behavior. The fact is, the very nature of the emerging crisis rules out such an approach. The capacity for *learning* enhances—indeed, may be essential to—the ability of a complex system to cope with stress and create and maintain a long-term equilibrium. The global social/ecological system, to achieve and maintain a state of equilibrium, must be capable not only of simple learning but even of the higher levels of Learning II and Learning III. A canonical education is simply inconsistent with this requirement.

To create a new model of the educated person. Historical concepts of the *educated person*—the philosopher king and the Renaissance man—are no longer applicable to the contemporary human and planetary condition. While no single unifying hypothesis of human nature has yet emerged to replace these earlier concepts,[1] a recent Stanford Research Institute study entitled "Changing Images of Man" found evidence that a new dominant image of man is coming.[2] More important, the SRI report argued that the "increasingly serious dilemmas of industrialized society appear to *require* for their ultimate resolution a drastically changed image of man-on-earth."[3]

In addition to the need for a new image of man, there is a need for new concepts and standards of *competence.* The general loss of public confidence in our political, economic, and social institutions and leadership has been widely documented and discussed. Our gods have developed a critical (and probably terminal) case of "clay feet."[4] Under these circumstances, Donald Michael says that we "have to

is only an initial attempt, and its ingredients are tenuous at best. A major goal for ecological educators must be the further development and clarification of such a model.

To develop the processes of an ecological education. Ultimately we need to develop an ecological education that can produce the transformers defined by the emerging new model. Further, we cannot wait for a perfect model of the transformer to be created before developing the instructional techniques and technology required to educate such people. No such final image is likely to be achieved, since the concept of *educated* will continuously evolve as the conditions of society change, as our understanding and knowledge of human potential expand, and as our standards of competency become more sophisticated. Even while our conception of the transformer is being developed, there will be a critical need for at least a *more* educated leadership and public. Even though we do not know exactly what a transformer is or what such a person needs to know, I hope I have demonstrated that we do have enough of an idea to start to put together the pieces of an adequate ecological education.

•

Many will say that the problems facing us now are too urgent for us to wait for the slow and inefficient processes of education to help solve them. Confronted with crisis, leaders will call for *action,* not for *learning.* It will be argued that government, business, and other institutions directly involved with the critical problems that concern us must act to solve them immediately. But will those institutions act to deal with these problems? And if so, will they be competent to deal with them? To say that our existing institutions and leadership *must* solve our problems is to say that a drowning man *must* swim to be saved. If the man does not know how to swim, the urgency of the situation may not be enough to make him learn. Even if he knows how to swim, and does, he may still be doomed if he does not know how to navigate, if he does not know in which direction to go. The alternative to swimming is sinking, and the alternative is no less real for being unthinkable. Our institutions and current leadership are responding slowly to the crisis of our times, and the response so far has been mainly *more of the same.* The problems facing us are enormously complex and difficult. "More of the same" is not going to make things better; in fact, it is likely to make things worse. We can survive the crisis and solve the problems that confront us, but only by learning to understand ourselves and our world in a new way and by learning to do things we have never done before in ways that we have never practiced before. The necessity of *learning* implies the necessity of *education,* albeit of a kind not generally represented by our conventional educational system. I will grant that education may not be able to solve our problems. In fact, our problems may turn out to be insoluble or at least unsolved. But if they can be solved, I believe that education can and must have an important role to play in finding the solutions.

There is another side to the coin, though. A huge educational system already exists. It represents both an enormous capital investment and the second largest item of national spending after defense. If we are going to spend scores of billions of dollars on education, we have the right and responsibility to demand that our educational system be as responsive as possible to the most critical problems facing our society, especially when these are problems that threaten the very survival of that society. The current system falls far short of this standard. Whether or not education can actually solve our urgent problems, shouldn't it at least do its share?

EPILOG

tion, there inevitably comes a critical turning point whose outcome determines the full birth or death of the inchoate global Mind. This turning point is experienced as an age (really just a moment in evolutionary time) of global ecological crisis. Passing through this great crisis, most planets harboring intelligent life either destroy themselves immediately or survive merely to decay slowly in the stagnant back waters of cosmic evolution. A few, however, break through the global crisis and make the quantum leap to the higher stages of planetary evolution. Their global Minds succeed in purging themselves of the subversive ideas that threaten to shatter them and go on to attain the next higher step up the ladder of cosmic consciousness. The fortunate planets that survive this great transformation achieve a level and kind of power of which few men even dream. They embark on a new journey of growth that makes the petty materialism of their adolescence seem the foolish game of a child.

I believe that the Earth is now on the threshold of that turning point.

Can our world survive its age of crisis? Can we halt the mindless plunder of the planet's limited stores? Can we protect our fellow living creatures from unnecessary extinction? Can we restore the purity and vitality of the air, water, and land? Can we end the scourge of violence and war? Can we cure the massive insanity that grips the global Mind? Can we achieve the great transformation to a higher level of planetary consciousness? I do not know. For all I have written here, I do not know the answers to these questions.

There was a time when I felt anger, hatred for the lunatic devastation and corruption I saw going on around me. I wanted to fight violence with force, insensitivity with hardness, greed with arrogance. I do not feel that way anymore. Then there was a time when I felt optimism, even euphoria. I felt confident that the collapse of the evil system of exploitation and destruction was built-in, inevitable. I do not feel that way anymore.

Then I came to feel despair, the complete loss of hope. I learned through bitter experience that the forces that enslave and progressively destroy human beings and life itself—fear, guilt, insecurity, the sense of inferiority, and the escape to materialism and willful apathy —were powerful forces that the greatest amount of determination, patience, wisdom, and love could not necessarily overcome. But I do not feel that way anymore either.

What I have come to feel is the certainty of uncertainty, that our present situation is so unstable that there is no way to anticipate what the final outcome will be. We are living at one of the few truly crucial moments in our planet's history, like the moment of creation, the moment when the first living cell was born, the moment when the first animal crawled out of the sea onto the land, the moment of man's emergence. We stand at the threshold of either utopia or oblivion, not knowing which. Pascal chose to believe in God because he believed that he was thereby covered for the hereafter. With neither optimism nor pessimism, I have decided to try to practice and pursue determination, patience, wisdom, and love because they seem to be the best bet for the future.

NOTES

PROLOG
1. G. De Bell, *Environmental Handbook*, 1970.

CHAPTER 1
1. Falk, *Endangered Planet*, 1971.
2. S. Brubaker, *To Live on Earth*, 1972.
3. *Webster's New Collegiate Dictionary*. Springfield, Mass., G. & C. Merriam Co., 1958.
4. Brubaker, *To Live on Earth*, 1972, p. 79.
5. Dubos, "The Limits of Adaptability," in G. De Bell, *Environmental Handbook*, 1970, p. 28.
6. Commoner, *Closing Circle*, 1971, pp. 15–17.
7. Commission on Population Growth and the American Future, *Population and the American Future*, 1972, pp. 1–2.
8. Hendricks, "Food from the Land," in Committee on Resources and Man, *Resources and Man*, 1969, p. 84.
9. Ryther, "Photosynthesis," pp. 72–76.
10. M. Overman, *Water*, p. 9.
11. Thomas Lovering, "Mineral Resources from the Land," in Committee on Resources and Man, *Resources and Man*, 1969, p. 117.
12. G. Hardin, *Exploring New Ethics*, p. 172.
13. Falk, *Endangered Planet*, p. 105.

CHAPTER 2

1. I am indebted to Dennis Meadows for suggesting most of the attributes in this list.
2. Commoner. *Closing Circle*, p. 29.
3. Curle, *Making Peace*, p. 1.
4. Ibid.
5. Ibid.
6. From *Steps to an Ecology of Mind* by Gregory Bateson. Copyright © 1972 by Chandler Publishing Company. Reprinted by permission of Chandler Publishing Company, New York. p. 109.
7. Ibid., pp. 462, 487; emphasis added.
8. Shepard, "Introduction: Ecology and Man—A Viewpoint," in P. Shepard and D. McKinley, *Subversive Science*, copyright © 1969, Houghton Mifflin Company, pp. 2–3; emphasis added.
9. From *Design with Nature* by Ian L. McHarg. Copyright © 1969 by Ian McHarg. Reprinted by permission of Doubleday & Company, Inc. pp. 26–27; emphasis added.
10. Mumford, *Myth of the Machine*, p. 413.
11. Illich, *Deschooling Society*, p. 114.
12. Lilly, *Center of the Cyclone*, p. 3.
13. Falk, *Endangered Planet*, p. 28; emphasis added.
14. D. H. Meadows et al., *Limits to Growth*, p. 195; emphasis added.

CHAPTER 3

1. Bateson, *Steps*, pp. 455–56.
2. Reprinted from *Urban Dynamics* by Forrester by permission of the M.I.T. Press, Cambridge, Massachusetts, p. 109.
3. Commoner, *Closing Circle*, pp. 75–77.
4. Ibid.
5. Teratogenesis is the generation of "birth defects" as a result of embryonic development, as distinguished from mutagenesis, where defects are of genetic origin.
6. L. Brown. "Rich Countries," pp. 158–59.
7. Ibid., p. 159.
8. *Time*, 26 November 1973; p. 26; emphasis added. Reprinted by permission from TIME, The Weekly Newsmagazine; Copyright Time Inc.

CHAPTER 4

1. D. H. Meadows et al., *The Limits to Growth.*
2. Reprinted with permission from *World Dynamics* Second Edition, by Jay W. Forrester. Copyright © 1973 Wright-Allen Press, Inc., Cambridge, Mass. 02142
3. The second requirement results from the assumption that it is desirable to maximize the lifetimes of people and capital. It is

11. G. Hardin, *Exploring New Ethics,* 1972; pp. 150–51.
12. Passell, Roberts, and Ross, review of *Limits to Growth.*
13. Schon, "Forecasting," p. 767.
14. Ibid.
15. Passell, Roberts, and Ross, review of *Limits to Growth.*
16. Lovering, "Mineral Resources," In Committee on Resources and Man, *Resources and Man,* 1969, pp. 124–25.
17. Ibid., p. 128.
18. Ibid.
19. Prices have been rising especially rapidly in recent years as many of the social and environmental costs of resource exploitation have become internalized.
20. A fivefold increase in petroleum prices over a two-year period has led to enormous growth in *talk* about conservation but relatively little automatic adjustment in consumption. In 1974 U.S. consumption of oil declined by about 2 percent, compared to the secular trend of several percent growth per annum. Much of this decline can be attributed to a general economic depression. So far, most of the cost of needed conservation has been unequally and unfairly allocated to those who are least well off, those who can least afford it, those who are least responsible for waste and inefficiency, and those on whom growth has traditionally conferred the smallest benefits and greatest costs.
21. Lovering, "Mineral Resources," p. 128.

CHAPTER 5
1. Chen, Lagler, et al., *Growth Policy*, 1974, pp. 4–5.
2. Kuhn, *Scientific Revolutions*, 1970, p. 150.
3. Ibid., pp. 157–58.
4. Ibid.

CHAPTER 6
1. This is a somewhat recursive statement since, as Forrester and Bateson and before them, Kant, among others, have emphasized, our only awareness of "physical" reality is via our conceptual models of of the systems that comprise it.
2. See V. Parsegian, *This Cybernetic World*, 1966.
3. J. Singh, *Great Ideas in Information Theory*, 1966, Dover Publications, Inc. pp. 8–9.
4. If we have three messages—m_1, m_2, and m_3—whose individual probabilities of occurrence are p_1, p_2, and p_3, the probability of occurrence of the sequence of all three messages ($m_s = m_1 m_2 m_3$) is equal to the *product* of the three separate probabilities: $p_s = p_1 \times p_2 \times p_3$. But the logarithm of this equation becomes a *sum:* $\log(p_s) = \log(p_1) + \log(p_2) + \log(p_3)$.
5. Bateson, *Steps*, 1972, p. 250.
6. Note that a message could result in an *increase* in entropy going from state X to X', which would imply that the message conveyed negative information; indeed, this kind of message is precisely what the communications engineer refers to as "noise."
7. The classic illustration of this is Sherlock Holmes, who was always capable of extracting vastly greater amounts of information from a given clue than his colleagues, Dr. Watson or Inspector Lastrade.
8. See J. Singh, *Great Ideas*, 1966; G. Bateson, *Steps*, 1972; M. Tribus and C. McIrvine, "Energy and Information," 1971; and E. Fermi, *Thermodynamics*, 1956.
9. The fact that the term "information source" is used in this diagram should not be taken as contradicting the earlier assertion that it is messages, not information, that flow from point to point. As noted in the discussion of information and entropy, some messages convey negative entropy to the recipient; we call this *information*. Other messages convey positive entropy, which we call noise. It is necessary in this diagram to discriminate between the sources of messages that convey information and those that convey noise. For brevity, these are

simply labeled "information source" and "noise sources," re-spectively.

10. See J. Singh, *Great Ideas,* 1966; and J. Pierce, "Communica-tion," 1972.
11. Powers, "Feedback," 1973.
12. Ibid.
13. See G. Bateson, *Steps,* 1972; W. Powers, "Feedback," 1973· V

18. A. Whitehead and B. Russell, *Principia Mathematica,* 1919.
19. We assume that the learning system does not receive signals from the comparators of the control system until these are actually translated into output by the effector functions, which output is then detected by the sensor functions. This assump-tion is consistent with Wiener's assertion that learning—in the cybernetic sense—results from *actual* and not merely *expected* performance.
20. Bateson, *Steps,* 1972, p. 289.
21. Ibid., p. 217; emphasis added.
22. Ibid., p. 218.
23. Ibid., p. 208.
24. Ibid., p. 300.
25. Ibid., pp. 303–304.
26. Ibid.
27. See G. Bateson, *Steps,* 1972; and N. Weiner, *Human Use,* 1971.
28. A. Bandura, *Principles,* 1969, p. 72.
29. It is also the basic purpose of this discussion to reduce or elimi-nate the distinction between "eco" and "psycho."

CHAPTER 7
1. Ian McHarg, "Values, Process and Form," in R. Disch, *Ecologi-cal Conscience,* 1970, pp. 27–28; emphasis added.
2. Becker, *Heavenly City,* 1958.
3. Einstein and Infeld, *Evolution of Physics,* 1938, p. 295.
4. McHarg, "Values," in R. Disch, *Ecological Conscience,* 1970, pp. 29–31; emphasis added.

5. Ibid., p. 31; emphasis added.
6. Sometimes McHarg also calls this "fitness."
7. Brostow, "Between Laws of Thermodynamics", 1972, pp. 124–25.
8. Monod, *Chance and Necessity*, translated by Austryn Wainhouse, published by Alfred A. Knopf, Inc., 1971, p. 19.
9. Brostow, "Between Laws," 1972.
10. J. Singh, *Great Ideas*, 1966, p. 81.
11. V. Parsegian, *This Cybernetic World*, 1973, p. 201.
12. Ibid.
13. Monod, *Chance and Necessity*, p. 94.
14. Ibid., pp. 20–21.
15. In addition, Monod cites the phenomenon of *autonomous morphogenesis*. I felt that this third aspect was not important to the discussion here.
16. Monod, *Chance and Necessity*, pp. 21–22.
17. Ibid., pp. 23–24.
18. Ibid., pp. 116–17.
19. Ibid., p. 43.
20. Ibid., p. 44.
21. In the hardworld, *nothing* may be *no thing*, but in the softworld, *nothing* is a message.
22. Monod, *Chance and Necessity*, pp. 165–66.
23. Skinner, *Beyond Freedom and Dignity*, 1971, published by Alfred A. Knopf, Inc., p. 123.
24. Ibid.
25. Bateson, *Steps*, p. 444.
26. Ibid.
27. Skinner, *Beyond*, p. 124.
28. Bateson, *Steps*, p. 482.
29. Ibid.
30. Ibid., p. 483.
31. L. White, "The Historical Roots," 1967; Reprinted in G. De Bell, *Environmental Handbook*, 1970; also in P. Shepard and D. McKinley, *Subversive Science*, 1969.
32. G. Bateson, *Steps*, p. 462.
33. Dubos, "Humanizing the Earth," 1973, p. 769.
34. I. Velikovsky, *Worlds in Collision*, 1950.

CHAPTER 8
1. Niehardt, *Black Elk Speaks*, 1972, copyright John G. Neihardt 1932, 1959, 1961, p. 181; emphasis added.
2. Festinger, *Theory*, 1957.

3. Toffler, *Future Shock*, 1970.
4. Commission on Population Growth and the American Future, *Population*, 1972, p. 36.
5. Cantril and Roll, *Hopes and Fears*, 1971.
6. Falk, *Endangered Planet*, 1971, p. 46.
7. Kenneth Boulding, "Economics of the Coming Spaceship Earth." in G. De Bell, *Environmental Handbook*, 1970, p. 100.

Bell, *Environmental Handbook*, 1970, p. 36.
15. Ibid., p. 37.
16. Ibid., pp. 43–44.
17. Crowe, "Tragedy Revisited," 1969.
18. Schelling, "Ecology of Micromotives," 1971.
19. Rawls, *A Theory of Justice*, 1972.
20. Schelling, "Ecology," p. 77.
21. Kagan, "Magical Aura," 1971, p. 93.
22. Laing, *The Politics of Experience*, 1967, p. 118.
23. Ibid., p. 121.
24. Rosenhan, "Reply," April 1973, p. 366.
25. Rosenhan, "On Being Sane," January 1973, p. 257.
26. Ibid.
27. Weil, *Natural Mind*, 1972, p. 127.
28. Castaneda, *Teachings of Don Juan*, 1969, pp. 127–32. Originally published by the University of California Press; reprinted by permission of The Regents of the University of California.
29. I learned this question from Dr. Zev Wanderer of the Center for Behavior Therapy in Los Angeles. This was Wanderer's standard reply to his clients' inevitable question, "What's wrong with me?"
30. Hunter, *Storming of the Mind*, 1972, pp. 19–20.
31. From *The Storming of the Mind: Inside the Consciousness Revolution* by Robert Hunter. Copyright © 1971 by Robert Hunter. Reprinted by permission of Doubleday & Company, Inc.; A. Weil, *Natural Mind*, 1972; C. Castaneda, *Teachings*, 1969, *Separate Reality*, 1972, *Journey to Ixtlan*, 1972; J. Lilly,

Center of the Cyclone, 1972; W. Thompson, *Edge of History*, 1972, *Passages about Earth*, 1974; R. Laing, *Politics*, 1967; A. Watts, *Psychotherapy*, 1971; Baba Ram Dass, *Remember*, 1971; G. Bateson, *Steps*, 1972.

32. C. Tart, "States of Consciousness," 1972.
33. Ornstein, *Psychology of Consciousness*, 1973.
34. Weil, *Natural Mind*, 1972.
35. Hunter, *Storming of the Mind*, 1972, pp. 111–12.
36. Kuhn, *Scientific Revolutions*, 1970.
37. A paradoxical question like "What is the sound of one hand clapping?"

CHAPTER 9
1. W. Francis, *A Report*, 1973.
2. Spilhaus, "Ecolibrium," 1972.
3. Rawls, *Theory*, 1972.
4. Callahan, "Ethics," 1972.
5. Skinner, *Walden Two*, Macmillan Publishing Co., Inc. p. 136.
6. Ibid., p. 196.
7. Ibid., p. 255.
8. R. Boguslaw, *New Utopians*, 1965.
9. Dostoevski, *Notes from Underground*, in P. Richter, *Utopias*, 1971, p. 191.
10. Bateson, *Steps*, 1972, p. 486.
11. Quoted by H. Daly, "Towards a New Economics."
12. Commission on Population Growth and the American Future, *Population*, p. 110; P. Passell and L. Ross, "Don't Knock," 1972, p. 64.
13. Quoted by H. Daly in "Towards a New Economics."
14. Recall that Norbert Weiner decreed that the purpose of "control" *is* the control—prevention or reduction—of entropy. See Weiner, *Human Use*, 1971.
15. Skinner, *Beyond*, p. 136.
16. Quoted by G. Hardin, *Exploring*, 1972, p. 103.
17. Boguslaw, *New Utopians*, 1965.
18. The difference between algorithmic and heuristic rules can be illustrated by the game of chess. The algorithmic rules of the game are those which define the allowable moves of the various pieces, the nature of checkmate, stalemate, and so forth. The heuristic rules are actually strategic themes: control the center, don't sacrifice the queen, beware of the "poisoned pawn," and so on.
19. Leiss, *Domination*, 1972, p. 194; emphasis added.

20. E. Schumacher, *Small Is Beautiful,* 1973.
21. P. Goldmark, "Communication and Community," 1972.

CHAPTER 10
1. Bell, *The Coming of Post-Industrial Society; A Venture in Social Forecasting,* New York, 1973.
2. I am indebted to William Bergquist for suggesting this disti...

9. Ibid., pp. 189–90.
10. Ibid., p. 30; emphasis added.
11. Ibid., p. 190.
12. Ibid.
13. Adapted from Schon, *Beyond,* p. 114.

CHAPTER 11
1. Sarason, *Creation of Settings.*
2. Boulding, "Intersects."
3. Michael, *On Learning to Plan.*
4. K. Chen, K. Lagler, et al., *Growth Policy.*
5. Michael, *On Learning.*
6. Thompson, *Passages.*
7. Castro, "We Have Failed," reprinted with an introduction by Lee Lockwood in the *New York Review of Books,* 24 September 1970.
8. Sarason, *Creation,* p. 10.
9. Ibid.
10. Ibid.
11. Watzlawick, Weakland, and Fisch, *Change,* p. 19.
12. Quoted by S. Sarason, *Creation,* p. 10.
13. The first six roles in this table come from Schon, *Beyond.*
14. Michael, *On Learning.*

CHAPTER 12
1. Straus, "Departments and Disciplines."
2. See Markley et al., *Changing Images;* and Elgin, "Third American Frontier."

3. *Postsecondary Education:* This includes not only formal under-graduate, graduate, and professional degree programs, but also fellowships, internships, in-service training, institutes, work-shops, adult and extension education, and educational pro-grams carried on through various nonschool organizations and mass media. Postsecondary education can be divided into two main sectors: collegiate and noncollegiate. The collegiate sector includes all two- and four-year, public and private colleges and universities. The noncollegiate sector consists of all other insti-tutions that offer educational programs beyond the secondary school level, including libraries, museums, recreational pro-grams, proprietary schools, and vocational and professional in-house training programs.

4. This depends on subsequent reinforcement. Reading is a skill that is retained because it is continually used and reinforced; high school French doesn't last long if you never use it again.

5. Torbert, *Learning from Experience,* p. 33.

6. The only Learning IV objective which we can identify is the cultivation or evolution of those systems or minds which achieve Learning III. On the other hand, Learning 0 objectives would be those already built into existing control or informa-tion-processing systems; since ecological education is implicitly concerned with change, it has no particular Learning 0 objec-tives.

7. This is not to imply that the constituents of a pattern of be-havior are causally connected to the pattern as a whole in a simple or strict way. Rather, the constituents are merely ele-ments in the gestalt of behavior-in-context; the absence or limitation of some desirable behavior pattern within a given area or among a given group may result from deficiencies in any or all of the constituents. Thus, for example, in a given area, attitudes toward family planning might be favorable, while the actual practice of effective birth control might be low because of widespread ignorance of the best methods or how to acquire them. Or, among a given group, practice of effective birth control might be fairly high, while the pre-vailing attitude toward family planning might not be ex-pressed very enthusiastically or favorably, the result being a negative, or at least neutral, spillover effect on other groups.

8. Events that threaten existing *learning* functions constitute *metaproblems.* Metaproblems cannot be solved by problem-solving, but only by metaproblem-solving. The phases of meta-problem-solving are probably similar to those of problem-solv-

ing, but they occur at the next higher order of logical type; that is, they would overlap Learning II and Learning III. In a sense, Castaneda's "problem" resulting from his conversation with Don Juan, depicted in the latter part of Chapter 9, is actually a metaproblem, which explains why his efforts at problem-solving were unsuccessful.

9. Schon, *Beyond*, p. 201.

17. Perhaps the ethos of ecological education should be "picaresque." See Meeker, *Comedy of Survival.*
18. Personal communication.
19. Alinsky, *Rules for Radicals,* pp. 68–69.
20. Center for Continuing Education, *Learning Society.*
21. Shane, *Educational Significance.*
22. In one survey of self-proclaimed "futurists," 90 percent were male and 97 percent were white.

CHAPTER 13

1. Note that the Environmental Education Act provides federal money for certain activities related to curriculum development at the elementary and secondary level, but not at the post-secondary level; nor does any other federal program provide such support.
2. A few innovative model settings do exist: the College of the Atlantic; the University of Wisconsin at Green Bay; the new College VIII at the University of California at Santa Cruz; Evergreen State College; Hampshire College; and Worcester Polytechnic Institute. Also the Lindisfarne Association; Empire State College; the University of California at San Diego's courses through newspapers; the University Without Walls; Esalen Institute; the Aspen Institute for Humanistic Studies; the Committee for the Future's New Worlds Training and Education Center, and "Syncons"; the Futures Lab of Earthrise, Inc. and Roger Williams College; the United Nations University; Habitat Institute.
3. Huckfeldt, *Forecast of Changes.*

4. One way this could be done would be for the U.S. Office of Education to require higher education institutions receiving federal funds to demonstrate their consideration of "environmental impact" in both their curricula and institutional management practices. To my knowledge, OE does not now do this, but the National Environmental Policy Act suggests that it has both a mandate and an obligation to do so.
5. A system dynamics approach could be very useful. See M. Garet, "Educational Policy"; and Fey and Knight, "Dynamics."
6. Schon, *Beyond,* pp. 189, 199.

CHAPTER 14

1. Aspen Institute for Humanistic Studies, Prospectus for a conference on "The Educated Person in the Contemporary World." For a report on this conference see *New York Times,* 10 August 1974.
2. Markley et al., *Changing Images,* 1974.
3. Ibid.; emphasis added.
4. See "Theory Deserts the Forecasters," *Business Week,* 29 June 1974.
5. Personal communication.

BIBLIOGRAPHY

ing, 1971.

Bandura, Albert. *Principles of Behavior Modification*. New York: Holt, Rinehart & Winston, 1969.

Bateson, Gregory. *Steps to an Ecology of Mind*. New York: Ballantine, 1972.

Becker, Carl. *The Heavenly City of the Eighteenth Century Philosophers*. New Haven: Yale Univ. Press, 1958.

Bell, Daniel. *The Coming of Post-Industrial Society; A Venture in Social Forecasting*. New York: Basic Books, 1973.

Boguslaw, Robert. *The New Utopians; A Study of System Design and Social Change*. Englewood Cliffs: Prentice-Hall, 1965.

Boulding, Kenneth. "Intersects," in The Conference Board. *Challenge to Leadership; Managing in a Changing World*. New York: Free Press, 1973.

Brostow, Witold. "Between Laws of Thermodynamics and Coding Information." *Science*, 13 October 1972.

Brown, Lester. "Rich Countries and Poor." *Daedalus*, Fall 1973.

Brubaker, Sterling. *To Live on Earth*. New York: Mentor, 1972.

Burgess, Anthony. *A Clockwork Orange*. New York: Ballantine, 1971.

Callahan, Daniel. "Ethics and Population Limitation." *Science*, 4 February 1972.

Cantril, Albert H., and Charles W. Roll. *The Hopes and Fears of the American People*. New York: Universe Books, 1971.

Carson, Rachel. *Silent Spring*. Boston: Houghton-Mifflin, 1962.

Castaneda, Carlos. *The Teachings of Don Juan; A Yaqui Way of Knowledge*. New York: Ballantine, 1969.

_____. *A Separate Reality; Further Conversations with Don Juan*. New York: Pocket Books, 1972.

_____. *Journey to Ixtlan; The Lessons of Don Juan*. New York: Simon & Schuster, 1972.

Center for Continuing Education. *The Learning Society*. South Bend: Notre Dame Univ., 1973.

Chen, Kan; Karl F. Lagler et al. *Growth Policy; Population, Environment, and Beyond*. Ann Arbor: Univ. of Michigan Press, 1974.

Clarke, Arthur C. *Childhood's End*. New York: Ballantine, 1972.

Commission on Population Growth and the American Future. *Population and the American Future*. New York: Signet, 1972.

Committee on Resources and Man. National Academy of Sciences/ National Research Council. *Resources and Man*. San Francisco: Freeman, 1969.

Commoner, Barry. *The Closing Circle*. New York: Knopf, 1971.

Crowe, Beryl. "The Tragedy of the Commons Revisited." *Science*, 28 November 1969.

Curle, Adam. *Making Peace*. London: Tavistock, 1972.

Daly, Herman. "Toward a New Economics: Questioning Growth." *ZPG National Reporter*, III, 3.

De Bell, Garrett, ed. *The Environmental Handbook*. New York: Ballantine, 1970.

Disch, Robert, ed. *The Ecological Conscience; Values for Survival*. Englewood Cliffs: Prentice-Hall, 1970.

Dubos, René. "Humanizing the Earth." *Science*, 23 February 1973.

Einstein, Albert, and Leopold Infeld. *The Evolution of Physics*. New York: Simon & Schuster, 1938.

Elgin, Duane S. *The Third American Frontier—Proposed Strategies for Exploring Human Potentials*. Menlo Park, Cal.: Duane S. Elgin, Stanford Research Institute, 1974.

Falk, Richard. *This Endangered Planet*. New York: Random House, 1971.

Fermi, Enrico. *Thermodynamics*. New York: Dover, 1956.

Festinger, Leon. *A Theory of Cognitive Dissonance*. Evanston: Row, Peterson, 1957.

Fey, Willard R., and John E. Knight. "The Dynamics of Educational Institutions." *Proceedings of Summer Simulation Conferences*. La Jolla, Cal.: Simulation Councils, Inc., 1973.

Forrester, Jay. *Urban Dynamics*. Cambridge: MIT Press, 1969.

Forrester, Jay. *World Dynamics*. Cambridge: Wright-Allen Press, 1971.

Francis, Walton J. *A Report on Measurement and the Quality of Life,* and *The Implications for Government of the Limits to Growth.* U.S. Dept. of H.E.W., January 1973.

Garet, Michael S. "Educational Policy and System Dynamics." *Journal of Research and Development in Education,* Winter 1974.

Goldmark, Peter C. "Communication and Community." *Scientific American,* September 1972.

tion. Boulder: Western Interstate Commission for Higher Education, 1973.

Hunter, Robert. *The Storming of the Mind; Inside the Consciousness Revolution.* Garden City, N.Y.: Anchor Books, 1972.

Huxley, Aldous. *Brave New World.* Garden City: Doubleday, 1932.

Illich, Ivan. *Deschooling Society.* New York: Harper & Row, 1971.

Janov, Arthur. *The Primal Scream.* New York: Putnam, 1970.

Kagan, Jerome. "The Magical Aura of IQ." *Saturday Review,* 4 December 1971.

Kuhn, Thomas. *The Structure of Scientific Revolutions.* Chicago: Univ. of Chicago Press, 1970.

Laing, Ronald D. *The Politics of Experience.* New York: Ballantine, 1967.

Leiss, William. *The Domination of Nature.* New York: Braziller, 1972.

Lilly, John C. *The Center of the Cyclone; An Autobiography of Inner Space.* New York: Julian Press, 1972.

Lowry, Ritchie P. "Towards a Radical View of the Ecological Crisis." *Environmental Affairs,* I, 2.

Marien, Michael. "Daniel Bell and the End of Normal Science." *The Futurist,* December 1973.

Markley, O.W. et al. *Changing Images of Man.* Policy Research Report 4. Menlo Park, Cal.: Stanford Research Institute, 1974.

McHarg, Ian L. *Design with Nature.* Garden City: Doubleday, 1971.

Meadows, Donella H.; Dennis L. Meadows; Jorgen Randers; and William Behrens. *The Limits to Growth.* New York: Universe Books, 1972.

Meeker, Joseph W. *The Comedy of Survival.* New York: Scribner's, 1974.

Michael, Donald. *On Learning to Plan—and Planning to Learn.* San Francisco: Jossey-Bass, 1973.

Moncrief, Lewis. "The Cultural Basis for Our Environmental Crisis." *Science,* 30 October 1970.

Monod, Jacques. *Chance and Necessity.* New York: Knopf, 1971.

Mumford, Lewis. *The Myth of the Machine; The Pentagon of Power.* New York: Harcourt, Brace & Jovanovich, 1970.

Niehardt, John G. *Black Elk Speaks.* New York: Pocket Books, 1972.

Ornstein, Robert. *The Psychology of Consciousness.* San Francisco: W. H. Freeman, 1973.

Orwell, George. *1984.* New York: Harcourt, Brace, 1949.

Overman, Michael. *Water.* Garden City: Doubleday, 1969.

Parsegian, V. L. *This Cybernetic World of Men, Machines, and Earth Systems.* Garden City: Anchor Books, 1973.

Passell, Peter; Marc Roberts; and Leonard Ross. "The Limits to Growth." *New York Times Book Review,* 2 April 1972.

Passell, Peter; and Leonard Ross. "Don't Knock the Two Trillion Dollar Economy." *New York Times Magazine,* 5 March 1972.

Pierce, John R. "Communication." *Scientific American,* September 1972.

Powers, W.T. "Feedback: Beyond Behaviorism." *Science,* 26 January 1973.

Rawls, John. *A Theory of Justice.* Cambridge: Harvard Univ. Press, 1971.

Reich, Charles. *The Greening of America.* New York: Bantam Books, 1971.

Richter, Peyton E. *Utopias, Social Ideals and Communal Experiments.* Boston: Holbrook Press, 1971.

Rogers, Everett. *Diffusion of Innovations.* New York: Free Press, 1969.

Rosenhan, D.L. "On Being Sane in Insane Places." *Science,* 19 January 1973.

——————. "Reply to Letters." *Science,* 27 April 1973.

Ryther, John H. "Photosynthesis and Fish Production in the Sea." *Science,* 30 October 1969.

Sarason, Seymour. *The Creation of Settings and the Future Societies.* San Francisco: Jossey-Bass, 1973.

Schelling, Thomas C. "On the Ecology of Micromotives." *The Public Interest,* Fall 1971.

Schon, Donald A. "Forecasting and Technological Forecasting." *Daedalus,* Summer 1967.

_____. *Beyond the Stable State.* New York: Random House, 1971.

Schumacher, E. F. *Small is Beautiful; Economics as if People Mattered.* New York: Harper & Row, 1973.

Shane, Harold G. *The Educational Significance of the Future.* Washington: World Future Society, 1972.

~~Sh___ _ R___ ___ _ D____ M_K____ _The S_b____ _ S_____ E____~~

Straus, Robert. "Departments and Disciplines: Stasis and Change." *Science,* 30 November 1973.

Tart, C.T. "States of Consciousness and State-Specific Sciences." *Science,* 16 June 1972.

Thompson, William Irwin. *At the Edge of History; Speculations on the Transformation of Culture.* New York: Harper & Row, 1971.
_____. *Passages About Earth.* New York: Harper & Row, 1974.

Toffler, Alvin. *Future Shock.* New York: Random House, 1970.

Torbert, William. *Learning from Experience; Toward Consciousness.* New York: Columbia Univ. Press, 1972.

Tribus, Myron and Edward C. McIrvine. "Energy and Information." *Scientific American,* September 1971.

Velikovsky, Immanuel. *Worlds in Collision.* Garden City: Doubleday, 1950.

Watts, Alan. *Psychotherapy East and West.* New York: Ballantine, 1971.

Watzlawick, Paul; John H. Weakland; and Richard Fisch. *Change; Principles of Problem Formation and Problem Resolution.* New York: Norton, 1974.

Weil, Andrew. *The Natural Mind.* Boston: Houghton-Mifflin, 1972.

Weiner, Norbert. *The Human Use of Human Beings.* New York: Avon Books, 1971.

Wells, H.G. *A Modern Utopia.* London: Chapman & Hall, 1905.

White, Lynn, Jr. "The Historical Roots of Our Ecologic Crisis." *Science,* 10 March 1967.

Whitehead, A.N., and Bertrand Russell. *Principia Mathematica.* Cambridge, Eng.: Cambridge Univ. Press, 1919.

INDEX

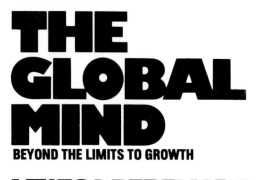

THE GLOBAL MIND

BEYOND THE LIMITS TO GROWTH

LEWIS J. PERELMAN

Man, as a determining factor of earth's destiny, has finally realized that the world is in a state of unprecedented instability and danger. We are in the throes of a global ecological crisis, the four chief dimensions of which are: the rampant degradation of environment; the explosive growth of population; the impending exhaustion of critical energy, mineral, and other resources; and the growing threats of violence and war.

Our leaders—politicians, business managers, militarists, and intellectuals—claim to be attacking the dangers that confront us. Yet their efforts seem to be without effect, except when they make matters worse still. Why such incompetence?

In *The Global Mind: Beyond the Limits to Growth,* Lewis J. Perelman theorizes that the Establishment has failed to realize that the ecological crisis is not a crisis of *things,* but of *ideas.* Modern industrial/technological civilization has been structured on a foundation of bad ideas, and the attendant errors are just now mani-